Joking Around

Tao insights into life

Joking Around

Tao insights into life

TALKS 11 TO 12 OF THE SERIES TAO THE GOLDEN GATE

OSHO

JAICO PUBLISHING HOUSE
Ahmedabad Bangalore Bhopal Bhubaneswar Chennai
Delhi Hyderabad Kolkata Lucknow Mumbai

Published by Jaico Publishing House
A-2 Jash Chambers, 7-A Sir Phirozshah Mehta Road
Fort, Mumbai - 400 001
jaicopub@jaicobooks.com
www.jaicobooks.com

Copyright © 2014 OSHO International Foundation.
All rights reserved

First Publication Copyright © 1981, OSHO International Foundation.
Copyright ©-all revisions 1953-2014 OSHO International Foundation.
All rights reserved

OSHO is a registered trademark of
OSHO International Foundation, used under license.

www.osho.com

JOKING AROUND
ISBN 81-7992-575-7

First Jaico Impression: 2006
Eighth Jaico Impression: 2014

No part of this book may be reproduced or utilized in
any form or by any means, electronic or
mechanical including photocopying, recording or by any
information storage and retrieval system,
without permission in writing from the publishers.

Printed by
Anubha Printers
Plot No. 19, Udyog Kendra Extn. 1
Ecotech-III, Greater Noida, U.P. 201308

CONTENTS

1. Man Is a Becoming — 1
2. It Is Always Today — 23
3. Transcending the Transcendental — 45
4. Just Joking Around — 66
5. This Moment Is All — 86
6. I Really Mean Business — 107
7. I Have Heard — 131
8. We Can Share — 154
9. Mind Is the Only Problem — 176
10. Religion: The Ultimate Luxury — 196

INTRODUCTION

Every few thousand years an individual appears who irrevocably changes the world around them in ways that are never immediately apparent, except to the most perceptive.

Osho is one such individual: his spoken words will resonate for centuries to come.

All those words have been recorded and transcribed into books like this one, written words that can carry a transforming message to the reader.

For Osho, all change is individual. There is no "society" to change – it can only happen to each one of us, one at a time.

So, no matter what the subject matter of the book, the thread that runs through all Osho's words is like a love song that we can suddenly, mysteriously, hear at just the right moment. And strangely, no matter what the words seem to be referring to, they are really only referring to us.

And this is no ordinary love song, more an invitation to open our hearts to hear something beyond the words, beyond the heart...a silence beyond all understanding.

Man Is a Becoming

The first question:

Osho,
Why is it that only humans repress, manipulate, kill, try to conquer the natural flow in nature, the Tao? Why are we so stupid?

Man is not a being, man is a becoming. This is one of the most fundamental things to be understood. The trees, the animals, they are all beings. Man is different: he is a becoming, he is a process. And with the process the problem arises: you can fall below the animals, you can rise above the gods. No dog can fall below dog-hood, neither he can become a Buddha; both are impossible. He is neither stupid nor a genius; he has no growth. He is born the way he is born; he will live, he will die the same – between his birth and death there is going to happen no evolution.

Man is different. That is man's privilege, his prerogative, but there lies also great danger. Man is not born fully complete; he is not born entire – birth is only a beginning of a process. Now, the process can take any form: it can become deformed, it can take a wrong route, it can go astray. Man begins his life as freedom but freedom has its price; you can't have it free. No other animal has any freedom except man.

Hence for centuries the mystics have said that man is a bridge between two eternities: the eternity of the unconscious and the eternity of the conscious, and man is always moving between these two polarities. He is like a tightrope walker.

Each moment is full of danger, but full of possibilities too. No possibility comes alone; it has its own danger. You can miss – you can fall from the rope into the abyss.

Man has been called by the mystics a ladder. Now, the ladder can do two things: you can use it to go upwards, and the same ladder can be used to go downwards. You use the same ladder for both the purposes, just your direction changes. When you are moving upwards your direction is different; when you are moving downwards your direction is just the opposite of it. But the ladder is the same, the result will be totally different. Man is a ladder between heaven and hell.

That's why, it is only human beings who repress, who manipulate, who kill, who try to conquer the natural flow in nature, who are stupid – because they can be Buddhas. Because man has intelligence, that's why he can be stupid. Stupidity simply means you have not used your intelligence; it does not mean absence of intelligence. If there is no presence of intelligence you cannot call man stupid. You cannot call a rock stupid; a rock is a rock – no question of stupidity.

But you can call man stupid because with man there is hope, a ray of great light. With man, a door opens towards the beyond. He can transcend himself and he is not transcending – that's his stupidity. He can grow and he is not growing, he is clinging to all kinds of immaturity – that is his stupidity. He goes on and on living in the past, which is no more – that is his stupidity. Or he starts projecting in the future, which is not yet – that is his stupidity.

He should live in the present with deep passion, with great love, with intensity, with awareness, and that will become his intelligence. It is the same energy: upside down it is stupidity; put it right, rearrange it, and it becomes intelligence.

Intelligence and stupidity are not separate energies. The same energy functioning in harmony is intelligence, functioning in contradictions is stupidity. Man can be stupid – don't think that it is unfortunate. It looks on the surface that it is unfortunate, but hidden behind it is great glory, great splendor which can be discovered.

But the society, the so-called religions, the state, the crowd, they all want you to be stupid; nobody wants you to be intelligent. They all condition you to remain stupid your whole life for the simple reason that stupid people are obedient. Intelligent people start thinking on their own; they start becoming individuals. They start having their own life, their own lifestyle, their own way of seeing, of being, of growing. They are no more parts of the crowd – they cannot be. They have to leave the crowd behind, only then they can grow. And the crowd feels offended; the crowd does not want anybody to be more than the average person – it is against the average person's ego. The crowd, the collectivity, has a great involvement: the involvement is that anybody becoming more intelligent, more individual, more aware, will not be any longer part of the mob psychology.

You cannot force Buddha to follow the stupid people. And the stupid people are many, the majority, ninety-nine point nine per cent. They have a great power with them – the power of violence – and they show it whenever it is needed. They showed it to Jesus, they showed it to Socrates, they showed it to Mansoor...they would like to show it to me.

The man who threw a knife to kill me just few days before was simply a representative of the ninety-nine point nine per cent people. He was not a single individual; the whole crowd psychology is behind him, he has the support of the crowd. The crowd also thinks in the same way; there is no difference about it. He is a leader; he is fulfilling the desires of many. They would like to remove me from the scene; I am becoming a disturbing factor to them. I am going against their taboos, I am going against their inhibitions, I am going against their past. They call it their culture, their heritage, their religion.

The man who threw the knife, before he threw the knife he shouted, "You are talking against our religion, our culture! We cannot tolerate it!" He is simply a mouthpiece. He is trying to show that the crowd can be violent if you try to be an individual; it will not tolerate your existence even. All the vested interests would like everybody to be stupid.

You will be surprised to know that your schools, colleges, universities don't exist, in fact, to help you to become intelligent – no, not at all. I have been associated with universities as a student, then as a professor, for many years. I know the very inner structure of your educational system: it is not concerned with creating intelligence in people. Of course it wants to create efficiency, but efficiency is not intelligence, efficiency is mechanical. A computer can be very efficient, but a computer is not intelligent.

Never think that intelligence and efficiency are synonymous; intelligence is a totally different phenomenon. Efficiency is not intelligence, it is mechanical expertise. The universities are concerned to create efficiency so that you can be better clerks and better collectors and better stationmasters and better postmasters, et cetera. But they are not concerned to create intelligence in fact they are all against intelligence. The whole structure of your educational system all over the world is to make you more and more capable of memorizing things because memory is a bio-computer.

Intelligence is a totally different phenomenon. Intelligence arises out of meditation, intelligence arises out of rebellion intelligence arises not out of memory. But your examinations only take care about your memory. Whosoever has better memory is thought to be more intelligent. But it happens many times that stupid people have beautiful memories, and intelligent people are not so good as far as memory is concerned.

Edison was not good as far as memory is concerned. He discovered one thousand scientific gadgets; nobody else had discovered so many things. Just the quantity of his discoveries is enormous, unbelievable. You may not be aware that you are using Edison's discoveries every day: the gramophone record, the radio, the electric bulb the fan, the loudspeaker; everything that you are using comes from one single person, Edison. But as far as memory is concerned, his memory was very lousy, very sloppy, so much so that once he forgot his own name which is really very difficult; almost impossible to forget your own name. If you can forget your own name you can forget anything! This seems to be the last thing. He managed to do the last thing.

In the First World War rationing came for the first time into existence, and he was standing in a queue to take his ration card. Slowly, slowly he came closer to the window. Then the last person in front of him moved and they called his name: "Thomas Alva Edison!" And he looked around as if they are calling somebody else; he looked in the queue.

One man recognized his face because many times he had seen his pictures in the newspapers. He said, "As far as I remember, you seem to be Thomas Alva Edison. Why you are looking here and there?"

He said, "You are right! I had completely forgotten! Many many thanks that you reminded me. Yes, I am Thomas Alva Edison."

His wife used to keep everything in order because his whole room was in constant chaos: thousands of papers, research papers, and whenever he would like a single thing it will take days to find it out, where it is. He will go on forgetting everything. He may have discovered something and he may start discovering again. And his wife will remind that, "You have done it! It is already in the market!"

He used to keep loose papers and will go on writing whatsoever thought will come to his mind. Then those loose papers will be lost here and there. His wife told him, "You better keep a notebook."

He said, "That's beautiful idea! Why it never happened to me?" But then he lost his whole book! He said, "Look, your suggestion I followed. With loose papers one thing was good: once in a while I used to lose few papers, but not all; now all papers are lost!"

Albert Einstein was not a man of memory. He failed in his matriculation simply because he could not memorize anything. This greatest mathematician of all the ages, and for ages to come, was incapable of counting small amounts of money; he will have to count again and again.

Once he was traveling in a bus. He gave the conductor some money; the remaining money was returned to him. He counted it once, twice, thrice, and each time the result was different, so he started counting the fourth time.

The conductor was looking and he said, "What is the matter with you? Don't you know figures? Thrice you have counted, now you are counting fourth time! Don't you know figures?"

He said, "Yes, I am a little lousy about figures!"

This man who has worked out greatest figures possible was incapable of counting small amounts of money. He will go into his bathroom and will not come out for hours because he will forget that he has to come out.

One of my friends, Doctor Ram Manohar Lohia, went to see him. He was telling me that, "I had to wait six hours because he was in the bathroom! And his wife started apologizing again and again and she said, 'He is in the bathroom, he is in the bathroom.' I said, 'But what he is doing in the bathroom?' The wife said, 'Nobody knows but if you disturb him he becomes very angry – he starts throwing things! But he always forgets; whenever he goes in he forgets to come out. Now we have to wait, whenever he comes out...When he will feel hungry or thirsty or something, then he will remember.'"

Doctor Lohia asked, "But what he goes on doing there?"

The wife said, "Yes, I have also been curious my whole life what he goes on doing. So in the beginning I used to peep through the keyhole – what he is doing? He sits in his bathtub and goes on playing with soap bubbles! And when I asked him, 'What are you doing?' he said, 'Don't disturb me, never disturb me, because it is playing with soap bubbles that I have discovered the Theory of Relativity, and the theory that the universe is expanding just like a soap bubble: it goes on expanding and one day it will burst – just like a soap bubble!'"

Down the ages you will find thousands of geniuses with very bad memory and thousands of people who had tremendous memory with no intelligence at all, because memory and intelligence come from different sources. Memory is part of the mind, intelligence is part of no-mind. Intelligence is part of your consciousness and memory is part of your brain. The brain can be trained – that's what universities go on doing. All your examinations are tests for your memory, not for your intelligence. But universities give you the wrong impression – as if memory is intelligence. It is not.

This whole educational system exists to destroy intelligence or to divert you from intelligence towards memory. Memory is useful, utilitarian. Intelligence is dangerous; it has no utility for the status quo, it has no utility for the vested interest. Intelligent people have always proved to be difficult people just because of their intelligence; they cannot bow down to any stupid thing. And our society is full of superstitions, stupidities; all kinds of nonsense prevails in the name of religion, in the name of politics, in the name of literature, art.

Each child is distracted, is diverted. Hence so much stupidity. It is really a miracle how few people have escaped from this prison – a Buddha, a Zarathustra, a Lao Tzu, a Jesus, a Pythagoras – very few people. It is almost impossible to escape from this prison because the prison is all around and it begins from the very beginning; from your very childhood you are conditioned to be a prisoner: a Christian, a Hindu, a Mohammedan – these are all prisons. And when you are prisoners of churches, nations, races, then naturally there is going to be violence.

No animal is as violent as man. Animals kill but they kill only when they are hungry, otherwise not. Man is the only animal who enjoys killing for no reason at all, as if killing in itself is a blissful activity.

One day in a restaurant a lion and a hare entered. The manager was shocked; they could not believe their eyes. A great silence fell over the restaurant. Many people were there eating, talking, gossiping; all became absolutely silent. What is happening? The manager rushed to the new customers. Somehow he managed to stammer to the hare, "What would you like, sir?"

The hare asked for coffee. The manager asked, "And what your friend would like to have?"

The hare laughed and he said, "Do you think if he was hungry I will be here? He is not hungry; otherwise he would have taken his breakfast – I would be gone! We can be together only when he is not hungry."

In a zoo in Moscow they have kept a lion and a sheep in one cage to show the philosophy of peaceful coexistence. Everybody goes to see the cage. It is a miracle! The sheep and the lion sitting side by side – sometimes the sheep fast asleep –

just so close to the lion, her head resting on lion's belly. This is something!

A very curious young boy asked the zoo-keeper that, "How do you manage? How you have trained them?"

The manager was getting retired that very day, so he told the truth. He said, "There is no miracle in it. All that we have to do is to change the sheep every day – a new sheep every day, that's all. There is no miracle. And when the lion is no more hungry there is peaceful coexistence."

But a lion won't kill if he is not hungry. It is only man who kills for no reason at all – for stupid ideas. One can understand if somebody is hungry, one can understand, but one cannot understand Hiroshima and Nagasaki – destroying one hundred thousand people within three minutes, a sheer joy of destruction.

This is happening because we have not allowed man's intelligence to flower. And whenever it has happened in any society that intelligence was allowed a little freedom, that society becomes weaker than other societies. It happened in India: India remained a slave for two thousand years for many reasons. One of the reasons was the great revolution that was brought by Krishna, Patanjali, Saraha, Mahavira, Buddha. These people brought such a great revolution, such a radical change in the consciousness of this country that many people were released from the bondage of stupidity; a great intelligence was released. The result was this: that the intelligent people stopped killing, they became non-violent; they refused to be recruited in the army. Buddhists and Jainas refused to be recruited in the army, the *brahmins* refused to be recruited in the army. Now, this was the cream, and the cream refused to fight. Then very stupid countries and very ordinary people – Hunas, Turks, Moghuls, who were far backward in every possible way – ran over the country. And because the most intelligent part of the younger generation was no more interested in killing and violence there was no resistance, no fight. They conquered the country. A big country was conquered by very small countries. For two thousand years this country remained in slavery for the simple reason...

The same thing happened in Athens. Socrates, Plato,

Aristotle, Pythagoras, Heraclitus, these were the people who released great intelligence, and a climate was created of freedom, of free thinking. And the whole Greek civilization disappeared. It was destroyed by stupid people who were surrounding the civilization. It was one of the most beautiful phenomena that was happening on the earth.

Now the same thing is happening again in America. If America and Russia are ever in conflict, there is every possibility America will be defeated for the simple reason because American youth is far more intelligent than the Russian youth. American youth has started thinking; Russian youth is absolutely conditioned – they function like machines. In these two world wars and in many small wars it has been noted down that American young soldiers are very disinterested in fighting. Otherwise, how you can explain the phenomenon of Vietnam? America with all its sophisticated arms could not win a poor country with no scientific sophistication at all.

It has been found that thirty to forty per cent American soldiers never used their weapons. They will go to the war field every day but they will not kill. It is beautiful, it is something to be appreciated, but dangerous too because thirty to forty per cent is a big percentage and soon it will be fifty to sixty per cent.

If Russia and America are ever in conflict, if the clash ever happens, there is every possibility that America will be the first to lose. The difference will not be much, maybe ten to fifteen minutes' difference, because now the question is not of human beings fighting, the question is of releasing atomic energy, hydrogen bombs and missiles, and they are all controlled by computers. If Russians attack America, then it will take ten minutes for American computers to react and reach Russia. And the same will happen if America attacks Russia: it will take ten minutes for Russian computers to react and to reach America. The difference will be only of ten to fifteen minutes; both will be destroyed. But if it ever happens, then that difference of fifteen minutes will be predictable. America will be the first to go for the simple reason that great intelligence is being released. Always higher cultures have been defeated blower cultures, hence no culture can afford to release intelligence.

My own suggestion is, unless we create a world government, intelligence cannot be allowed. And the time has come for a world government. National governments are no more needed: they are things of the past, they are part of our stupid past. Nations are no more needed, just a world government. And if there is a world government it will have a totally different quality for the simple reason because armies will have to be reduced, because there will be no question of fighting with anybody.

Now seventy per cent money, wealth, income goes to the army – seventy per cent; only thirty per cent is left for other purposes. That means seventy per cent of our energy is to kill, to be violent, to be destructive. A world government is an absolute necessity to save humanity. And the quality of the world government will be totally different because it won't need great armies; just small police forces will be enough. It will have all the functions – the post office, the railway, the airplanes, et cetera – but they are not destructive; they serve people.

And once army disappears from the world great intelligence will be released because it is army that is destructive of intelligence. It recruits the most healthy people and destroys their mind, because a real soldier is possible only if one becomes just absolutely mechanical.

Man kills for no reason. Man tries to repress rather than to understand, manipulate rather than to relate, because to relate with somebody needs great understanding; manipulation needs no understanding. Repression is easy, very easy – any fool can do it.

That's why if you go to the monasteries you will find all kinds of repressions and you will find all kinds of fools gathered together there. I have never come across intelligent monks and nuns; if they are intelligent they will not be monks and nuns anymore. They will renounce that nonsense, they will come out of their so-called religious prisons. But repression needs no wisdom; it simply needs a powerful ego, so you go on suppressing everything into the unconscious. But whatsoever you suppress will have to be suppressed again and again, and still it will never be eliminated. It will become more and more powerful as you grow older because you will become weaker. The suppresser will become weaker and the suppressed will remain fresh and young because it has never been used.

The real problem arises in old age when suppression starts exploding and creates all kinds of ugliness. It is five thousand years suppression that is creating all our neurosis, all our perversions. Suppress sex and you will become more sexual; your whole life will be colored with sex. You will think always in terms of sexuality and nothing else. Suppress sex and the ugly institution of prostitution will arise, is *bound* to arise. More suppressive a society is, more prostitutes will be found there; the proportion is always the same. You can count your nuns and monks and you can know by counting them how many male and female prostitutes will be in the country. It will be exactly the same number because nature keeps a balance. And perversions...because sexual energy will find its ways, its own ways. Either it will create neurosis or hypocrisy; both are ill states. The poor will become neurotic and the rich will become hypocrites.

It is told that when Moses in his rage smashed the tablets of the Ten Commandments, everybody rushed to grab a piece.

Of course the rich and the politicians were the first. They got all the good pieces on which was inscribed, "Commit adultery," "lie," "steal." The poor and all the rest got only the pieces that said, "Thou shalt not," "Thou shalt not."

Repression creates cunningness. You lose authenticity, you lose naturalness, spontaneity, you lose truth. You start lying to others, you start lying to yourself. You start finding ways how to lie and how to go on lying. And a single lie will need thousand other lies to protect it, to support it.

Two mediaeval knights are leaving on a crusade. Since they are old friends, the one asks the other, "Explain something to me. You are always complaining that your marriage is finished, that your wife is a bore, and that she has become as ugly as a witch. Is that right?"

"That's right," answers the other.

"So then tell me," says the first, "why did you lock her in a chastity belt?"

"Because on my way back," he explains, "I am going to tell her that I lost the key!"

Either lying, hypocrisy, deception, or madness...

The safari had been in the remote African jungle for months, capturing animals for the zoo. Smedley's sexual frustration had risen to a point where he decided to try sex with a huge, ferocious female gorilla.

His friend helped chain her down and put a bucket over her head, and Smedley started making love right away, when suddenly the gorilla broke the chains and wrapped her arms around Smedley.

The others grabbed her arms to rescue him, as Smedley moaned incoherently. When, with three men on each arm, they finally freed him, he shouted, "No. The bucket, you fools! Take off the bucket! I want to kiss her!"

In madness you can do anything!

Repression means a method of creating conscience instead of consciousness. Consciousness is non-repressive; it depends on understanding, it depends on meditativeness, awareness. Conscience is repressive: it simply goes on giving you orders, "Do this. Don't do that." It does not change you but it poisons your life.

Friedrich Nietzsche is right when he says, "Religions have not been able to transform man but only to poison his joys." I perfectly agree with this man about this – religions have really poisoned all your joys. If you are eating, religions there are which condemn everything that you eat, and great guilt arises about sex, about food, about clothes, about everything.

Jainism even teaches...particularly its monks and nuns don't take any baths; they are not allowed to take a bath because to take a bath means you are trying to make your body look beautiful. That is sex, nothing else. You may never have thought about it that taking a bath has something to do with sex, but perversions know no limits. Jaina monks and nuns are not allowed to brush their teeth because that means you are trying to make yourself beautiful. There is no need – the body is dirty.

There is no need to give it an appearance of beauty, freshness, fragrance – no need. It has to be hated: it is disgusting. it is nauseating.

But then I have come across Jaina monks and Jaina nuns who will take a sponge bath, but they have to lie about it. They will keep their toothpaste hidden in their bags – they have to hide it; nobody should know about it. They used to come to see me when I used to travel around the country and I will immediately know in whose bag there is toothpaste because their mouth smells so foul if they don't use any toothpaste or any kind of cleaning their teeth. Then to talk with them is almost a torture. So I will immediately know if some nun...particularly nuns because women after all are women; even if they are Jaina nuns it makes no difference. They are more body-oriented, and nothing is wrong about it; it is perfectly good, it is perfectly healthy. So I will immediately know – if the foul smell is not coming I will immediately know – and I will tell them that "I know that your bag has toothpaste in it!"

And they will be surprised. They will say, "How you came to know about it? Nobody knows about it! Can you see inside our bags?"

I said, "Yes! I can see inside you; what about your bag?"

They will say, "You are the first person who has immediately discovered."

I said, "There is nothing much in it. Don't think that there is some miracle or anything. Just I am so tortured by Jaina monks and nuns that whenever somebody from your company comes and is not smelling bad I immediately know that there is something in the bag. You must be taking a sponge bath."

Now, even to take a sponge bath seems to be doing a crime. Cleaning your teeth looks like you are getting ready for hell. It has poisoned your life, it has not transformed your life.

Repression cannot transform. Either it makes you hypocrites...if you are a little intelligent, just even a little intelligent, you will be a hypocrite. If you are utterly stupid then you will go insane.

"How was your boat trip to Europe?" asks Pedro to his friend.

"Fantastic! Imagine, on the first night I met a girl, one of the most beautiful I ever seen. We chitchatted for a while and it was love at first sight. We were soon in each other's arms. It was only the next morning as I held her in my arms that I found she was the wife of one of my best friends. It was such a shock that we both felt tremendously guilty, both cried and cried and cried."

"That's really something! But how was the rest of the trip?"

"Well, you know, it was just fucking and crying, fucking and crying, fucking and crying!"

That's what is going to happen.

Repression is one of...the greatest calamity that has happened to humanity. And it is because of repression manipulation comes in. Because you cannot be true with yourself, you cannot be naked with others. You lose all truth, all respect for truth. You lose all authenticity and you start being deceptive. Manipulation is a deceptive way of exploiting the other. You lose all respect for humanity because you have lost respect for yourself. How can you respect yourself if you are lying, if you are not authentic, if you are not sincere? And if you don't respect yourself you cannot respect anybody else in the world. When you lose respect for others you manipulate, you start using them as means.

Respect means each individual is an end unto himself; disrespect means nobody is an end and you can use everybody as a means for your own purposes, for your own ends. The husband uses the wife as a means, the wife uses the husband as a means; this is manipulation. And because you use each other as means...even parents use their children as means and children use their parents as means. Religious people are using God as a means, what to say about others? Everybody is using everybody else as a means.

Then you are constantly afraid: somebody may take your means. Somebody may take your wife away from you so you have to create a wall around her, you have to put her in chains; you have to make her such deeply dependent on you that she cannot move even an inch beyond you, without you. And of course in return she does the same to you; it is tit for tat. She starts becoming jealous, very possessive. She is constantly curious about you. what you are doing, where you are going.

One day I saw Mulla Nasruddin almost crying, he was so sad. I said, "What is the matter? Why you are so sad?"

He said, "I am really sad. My wife has appointed a new secretary for me."

I said, "So what? What is there to be so sad about it? Is she blonde or brunette?"

He said, "Forget all about blondes and brunettes. He is bald! That's why I am crying!"

The wives keep an eye about everything...what is going on in the office. Many times they will phone: "Where you are? What you are doing?" Continuously suspicious of each other, how can love grow? It is impossible in such a poisoned atmosphere for love to grow. And when love is missing, all your love energies turn into hatred – your love energies go sour, that's what hate is – then you become destructive. Love is creative, hate is destructive. Then you go on finding excuses how to destroy.

Have you watched it? Whenever there is a war people seem to be more joyous than ever. In India it has happened: When India and Pakistan went to war there was great life all over the country; otherwise this country is almost dead. People are dragging themselves somehow, tolerating life somehow; there is nothing for them to enjoy. But once the war was there and they were destroying each other, suddenly they became alive. There was life on people's faces – something was happening. Their talk became lively, their conversation became juicy. From the morning to the night they were continuously watching: "What is happening? Who is winning? How far we have entered into Pakistan? How far we have reached into Bangladesh? How our armies are winning?" Whenever there is a war you will see people becoming alive, coming to life. Otherwise they go dull; their life loses all joy.

Why in destruction we are so much interested? And it is not only nations. If Christians and Mohammedans are in a crusade, in a *jihad*, in a religious war, see both are very alive. Then Christians feel a great brotherhood with all other Christians. Then the Protestants and the Catholics are no more enemies;

then they are all Christians, followers of Christ. And Christianity is in danger, so who bothers about small theological matters? Mohammedans have to be destroyed! And when Mohammedans are at war with the Christians and killing Christians they lose all their inner conflicts; they become united. Then the Shias and Sunnis are no more enemies; they are friends, brothers, followers of the same religion, worshippers of the same prophet, of the same book, the holy Koran. And Islam is in danger so there are no more any theological problems to be discussed.

Hindus and Mohammedans, whenever they are in a murderous mood, become united amongst themselves; otherwise they go dull, dead – they start vegetating again. It is very strange. Why people are so much interested in destruction? If you are going on the street and you see two people fighting – you may be going for a very urgent work – you will forget all about the urgent work; you will stop there. First you will see the fight; you cannot leave that place. The urgent work can wait; in fact there is no more any urgency than to watch the fight. Why? Why a crowd gathers when two persons are fighting? You become identified with the fight. And this happens in many ways. Just a football match or a hockey match and you see thousands of people shouting, going almost mad, jumping, ready to kill each other. Why so much interest? What is happening there?

If somebody comes from some other planet and watches a football match he will be puzzled. What is going on? People are throwing a football from this side to that side, kicking it and thousands of people are watching. Just a football is being kicked!

I was never interested in any game. When I was in my high school my principal called me. He said, "You never participate in any game."

I said, "You show me any intelligent game and I will participate."

He said, "What do you mean, 'intelligent game'?"

I said, "This is so foolish, volleyball. Why should I throw the ball over the net to the other side and they throw it to my side?

They can have one ball, I can have one ball. They go home, I go home. Keep your balls and do whatsoever you want to do with them – hug them, kiss them! Why this nonsense? And what is so much excitement about? I can't see any point!"

He looked at me, puzzled. He said, "Your point is right but I have never looked from this angle. Yes, what exactly is the excitement? But please don't say it to anybody. If you don't want to participate, don't participate, but keep quiet. Don't destroy others' joys."

So I was the only one in my school who was freed on the condition that I will not tell anybody that this is all nonsense, I will not propagate my idea.

In the university it was compulsory to have a certain military training. I refused. I said, "I am not that stupid! Some fool tells me, 'Right turn! Left turn!' Why? I don't have any need to turn to right or to left. I refuse on the grounds that this is stupid! And unless I am proved wrong I am not going to participate."

My vice-chancellor said, "You do one thing. We can free you only on health grounds; there is no other possibility. And I will tell the university doctor to give you a certificate, that your health does not permit you to participate in the military training."

I said, "Do whatsoever you want to do, but I am not going to participate and if you make trouble for me, I will create much trouble for you. I am going to convince others."

He knew me...He said, "You don't worry. You don't go to the doctor, I will manage. I will take the certificate from the doctor and I will do everything that is needed. You are freed, but don't say it to anybody. I can understand your point – you are right."

People can see, but still this goes on and on for the simple reason that so much energy is boiling within, it has to be thrown out somewhere. Now, a stupid game, a silly game like football, and thousands of people get so excited – so much ado about nothing! They start fighting...after each football match there is a riot. The police have to be called, tear bombs have to be thrown, the mob has to be somehow dispersed.

What is happening to humanity? It is a simple phenomenon,

we have repressed everybody so much that the energy is ready to throw the lid any moment. It is like boiling your kettle and not allowing the vapor to get out any outlet, and sitting holding the lid tight. Then instead of making tea you may destroy the whole family! The tea kettle may explode; it may destroy. That's what is happening. For thousands of years man has been sitting on repressed energies. Now it is time: either a Third World War or a new birth of man, either a Third World War or a new style of life has to be introduced.

And my work here consists in introducing a new life style.

You ask: *"Why is it that only humans repress, manipulate, kill, try to conquer the natural flow in nature, the Tao? Why are we so stupid?"*

We have been made to function stupidly. We need a totally different gestalt, a different social structure, a different world view, a different philosophy of life in which intelligence is respected, in which intelligence is supported, individuality is nourished. But we go on doing just the opposite.

The second question will show you what we go on doing...

The second question:

Osho,

I am a priest. I don't agree with your observation that religion creates sexual perversions. Please don't ask for my name, but I hope that you will answer my question.

Okay, Sir. I will call you Reverend Banana! I hope that you won't feel offended – no offense is meant. It is only that I can't take anything seriously, particularly priests. And you will feel happy that you are nothing compared to one of my sannyasins. I had given him the name Swami Parinirvana; *parinirvana* means transcendental freedom. But my sannyasins are so beautiful people, they have changed his name to Paribanana. Now it means "a transcendental banana"! So you are nothing compared to Paribanana. And to show respect I will call you Reverend Banana.

The first perversion is that you are so coward you cannot

even write your name. What kind of truth-seeker you are? You cannot write to what religion you belong; you want to hide all these facts. You must be living a very cowardly life behind masks, behind a facade, a beautiful facade. But a man who is coward can never be religious; religion needs courage. A man who is coward can never be intelligent; intelligence needs courage, it needs guts, because intelligence will lead you into rebellion, into insecurity, into the unknown and finally into the unknowable.

You say: "I am a priest. I don't agree with your observation that religion creates sexual perversions."

Then from where sexual perversions come? There are aboriginal tribes where no sexual perversion exists. I have lived with an aboriginal tribe in Bastar – no sexual perversion. You will not hear any homosexuality there, no masturbation; people have not heard even about these things. But missionaries are corrupting them; missionaries call them immoral. Just the opposite is the case because these simple people who live in the thick jungles of Bastar have in their villages – small villages they have – a special place for youngsters.

The moment a boy or girl shows any sexual interest he starts living in a special house, a communal house where all the kids of the commune live – a kids' house; girls, boys, all live together. The moment any child shows any sexual interest he is transferred from the family to the communal house where girls and boys live together. The house is called *ghotul*. There is only one discipline to be followed: no boy or girl have to sleep with each other more than three days together. Again after few months they can sleep for three days, so that all the boys of the commune and all the girls of the commune can come in contact with everybody.

Now this missionaries call prostitution. It is not prostitution, it is just a beautiful training and a discipline: it makes them aware of all possible relationships. All the boys come to know about all the girls, all the girls come to know about all the boys, so when the question of choosing for a husband or a wife arises it is very simple. They know with whom they fit totally well, with whom they feel the most harmonious. They have experimented with all the girls, all the boys. And because they can live only three days together at a time, no jealousy is created – no jealousy is possible. You cannot say, "This is my girl, and what you are doing with her?" After three days she is no more your girl. Nobody is nobody's. It is a temporary friendship – for three days you experimented with each other. Once they are sexually mature they get married. There is no divorce, no extramarital relationship either, and there is great harmony in their married life – it is bound to be so.

But the Christian missionaries have reached there to transform them. The Christian missionaries think that they are very corrupted people: their children are being taught prostitution. These children are falling in the hands of priests because they are poor. You can supply them bread and butter and clothes and medicine, so now hospitals and schools – and the Bibles, and slowly, slowly...

I had visited Bastar twenty years before, but now I hear that things have almost completely changed. In many villages *ghotul* has disappeared, because of Christian missionaries, because they have condemned it so much. But perversions have entered: now the children will be masturbating, because a boy becomes sexually mature at the age thirteen or fourteen, and you allow him to get married at the age of twenty-four or twenty-five. These eleven years, what he has to do with his sexual energies? Either he learns masturbation, which is a perversion, or he becomes homosexual, which is a perversion; the girls become lesbians.

And you say to me that you don't agree with my observation. It is not an observation, it is simply a statement of the fact. It is religion, the so-called religion that has existed up to now on the earth, that has created all sexual perversion. Your monasteries, your nunneries are all sexually perverted; they are full of sexually perverted people.

The wife of a Brazilian diplomat to be transferred to Japan was talking to an old monk in Japan.

"Sir," she asked, "do you have elections in Japan?"

The monk hesitated a little and then said, "Yes, madam, every morning."

A new monk joins into the monastery. An old monk asks

MAN IS A BECOMING

him, "Do you enjoy a drink or two, old man?"
"Well, actually, I never touch the stuff, sir."
"Pity! But how about a good cigar, old chap?"
"Never smoked, actually."
"Pity! But you are a lady's man, eh what?"
"Could not say so, sir."
"Pity! Between you and me, are you – um – one of those?"
"No, sir!"
"Pity!"

Seven years of rigorous training and discipline had passed, and the ten young monks were about to take their final examination before being accepted into the Holy Order.

To test their control over earthly temptations, they were all lined up in a row, stripped completely naked, and a small bell was tied to each of the ten pricks.

Then out came a beautiful sensuous naked brunette who proceeded to walk along the line of the ten monks. Nothing happened until she got to the last monk, and then...ting-a-ling, ting-a-ling went his bell.

The poor embarrassed monk pleaded to his superior for another chance to prove his ability to control himself, and after some discussion it was agreed he would be given another opportunity to show he had risen above earthly temptations.

When the ten monks had again formed into a line, a lovely, naked, curvaceous blonde stepped out and sauntered along the line of men. Nothing happened until she got to the end of the line when again...ting-a-ling, ting-a-ling went the bell of the last monk, this time more excitedly than before.

It was only through the compassion of the Father Superior that number ten was allowed one final chance, but if he failed again he would be sent away with no further discussion.

When the ten monks lined up for the third time, a most beautiful naked redhead appeared and temptingly walked along the line. When she got to number ten it was more than he could bear, and his bell rang so violently that it broke its cord and fell to the ground.

Totally dejected, number ten had to accept his fate of being sent out of the Order.

As he stepped forward and bent over to pick up his bell, there was suddenly heard the sound of nine ringing bells – ting-a-ling, ting-a-ling, ting-a-ling...

It Is Always Today

The first question:

Osho,
Why is it so difficult to forgive, to stop clinging to hurts long since past?

The ego exists on misery – the more misery the more nourishment for it. In blissful moments the ego totally disappears, and vice versa: if the ego disappears, bliss starts showering on you. If you want the ego, you cannot forgive, you cannot forget – particularly the hurts, the wounds, the insults, the humiliations, the nightmares. Not only that you cannot forget, you will go on exaggerating them, you will emphasize them. You will tend to forget all that has been beautiful in your life, you will not remember joyous moments; they serve no purpose as far as the ego is concerned. Joy is like poison to the ego, and misery is like vitamins.

You will have to understand the whole mechanism of the ego. If you try to forgive, that is not real forgiveness. With effort, you will only repress. You can forgive only when you understand the stupidity of the whole game that goes on within your mind. The total absurdity of it all has to be seen through and through, otherwise you will repress from one side and it will start coming from another side. You will repress in one form; it will assert in another form – sometimes so subtle that it is almost impossible to recognize it, that it is the same old structure, so renovated, refurnished, redecorated, that it looks almost new.

The ego lives on the negative, because the ego is basically a negative phenomenon; it exists on saying no. No is the soul of the ego. And how can you say no to bliss? You can say no to misery, you can say no to the agony of life. How can you say no to the flowers and the stars and the sunsets and all that is beautiful, divine? And the whole existence is full of it – it is full of roses – but you go on picking the thorns; you have a great investment in those thorns. On the one hand you go on saying, "No, I don't want this misery," and on the other hand you go on clinging to it. And for centuries you have been told to forgive.

But the ego can live through forgiving, it can start having a new nourishment through the idea that, "I have forgiven. I have even forgiven my enemies. I am no ordinary person." And, remember perfectly well, one of the fundamentals of life is that the ordinary person is one who thinks that he is not; the average person is one who thinks that he is not. The moment you accept your ordinariness, you become extraordinary. The moment you accept your ignorance, the first ray of light has entered in your being, the first flower has bloomed. The spring is not far away.

Jesus says: Forgive your enemies, love your enemies. And he is right, because if you can forgive your enemies you will be free of them, otherwise they will go on haunting you. Enmity is a kind of relationship; it goes deeper than your so-called love.

Savita has asked a question that, "Osho, why a harmonious love affair seems to be dull and dying?"

For the simple reason because it is harmonious; it loses all attraction for the ego; it seems as if it is not. If it is absolutely harmonious you will completely forget about it. Some conflict is needed, some struggle is needed, some violence is needed, some hatred is needed. Love – your so-called love – does not go very deep; it is only skin-deep, or maybe not even so deep. But your hate goes very deep; it goes as deep as your ego.

Jesus is right when he says, "Forgive," but he has been misunderstood for centuries. Buddha says the same thing – all the awakened ones are bound to say the same thing. Their languages can differ, naturally – different ages, different times, different people – they have to speak different languages, but the essential core cannot be different. If you cannot forgive, that means you will live with your enemies, with your hurts, with your pains.

So on the one hand you want to forget and forgive, because the only way to forget is to forgive – if you do not forgive you cannot forget – but on the other hand there is a deeper involvement. Unless you see that involvement, Jesus and Buddha is not going to help. Their beautiful statements will be remembered by you, but they will not become part of your lifestyle, they will not circulate in your blood, in your bones, in your marrow. They will not be part of your spiritual climate; they will remain alien, something imposed from the outside; beautiful, at least it appeals intellectually, but existentially you will go on living the same old way.

The first thing to remember is: ego is the most negative phenomenon in existence. It is like darkness. Darkness has no positive existence; it is simply absence of light. Light has a positive existence; that's why you cannot do anything directly with darkness. If your room is full of darkness, you cannot put the darkness out of the room, you cannot throw it out, you cannot destroy it by any means directly. If you try to fight with it, you will be defeated. Darkness cannot be defeated by fighting. You may be a great wrestler but you will be surprised to know that you cannot defeat darkness. It is impossible, for the simple reason that darkness does not exist. If you want to do anything with darkness you will have to go via light. If you don't want darkness, bring light in. If you want darkness, then put the light off. But do something with light; nothing can be done with darkness directly. The negative does not exist – so is the ego.

That's why I don't say to you: Forgive. I don't say to you: Don't hate; love. I don't say to you that drop all your sins and become virtuous. Man has tried all that and it has failed completely. My work is totally different. I say: Bring light into your being. Don't be bothered by all these fragments of darkness.

And at the very center of darkness is ego. Ego is the center of darkness. You bring light – the method is meditation – you become more aware, you become more alert. Otherwise you will go on repressing, and whatsoever is repressed has to be repressed again and again and again. And it is an exercise in futility, utter futility. It will start coming up from somewhere else. It will find some other, weaker point in you.

I come across every day so many questions which show how negativity asserts, in how many subtle ways. Just the other day I was joking that Mukta has asked me: Can she bring a 1939 model Rolls Royce for me? I said, "I am no more interested in anything old and rotten. You can call it a vintage car, you can call it antique, and you can call it beautiful names, but the truth is: for forty years so many rotten people have used it...I don't want to use it any more."

Yatra immediately wrote a question to me: "Osho, don't you have any taste? Old things also have their beauty." Yatra may not be knowing, may not be aware that this is a form of negativity. I was simply joking, otherwise why I should be speaking on Ko Hsuan? Twenty-five centuries old...

But immediately...A chance cannot be missed. If you can say something against me, you will not miss the chance.

Just today I have received another question from Atta, that "You use so many times the words *I*, *me*, *my*, *my sannyasins*. You seem to be the greatest ego around."

I can stop using *I*, *me*, *my*, *my sannyasins* – that won't help. These are just words, and perfectly utilitarian. I also use the word *darkness*, although it does not exist. It has never existed, it cannot exist. Just by using the word *darkness*, darkness does not start existing. But Atta must be waiting for some opportunity to say something aggressive to me, to be in some way violent to me. This is natural, because sannyas means surrender, and when you surrender then more often than not you are repressing your ego. It will find its way from somewhere to assert.

It is not just a coincidence that Buddha's own brother, Devadatta, tried many times to kill him. His own cousin-brother...Why? Why he was so antagonistic to him? And he was also his disciple. But they were contemporaries, of the same age. They were brought up in the same palace, educated by the same teachers in the same academy, played together.

And then Buddha became enlightened, and there was deep jealousy in Devadatta. First he tried on his own to become enlightened; he could not. So, unwillingly, reluctantly, he surrendered to Buddha. He must have said with deep resistance, "*Buddham sharanam gachchhami*; I take shelter into the Buddha, into your feet." But deep down somewhere he must be thinking that, "We belong to the same royal family, the same blood, the same education. We have played together. So why I should surrender to this man?" And then, once he started going a little into meditation, just a little, few experiences of meditation, and he started gathering a following around himself He started to spread the rumor that he has also become enlightened.

Buddha called him, that "You *will* become enlightened; there is no problem about it. But right now you are just on the way. Don't miss this opportunity." This offended him very much. Immediately all repressed resistance asserted – he revolted. He took away few people those who had become his friends and followers, away from Buddha. And their whole effort was: How to kill this man?

Judas was the cause of Jesus' death, and Judas was the most intellectual disciple of Jesus. Remember it. Never forget it, that he was the most sophisticated disciple of Jesus. All others were very unsophisticated, simple people, almost primitive people: villagers, fishermen, carpenters, potters, weavers; except Judas nobody was educated. Judas was really far more educated than Jesus himself, far more informed. And he was waiting that sooner or later, he will be the head. Once Jesus is removed from the scene, he will be the head of the whole commune. And there seemed to be no possibility of Jesus ever dying before him. Finally he decided that it is time that this man should be removed forcibly.

Judas was the culprit, the real murderer. He sold Jesus only in thirty silver coins. He was thinking that this is the only way to remove Jesus from the scene, then he can take over the leadership of the group, of the commune. There must have been deep down a hurt ego.

It has always happened that way. Mahavira's own disciple, Makkhali Gosal, revolted against him and he started spreading the rumor that "Mahavira is not the true enlightened person, I am the true enlightened person." When Mahavira heard it he laughed. When Mahavira came to the place where Gosal was staying, he went to see him and he said, "Makkhali Gosal, have you gone mad? What are you doing?"

And the man must have been immensely cunning. He said, "I am not your disciple, remember; the man who used to be your disciple is dead. The body is of Makkhali Gosal, but a great spirit has entered into the body. The spirit of Makkhali Gosal has left. I am a totally different person, can't you see?"

Mahavira laughed and he said, "I can see perfectly well. You are the same stupid fellow, and you are still doing stupid things. Don't waste time! Put your energies in becoming enlightened yourself Why be worried about me — whether I am truly enlightened or not. If you are not my disciple, Makkhali Gosal, if you are a totally different spirit who has entered, I accept. If you say, I accept it. But then why you are concerned with me? Twenty-four hours you are speaking against me. That simply shows that you are still carrying some grudge against me."

It is very essential to understand because you are all disciples here, and you all will be carrying some grudge or other against me, for the simple reason because I am trying to destroy your ego. That I have to do; that's the function of the master, to destroy your ego. And you can become very revengeful, and you can carry deep wounds through it.

You ask me: *"Why is it so difficult to forgive, to stop clinging to hurts long since past?"*

For the simple reason that they are all that you have got. And you go on playing with your old wounds so that they keep fresh in your memory. You never allow them to heal.

A man was sitting in a compartment in a train. Across from him was sitting a Catholic priest who had a picnic basket beside him. The man had nothing else to do so he just watched the priest.

After a while the priest opened the picnic basket and took out a small cloth which he placed carefully on his knees. Then he took out a glass bowl and placed it on the cloth. Then he took out a knife and an apple, peeled the apple, cut it up, put the pieces of apple in the bowl. Then he picked up the bowl, leaned over and tipped the apple out of the window.

Then he took out a banana, peeled it, cut it up, put it in the bowl, and tipped it out of the window. The same with a pear and a little tin of cherries and a pineapple, and a pot of cream – he tipped them all out of the window after carefully preparing them. Then he cleaned the bowl dusted off the cloth, and put them back in the picnic basket.

The man who had been watching the priest in amazement, finally asked, "Excuse me, Father, but what are you doing there?"

To which the priest replied coolly making fruit salad."

"But you are tipping it all out of the window," said the man.

"Yes," said the priest. "I hate fruit salad."

People go on carrying things that they hate. They live in their hatred. They go on fingering their wounds so they don't heal; they don't *allow* them to heal – their whole life depends on their past.

Unless you start living in the present, you will not be able to forget and forgive the past. I don't say to you: Forget and forgive all that has happened in the past; that is not my approach. I say: Live in the present that is the positive way to approach existence. Live in the present. That is another way of saying: Be more meditative, more aware, more alert, because when you are alert, aware, you are in the present.

Awareness cannot be in the past and cannot be in the future. Awareness knows only the present. Awareness knows no past, no future; it has only one tense, the present. Be aware, and as you will start enjoying the present more and more, as you will feel the bliss of being in the present, you will stop doing this stupid thing that everybody goes on doing. You will stop going into the past. You will not have to forget and forgive, it will simply disappear on its own accord. You will be surprised – where it has gone? And once the past is no more there, future also disappears because future is only a projection of the past. To be free from past and future is to taste freedom for the first time, is to taste God. And in that experience one becomes whole, healthy; all wounds are healed. Suddenly there are no more any wounds; you start feeling a deep well-being arising in you. That well-being is the beginning of transformation.

The second question:

Osho,
What is your fundamental teaching to your sannyasins?

It seems you must be a total stranger to this place, otherwise such a question is not possible, because I have got no teaching. I am not a teacher at all; I don't teach you anything.

Teaching means imparting information. Teaching is basically indoctrination, giving you certain beliefs, conditioning your mind for a certain ideology. I am against all ideologies, I am against all doctrines, because they all help and strengthen your mind. My work here consists to help you to go beyond the mind. You are not supposed to learn something here but to unlearn; you have to go through an unconditioning process.

And I don't recondition you. That is what is being done by Christians, Hindus, Mohammedans and everybody else. If a Hindu wants to become a Christian he will have to go through two processes: one will be he will have to be unconditioned as a Hindu and then reconditioned as a Christian. But only conditioning changes, nothing else. Your garments change, your consciousness remains the same.

Consciousness is experienced only when you are unconditioned and not reconditioned again, when you are left alone to yourself, utterly innocent. I call it purity.

That's the essence of Ko Hsuan's Tao. These sutras of Ko Hsuan are called *The Classic of Purity.* Tao has no doctrines, no teachings. It believes in absolute emptiness of the mind, in nothingness. When you are utterly empty you come in contact with the beyond. The beyond is not far away, but you are so full of rubbish, so full of junk, that there is no space for the beyond to enter in you. It is like a room is full of furniture. Empty the room of all furniture: on the one hand the room is emptied, all furniture is removed from the room; on the other hand the room is becoming full of emptiness, the sky is entering, the space is entering – the room is becoming more spacious.

IT IS ALWAYS TODAY

That's what happens when your being is unconditioned and left alone.

I don't want to teach you anything at all. I don't want you to believe in God because what is the need to believe in God? When God can be experienced, why believe? Belief is a poor substitute. When you can have the real thing why go for plastic flowers? When you can grow the red roses, why hanker for something unreal and synthetic?

All beliefs are unreal. I would like you to be knowers, not believers. I would like you to be seers, not Hindus, not Christians, not Buddhists. Yes, I would like you to be a Buddha, an awakened being. I would like you to be a Christ, but not a Christian. And the difference is tremendous. Friedrich Nietzsche used to say that the first and the last Christian died two thousand years before on the cross. Let me repeat: the first and the last Christian. Friedrich Nietzsche himself was a madman, but sometimes mad people have great insights which the so-called sane go on missing. Nietzsche has many insights. This is one of...very significant statement that he has made.

Be a Christ. Why not be crowned by the experience of God himself? I don't teach you about God because all teachings are about. The word *about* means around. All teachings are about and about around and around; they go in circles. They make you knowledgeable but they don't make you knowers.

I don't have any teaching to teach. I have certainly a truth but it cannot be taught. Truth can only be caught, it can never be taught. That is the whole meaning of satsang, of being in the company of a master. That is the whole purpose of sannyas: being in tune with me.

Truth is a transmission beyond words. Words move from one mind to the other mind. What I am saying to you is from one mind to another mind. What is not said is far more important. Listen to my silences the pauses in between. Listen to the gaps. When you are in tune with me, in deep harmony with me, when there is no fight going on between you and me – no resistance, no conflict no argument...And there is no need of any argument because I am not trying to convince you of anything, I am not trying to persuade you to become followers, to become imitators. My effort is totally different: it is that of communion, not of communication.

When two hearts are beating together in rhythm, in a kind of synchronicity, when they are dancing together hand in hand, in a deep loving embrace, then something is transmitted, something jumps from one heart to the other heart. It is like bringing an unlit candle close to a lit candle. when you bring the unlit candle very close to the lit candle; the flame jumps from the lighted candle to the unlit candle. The lighted candle loses nothing, but the unlit candle gains infinity.

I have no teaching. I don't give any discipline to my sannyasins. I want them to be individuals, I don't want to make them carbon copies. I would like them to be themselves, authentically themselves. My whole longing is to create individuality in you, not a collective mind. Christianity is creating a collective mind. Mohammedans are creating another collectivity, Hindus still another, and so on and so forth.

My trust is not in the collective mind, my trust is in the individual. I am an individualist; I believe in the supreme value of the individual there is nothing higher than the individual.

There is a beautiful saying of a Baul mystic, Chandidas: *Sahar upar manusatya. Tahar upar nahin.* Chandidas says: The highest truth is the individual man, there is nothing higher than that, there is nothing more valuable than that.

The individual is not a means to anything – to communism, to socialism, to Hinduism, to Jainism, to Buddhism, to fascism. And up to now, hitherto, for thousands of years man has been treated always as a means to some end – any stupid end is enough excuse to sacrifice millions of individuals.

I don't want to sacrifice any individual, because there is nothing higher than the individual My respect for the individual is absolute, unconditional. The individual is an end unto himself. I want to help you to support you, so that you can be yourself.

You ask me: *"What is your fundamental teaching..."*

There is something fundamental, but it is not teaching. It is my love, not my ideology. It is my drunkenness that would like to impart to you, a spark that I would like to ignite your soul with it, a fire.

A dervish, a Catholic priest, and a sannyasin met in a railway station and got round to talking about religion.

"Well," said the dervish, "we Sufis are the vital force in Islam. We are the sap that keeps the tree green. We are constantly infusing the old traditions with fresh insights and energy. But, of course, Islam is a very conservative religion, and so we have to put the new wine in old bottles to make it acceptable."

The priest, who was an American Jesuit, said, "I can sure understand that. We Jesuits are the dynamic force in the Catholic Church. We are the ones who give it intellectual stature and keep the faith up-to-date with a rapidly changing world. Naturally our Lord's teachings remain eternally true and valid, but we have to give the Church new forms to deal with modern needs. You might say that we put old wine in old bottles to make it palatable."

The sannyasin remained silent until the dervish nudged him and asked, "And what do you do, my friend and this guru of yours?"

The sannyasin replied casually, "Oh, we drink the wine and break the bottles."

The third question:

Osho,
I am Michael Potato-Singh who wrote to you from Amritsar. I have arrived now. Here are a few of my questions.

This place is really becoming more and more beautiful!

You are welcome, Michael Potato-Singh. Reverend Banana is here. You have come, and I hope your friend Michael Tomato, who wrote to me from Bangalore, will be also coming soon.

It seems that Michael Potato and Michael Tomato are not two persons. Their handwriting is exactly alike. If it is a joke, it is beautiful. I love jokes. But it may not be a joke, it may be a serious affair. You may be a split personality, you may be a schizophrenic – one day Michael Potato, another day Michael Tomato. And who knows what else you are going to reveal to us in future!

But anyway, my sannyasins are all vegetarians. We need all the potatoes and tomatoes and the bananas. So please remain here, and call all your friends also. We are not cannibals – pure vegetarians. So we will eat only that part of you – the cabbage part, the cauliflower part, the banana part. I don't think that there is anybody here like Idi Amin who would like to eat you totally.

I have heard:

Idi Amin was on an airplane flight, and the air hostess brought the menu. He looked at the menu, threw it away, and said, "Please bring me the passenger list."

It is good that you were not there. In fact, I myself like potato chips once in a while. Good that you have arrived. You are welcome.

Michael Potato's first question is:

Do you know why the Jews are angry with Moses?

I have been a Jew in my past life, so I know. They are angry because if Moses had taken a left instead of right, they would have had the oil.

And Michael Potato asks – second question:

Can you tell me what storks do on their days off?

Yes, Michael Potato. I am tremendously interested in such metaphysical questions...They circle around the convents and make the nuns nervous.

And Michael Potato's third question is:

What question can never be answered by yes or no?

Only one question, Michael Potato: *Are you asleep?*

And the fourth question:

Osho,

Michael Potato asks,

Do life's ups and downs bother you?

IT IS ALWAYS TODAY

No, just the jerks like you!

The fourth question:

Osho,
I have come here in search of nirvana but now all that I want is to be a part of your Buddhafield, I don't care a bit about nirvana anymore. Please accept me, although I'm not worthy of it.

It is one of the most significant things to understand that the very desire for *nirvana* is the only hindrance. You can desire money, you can desire power, you can desire prestige, but you cannot desire nirvana; that is a contradiction in terms. *Nirvana* simply means the understanding that all desires are futile – the desire for *nirvana* included.

Desire as such is absurd. To be in a desireless state is what *nirvana* is all about. Everybody who comes here comes with a certain desire. The people who come always come with a background. If they have been brought up to believe in God, they come in search of God. If they have been brought up with the belief in self-realization, if they have been taught that the most important thing in life is to know thyself, they come here to know their innermost being, their supreme self. If they have been brought up and conditioned that the ultimate search is for *moksha*, *nirvana*, enlightenment, then they come with that desire.

Everybody who comes is bound to come with a certain desire. That is natural, otherwise you would not be here. But once you are here, as you start getting deeper and deeper into understanding me and what is happening here, you start seeing that desiring is the root cause of all misery. There is no other misery than desiring. It is desiring that is covering your eyes like a veil. It does not allow you to see that which is because you are always concerned about that which should be. Desire leads you into the future, and the future is not yet. And whatsoever you desire comes from the past.

You must have been brought up with a Buddhist conditioning,

otherwise why *nirvana*? Why not God? Why not moksha? Why not truth? You have come here to seek and search for *nirvana* for the simple reason that you have been told from the very beginning that unless one finds *nirvana* there is no fulfillment, there is no bliss, there is no joy, life remains a misery.

But that is a basic misunderstanding. Buddha's whole effort was to help people see that desiring...it is not the question *what* you desire, the question is that you desire. Desiring in itself is the cause of misery because it takes you away from the present, from the now, from the here. The very word *nirvana* means cessation of desire, so how can you desire *nirvana*? That is impossible; that is getting into a contradiction.

Many Buddhist monks have come to me, and they have asked how to attain *nirvana*. And I have to tell them that don't be stupid. The very idea of attainment is egoistic, the very idea of attaining any goal whatsoever, of achieving any goal whatsoever is a mind game; it is a mind trip, it is an ego number. And *nirvana* simply means seeing all this and through seeing it, it drops. Not that you have to drop...Remember this: if you drop, you will always drop for some other desire. You can drop, but then immediately your mind will say, "Why you are dropping this?" It will ask for another desire to be replaced.

Many times it has happened: People come here to meditate, to attain peace of mind, and they don't know that the very idea of attaining anything is the cause of remaining into a turmoil. Peace of mind simply means you have dropped the whole nonsense of achieving, attaining, you have dropped the very idea of being ambitious about anything, worldly or other-worldly. And of course, desire is always impatient. They want it quick, like instant coffee, because why waste time? So they come to me and they ask, "How long it will take to attain peace of mind?

I say, "If you are asking how long, then you will make it very difficult; it will become almost impossible to attain. You forget about time. Time is mind. You forget about time." Present is not part of time – time consists only of past and future; present is beyond time. "You forget about time," I say to them, "and don't be impatient."

They say, "Okay. If we are not impatient, if we forget time, how long it will take to attain?"

Do you see the contradiction? They are again in the same rut; from the back door...Now such a person cannot meditate because constantly he will be thinking, "When it is going to happen? When? One hour has passed and it has not happened yet. Two days have passed and it has not happened yet. Seven days have passed and it has not happened yet." He will be constantly looking at his clock. Again and again, "When? So much time has gone." He will remain tense, he will not relax. Desires don't allow you to relax; they keep you tense, they keep you anxious.

It is good that you say: "I have come here in search of nirvana. But now all that I want is to be a part of your Buddhafield."

It is good that the desire for *nirvana* has disappeared. But remember, this wanting to be part of a Buddhafield may be just another way of the same desire – a new name, with a new label. Let this also go. You are here. While you are here be totally here. Why bother about the tomorrow? The tomorrow never comes, it is always today. Have you not experienced it? The tomorrow never comes. Your whole life is the experience that the tomorrow is nonexistential. It is always today. Be here now, and you are part of the buddhafield. Now don't create a new desire, otherwise it will create the same misery.

You say: "I don't care a bit about *nirvana* anymore."

No, you must be caring a little bit. Otherwise why you say, "I don't care a bit about *nirvana* anymore"?

When one is finished with something, one is so totally finished that one forgets all about it; one does not move to the opposite extreme. The opposite extreme is also part of the same desire. First you are too much attached, then you start becoming too much detached – another extreme. A man is running after money, then one day he gets tired, then he starts running away from money. He says, "I don't want even to see money, I don't want even to touch money." But this is the same man.

The greatest disciple of Mahatma Gandhi, Vinoba Bhave, does not look at money. If you take money in front of him he immediately closes his eyes. What does it mean? It simply means that still somewhere the attachment goes on lingering. Now, behind all this detachment it is the same attachment. Now attachment is standing on its head, it is doing *shirshasan*, a headstand. But it is the same attachment.

My approach is neither of attachment nor of detachment, but of simple understanding.

You say: *"Please accept me, although I'm not worthy of it."*

Who has said to you that you are not worthy of it? God never creates any unworthy people – he cannot: existence always creates the most beautiful people possible. The sinners are as much beautiful as the saints. They have their own beauty. I have been with saints, I have been with sinners, and my experience has been the sinners have more innocence than your so-called saints. Sinners are more simple people, more innocent people than your so-called saints.

Your saints are cunning, clever; in fact, their sainthood is nothing but cunningness and cleverness. They are very calculative; they are taking each step with deep calculation. They are very greedy – of course, they are greedy for the other world, but greed is greed; they are greedy for God, they are greedy for heavenly pleasures. But what pleasures they are imagining in heaven? The same pleasures; it is not going to be much different. All the religions say that there are beautiful women, very young, and they always remain young. Now the scriptures are five thousand years old, but the women there are still young.

There are religions which believe that there are streams of wine in heaven, trees of gold, and flowers of diamonds and emeralds. So what is wrong with this world? Here they teach: Renounce your family, your wife, your husband, your children. Here they say renounce, and there they allow you the same rewards millionfold. There are wish-fulfilling trees, *kalpavrikshas*: you just sit underneath the tree and any desire, any wish, and immediately it is fulfilled – not even a single

IT IS ALWAYS TODAY

moment is lost. Then there seems to be no difference at all.

Sinners are far more simple people.

A guy comes to heaven's door and asks Saint Peter for permission to enter.

"Do you really want to come in?" asks Saint Peter.

"Yes," answers the man.

"Your name?"

"Aristotle."

"Aristotle Onassis?" inquires Saint Peter.

"That's it," is the reply.

"Ah," says Saint Peter, "you are the famous shipowner from Greece who had that marvelous yacht that crosses the Mediterranean, and who gave incredible parties with lots of champagne and caviar?"

"Yes, that is me," says Onassis.

"You are the one who had that beautiful woman called Jacqueline, who once was the First Lady of America?" continues Saint Peter.

"Yes, that is me."

"Well, well. So you are the one who had that incredible island with a whole bunch of servants, pools, flowers and everything?"

"Yes, that is me."

"You are the one who had carte blanche in the best restaurants of the world, and was always seen with the most beautiful women?"

"Yes, that is me."

"Okay, okay," says Saint Peter. "You can come in, but you are going to find this place a shit, man!"

So why not be Aristotle Onassis here? Why bother about the paradise and the beautiful women and the streams of wine and wish-fulfilling trees? All these things are possible here.

The sinners are satisfied with the momentary, and the saints want the permanent. Then who is greedy?

It is good but drop this idea that you are not worthy. I have never come across any man who is not worthy of being blissful. It is up to you. If you want to be blissful, nothing hinders you except your own unintelligence. And that unintelligence can be dropped very easily. Except your ego, nothing hinders you and that ego is nonexistential. And that ego does not allow you to be intelligent because it lives on stupidity, it lives on misery, it lives on anguish. Everyone is worthy, otherwise you would not have been.

Such a beautiful gift of life has been given to you. How you can be unworthy? And I accept you totally as you are: worthy, unworthy, good, bad, saint, sinner. I never ask anybody, "Who you are? What are your qualifications? What are your virtues?" I never ask. Whosoever you are, if God accepts you, if existence accepts you, who I am to reject you?

People say to me, "You go on giving sannyas to everybody?" I say to them, "If God goes on giving life to everybody, then what is wrong in giving sannyas to everybody?" Life is far more valuable. And if God someday asks me, then it is between me and him. There is going to be a great argument, that "You go on giving life to everybody, so what is wrong in giving them sannyas? Sannyas simply means to help them to live life totally. You have given life, I am giving them just the art how to live it totally, intensely, passionately."

The fifth question:

Osho,
I am in tremendous love with your hands, moving, gesturing, dancing with the song that you sing every day.

There is nothing special about it. I just told you in one of my lives, past lives, I have been a Jew, and Jews cannot talk without moving their hands – impossible.

One thousand miles off the Brazilian shore, a boat full of sannyasins sunk. Unfortunately there was no lifeboat and no one on board could swim. For some mysterious reason however, the Jews were able to stay above the water, and only they survived.

When the Jews approached the shore, the village people, mostly fisherman, could not believe their eyes. They saw the strange people in the water moving towards the shore, all of them making strange arm gestures. Being superstitious the people of the village thought that the Jews must be black magicians thrown out by the sea. Once the Jews stepped into the shore the village priest cautiously approached them and asked, "How did you all arrive here without a lifeboat?"

And the Jews answered with sweeping arm gestures, "Talking, talking."

The sixth question:

Osho,
I cannot decide whether to become a sannyasin or not. Any suggestion from you will be welcome.

Do you really mean it will be welcome, or it is just politeness? If you cannot decide, how can you welcome something which I have not even uttered yet? I may say to you, "Take the jump and become a sannyasin." But I know you for ten years: indecisiveness is your very soul – you have never been able to decide anything about yourself I have seen you deciding many things, and by the time you decide the opportunity is gone. You wanted to marry a woman and by the time you decided, she was already married.

You are a politician and politicians are of wavering minds, otherwise they will not be politicians. Politicians are a little bit insane; they are not centered, hence they cannot decide. And this is not for the first time you have asked me about sannyas either. This must be at least the seventh time in these ten years – again and again you have asked, that you cannot decide.

Remember one thing: death is coming closer every day and death will not ask you whether you want to die or not – it won't leave the decision to you – it will simply take you away. Before that happens let something essential grow in your life.

And what can you lose by becoming a sannyasin? You don't have anything to lose. You cannot lose anything because, in the first place, to lose you have to have it. I know you are absolutely poor. By "poor" I don't mean that you don't have money; by "poor" I mean you don't have any inner richness.

Deep down, every politician suffers from inferiority complex, he suffers from inner poverty. He suffers from such inner emptiness, meaninglessness, that he wants to fill it up with some power, some prestige, some fame. And you have tried your whole life. And it is not that you have not succeeded – you have succeeded in your own way – but this is to be absolutely taken note of whether you fail in politics or succeed, you always fail. Those who trail, of course, they fail. And those who succeed, they also fail.

You have heard the proverb: "Nothing succeeds like success." I don't believe in it. I have changed it. I say, "Nothing fails like success," because once you have been successful in something then suddenly you become aware that success is there but your inner emptiness remains the same. In fact, now you feel it more – you feel it more because even the desire for success that was filling it somehow, keeping you occupied, is no more there. You have succeeded: you have the money, you have the power, you have name, you have fame, and the inner emptiness is still there, intact. Nothing has changed there.

If you ask me then it is time to take the jump. It is enough – ten years you have been thinking. How long one is going to think about it? Either take the jump and become a sannyasin or forget all about it. Never ask the question again.

A man in a ragged and frayed blue check suit approached a farmer for a job.

"I will do anything," he said, "just so long as you feed me."

Now the farmer did not really need any help, but he remembered the huge pile of cow manure in the barn that needed to be spread on the fields. He snickered to himself at the revolting task, and said, "Follow me. You see this huge pile of shit? Well, I want it spread deep and thick and even on the east forty."

The man in the checkered suit smiled amiably and set to work. It was a huge pile of shit. The farmer thought it would take him at least a week to complete the job, so he was very surprised at the end of the first day to find the manure pile completely gone and the east forty perfectly covered in a deep, thick, even layer of shit.

"Well, you are a wonderful worker," he exulted. "Come on in

for some roast beef, canned peas, mashed potatoes and gravy." They had a pleasant evening and went to bed early.

The next day the farmer took the man out to a little shack where he stored the potatoes. "You have got an easy job today," he said. "All you do is to go through this pile of potatoes one by one and put the big ones over here and the little ones in a pile over there. Have a good time, and I will see you just before dinner time." And off the farmer went.

Returning around five-thirty the farmer found the ragged man slumped on the original pile of potatoes, sobbing uncontrollably.

"What is the matter?" inquired the farmer. "Yesterday you moved a mountain of bullshit single-handedly, and today you did not even begin your work!"

"Well, you see, I used to be a politician before the great crash," said the man, "and you know how politicians are – we love to spread the shit around, but when it comes to making decisions..."

The last question:

Osho,
I have no idea what you are talking about. Do you?

Neither do I. I am a madman.

But you are not mad. You should be able to figure it out. What is wrong with you? Are you a Jew, or a Polack, or an Italian?

A man asked his Jewish boss for a raise in salary. The boss said, "What do you mean give you a raise? You don't work here at all. Listen. There are three hundred sixty-five days in the year, three hundred sixty-six this year because it is a leap year. The working day is eight hours. That is one-third of a day. So over the year that is one hundred twenty-two days. The office is shut on Sundays, so that is fifty-two off, making seventy days. Then you have two weeks holiday. Take off fourteen days, which leaves fifty-six. There are four bank holidays, which leaves fifty-two. Then the office is closed on Saturdays, is not it? Well there are fifty-two Saturdays in the year, so you don't do anything here at all. Yet you are asking me for a raise?"

Jews have their own ways of calculating things. If you are a Jew, very calculative, cunning, clever, then it will be difficult for you to understand what I am saying, because what I am saying is not comprehensible to cunning minds. Otherwise it is very simple. It is comprehensible only through innocence. If you are not innocent then it becomes difficult, then it becomes almost impossible to understand what I am saying. otherwise things are so simple that I am saying, that they have never been said in such a simple way.

Or maybe you are a Polack?

Three Europeans, an Englishman, a Frenchman and a Polack, got caught during a South American revolution, and after a quick trial, were all condemned to die in front of the firing squad. The three men agreed that in order to escape death each one would make the firing squad panic by shouting some natural disaster.

The Englishman was first, and when the guards were aiming at him, he shouted, "Earthquake!" The guards panicked and he escaped during the confusion.

Similarly the Frenchman, once against the wall, yelled "Tidal wave!" The guards ducked and he also got away.

Finally, it was the turn of the Polack. The officer in charge ordered, "Ready! Aim!" and the Polack shouted, "Fire!"

Or, if the worst comes to the worst you may be an Italian.

Arturo is in despair. "What a tragedy!" he cries. "I come back-a last-a night and found-a my wife in-a bed-a with a Chinese."

"What-a did-a you say?" asked his friend.

"What-a could-a I say?" says Arturo. "I don't-a know-a any Chinese!"

Transcending the Transcendental

The Venerable Master said:
When he has clearly thought about these three he perceives only a void, but when he contemplates the void, he realizes that the void is also void and has become a nothingness. The void having vanished into nothingness, he realizes that the nothingness of nothing is also nothing, and when the nethermost nothingness is reached, there is most truly to be found a deep and unchanging stillness.
In this profound stillness how can desires be begotten? When desires are no longer begotten, then there is essential and unchanging stillness.
Truth is essentially unchanging.
All things in heaven and earth are in essence unchanging.

The East has respected the master tremendously. The West is absolutely unaware of the phenomenon of the masters. It knows the teachers, it is perfectly aware about the teachers, but not about the masters. Even people write about Jesus as a great teacher – western scholars write about Buddha as a great teacher – not knowing the difference. The difference is immense; the difference is so immense that it is unbridgeable. The master is a totally different world.

The teacher is part of the ordinary, day-to-day existence. He knows more than you know: the difference is of quantity, not of quality. You can know more by just a little more effort. The teacher is just a little ahead of you as far as learning, knowledge, information, is concerned, but his being is the same as yours.

The master may not know more than you, he may not know even that much as you know, but he *is* more – he has more being. The difference is of quality: he exists on a different plane. He has entered a totally different dimension of which you are completely oblivious. He knows only one thing, that is his own inner being. And that knowing cannot be called knowledge for the simple reason because knowledge needs three things: the knower, the known and between the two exists the knowledge. The relationship between knower and the known: that is knowledge. But when you know yourself; the knower is the known, the knower is the knowledge; there is no distinction at all. There is no subject and no object. There is unity, not division.

The master is one who has become united in the fundamental sense of ultimate consciousness. He is simply conscious. This consciousness gives him a totally different world view; with this consciousness everything else changes. He sees things in a new light, his eyes are unclouded. He has clarity, he is transparent, he is a pure mirror, crystal clear – not even a thought moves in his consciousness. Hence there is no more any veil, no more any obstruction.

The teacher is so full of thoughts that he is just the opposite end of the master. Never call Buddha a teacher or Jesus a teacher or Lao Tzu a teacher – they are masters. Moreover, they don't teach at all – why call them teachers? They don't impart any new knowledge to the world. Albert Einstein can be called a great teacher, Newton can be called a great teacher. Darwin can be called a great teacher, Marx, Freud – these people can be called great teachers: they have taught many things. What Lao Tzu has taught? What Buddha has taught? What Zarathustra has taught? Nothing at all! But they have imparted a new vision, a new style of life. They have touched people's heart, and they have transformed those hearts. They don't give you information, they give you transformation. What they say is not important, what they are is important. What they say is only a device; their silence is important.

If you want to understand Buddha, Lao Tzu, Ko Hsuan, Kabir, Nanak, you will have to learn how to read between the lines. You will have to learn how to understand silence and the music of silence. You will have to be silent. It is a totally different kind of learning – in fact, it is unlearning. Whatsoever

TRANSCENDING THE TRANSCENDENTAL

you know you will have to drop. You will have to drop all your beliefs, ideologies, philosophies. All that has been given to you by your teachers from the kg to the university level, you will have to get rid of it, you will have to transcend it. You will have to transcend all your teachers; only then you will be able to understand a master. A master is against all teachers.

The East has not respected teachers; its total respect goes to the masters. The teachers are utilitarian; they are experts. If something goes wrong in your bathroom you call the plumber. He knows more than you as far as plumbing is concerned, but that is no reason to pay him great respect and call him "venerable." Something goes wrong with your body, you call the doctor. He is another kind of plumber: he fixes your body. If you want to learn mathematics you go to a teacher.

You go to a master only when you are tired of all this utilitarian existence. When you have come to see that there is something more, when you have felt a deep urge, a great longing, to know that which is non-utilitarian, which has intrinsic value, which can neither be sold nor purchased, which has no price but immense value, when you have come to feel the existence of the mysterious, of the miraculous, then only you are capable of contacting a master.

In fact, the ancient Egyptian scriptures say: When the disciple is ready the master appears himself. And when the disciple is ready? When he is tired of the utilitarian world. In the world everything has a utility; but God has no utility, truth has no utility, love has no utility, bliss has no utility, beauty has no utility. What is the utility of a rose Flower? An atom bomb has utility, a sword has utility. What is the utility of a beautiful sunset? There is no utility in it. Only when you start feeling the longing for the non-utilitarian you are capable of being with a master; otherwise you will go on moving from one teacher to another teacher.

To be with a master needs tremendous preparation. And the greatest thing required is the longing for the unknown, the longing for that which is not of this world. The longing seems to be almost mad to those who are concerned with money, power, prestige. They will think you have gone crazy if you become interested in meditation, if you become interested in silence. if you become interested in a master. But the East has paid tremendous respect to the masters.

Ko Hsuan starts each sutra with these beautiful words:

The Venerable Master said...

He does not mention the name of the master. In fact, names are of no use as far as a master is concerned because a single master represents all the masters of the past, of the present, and of the future, too, because the taste of a master is the same. Whether you come close to a Buddha or to a Mahavira or to a Moses or to Mohammed, it makes no difference. You will have the same taste, the same ecstasy, the same perfume. The same joy will pervade you; the same dance will start happening in your heart.

Buddha has said again and again that you can taste the sea from anywhere: you will always find it salty. So are the masters – names are irrelevant.

Ko Hsuan does not mention the name of the master – names are utilitarian. A master represents the ultimate, the nameless. He is the spokesman of the nameless experience – let him also be nameless. That is his message.

The Venerable Master said...

Remember few things before we enter into the sutra. Why the East respects the master and not the teacher? Why the master and not the scholar? Why the master and not the pundit? Because the East has known that the pundit is only a parrot: he repeats what others have known; he has not experienced it himself. And because he has not experienced it himself it has no validity. He may be able to argue well, he may be able to convince you, he may be able to masquerade many proofs for what he is saying, but still what he is saying is borrowed; it has no roots in his own being. He is only talking to you from his memory, not from his consciousness.

And truth is not in the scriptures. Truth is your very center of being, it is your essential core. You can become very clever with words – it is not difficult either – but those words are impotent, those words are empty, those words really don't have any meaning. Meaning comes through experience.

When Jesus says something it has meaning. You can repeat the same words; it cannot have the same meaning because your experience is not of that level, of that plane. You will put your own meaning into it, you will pour your own experience into it. You will use Jesus' words as containers, but the content will be yours. The bottle will be Jesus', but the wine will be yours.

And what have you got? You know nothing of importance. All that you know is simply rubbish – maybe useful in the world, maybe even necessarily needed in the world for a livelihood, but you don't know what life is. You know how to earn money and you know only how to waste life.

> There was an old professor of Darjeeling
> Who traveled from London to Ealing.
> It said on the door,
> "Please don't spit on the floor,"
> So he carefully spat on the ceiling.

"That philosopher really suffers for his beliefs," said Mulla Nasruddin one day to me.

"Why, what does he believe?" I asked him.

"That he can wear a size 8 shoe on a size 11 foot!"

All your beliefs are like that. You are wearing clothes which were perfectly good for a Buddha but are not good for you. You are wearing shoes which were perfectly good for Lao Tzu but are not good for you. You are living in houses made by others for a totally different purpose, which is not your purpose. Your whole life is a long, long misery for the simple reason that if you have a size 11 foot and you are wearing size 8 shoes, whatsoever you believe, your belief is not going to help; it will create misery for you.

Look at people's lives – no joy, no song, no celebration. And these are Christians: they believe in Christ. And these are Hindus: they believe in Krishna. And these are Buddhists: they believe in Buddha. Something very fundamental has gone wrong. They may say they believe in Buddha, but only the words can be of Buddha. Who is going to put the meaning in those words? You will put your own meaning – and unless your experience changes, your meaning is going to remain very ordinary.

A man and his son are driving in a taxi with a great scholar in Paris near Place de la Madeleine. They pass through a street full of prostitutes standing on the sidewalk. The taxi is almost stopped by the traffic.

"Daddy, Daddy, what are all these women doing standing there?"

"Well...hmm...these women must he waiting for their husbands. You see, it is six o'clock and offices are closing."

"Don't listen to your father! These are whores!" says the scholar who is a great believer of straight-forwardness with children.

"Daddy, what are whores?"

"Well,...hmm...you see...it means they have more than one husband."

"You mean like movie actresses?"

"Yes, but more – lots, hundreds, thousands of husbands!"

"Gee! But all these thousands husbands...then they must have lots of children too!"

"It is quite rare, but it happens, of course."

"And these children, Daddy, what do they become?"

"They become...scholars!"

The East has never paid any respect to the scholars. They are intellectual laborers, they are not real intelligentsia – the West has always misunderstood them for real intelligentsia. They are intellectuals, but they are not intelligent people. Sometimes you will find the so-called intellectuals more stupid than the farmers and the gardeners and the fishermen, for the simple reason because the farmers and the gardeners and the fishermen and the carpenters, they live close to nature, to life, to existence. They have a far truer experience, far closer, intimate contact with reality than your so-called professors, pundits and scholars. They live surrounded with words – big words, bombastic words – but they live in prisons of words. You can be very easily deceived by them because they talk in the same way as the masters. They are pseudo, they are pretenders. Beware of it and beware of their stupidity.

An Englishman is walking up a mountain when he sees a famous professor of philosophy passing in a car, driving backwards up the hill.

"Hey, professor!" the surprised Englishman calls out. "What are you doing?"

"Well," the professor answers, "I have to deliver a package up the mountain and I was told it was impossible to turn around up there."

After this both continued their trip up the hill. Fifteen minutes later the Englishman sees the car coming down the hill backwards again.

"Hey, professor, stop!" he says, "What is the matter?"

"Oh!" the professor replies smiling. "I was wrong – I could turn anyway!"

The master is one who lives the truth. Not that he knows about it, not that he has heard about it, not that he philosophizes about it, but he lives it, he knows it – he has become truth itself. His being is his teaching; everything else is just a device to bring awakening to the sleeping ones. If he uses words it is not to convey the truth, he uses words like alarm clocks to wake you. The teacher uses the words to convey truth. And truth can never be conveyed by words. The master also uses the words, but never to convey the truth. He knows perfectly well truth cannot be conveyed; it is untransferable. It cannot be communicated by any means, but *you* can be awakened to it.

The real thing is not to tell you the truth; the real thing is to make you aware. The moment you are aware you know the truth because truth is already within you. It is not something that comes from the outside; it is something that is asleep within you and has to be awakened.

The master uses words and because he uses words, scholars go on repeating the same words for centuries, thinking that they are important words, very important words. They must be containing truth because Buddha used them, Ko Hsuan used them, Bodhidharma used them, Rinzai used them, Bahauddin used them. Such great masters have used them – those words must contain something of immense value. They contain nothing. They were used for a totally different purpose. The purpose was to awaken the sleeping ones.

Brigitte Bardot was given a parrot as a gift and she put it in her bedroom. Every night she would bring a new lover to her bed and from his cage the parrot would encourage all her lovemaking with words like, "Go on! Go on! You are coming!"

After a few days Brigitte Bardot got rather annoyed with him and when one morning, while she was walking around naked, the parrot shouted, "Come here, beloved, I want to make love to you!" she got infuriated and beat the parrot up.

While smoothing his feathers the parrot sadly said, "But you did not treat the other cocks like this!"

The pundit is a parrot. He thinks Buddha influenced millions of people by these words, Krishna transformed thousands of people by these words, Bhagavadgita, and Mohammed has inspired thousands of souls for centuries by Koran and the words that it contains – these words must be of great potential. So he goes on repeating those words. But those words contain nothing. He is simply imitating a device not knowing the exact purpose of it.

A corporal is instructing his platoon. He calls a newly-arrived soldier and asks him, "You, Gino! What is the flag for you?"

"The flag," answers the soldier, "is a piece of cloth of different colors."

"What! What are you saying? You idiot! The flag is everything. The flag is your mother, remember, your mother!"

Then he turns to the next soldier and asks, "Tell me what is a flag?"

"Gino's mother," replies the soldier.

Beware of the scholars; they are the most stupid people around. But they talk beautifully, and if you are not alert you can be very easily deceived by them. They recite Koran, they recite Bhagavadgita, they quote the Vedas, the Upanishads, they comment and they interpret, and in a very logical way, in a convincing way – it will appeal to your mind. But, in fact, Buddha never wanted to appeal to your mind, neither Krishna wanted to appeal to your mind. They wanted to help you to go beyond the mind. They were not to convince your mind, because if you are convinced about a certain idea you will remain *in* the mind. They were trying to unhinge you from the mind.

Can you see the totally different purpose? The purpose of a master is to push you beyond the boundaries of the mind, and the purpose of the scholar is to convince you intellectually about the rightness, about the validity of a certain ideology, philosophy. He makes your mind more strengthened, he gives you more mind. The master takes away your mind, the master destroys your mind. The teacher nourishes your mind. So many times the teacher will look more appealing to you, more convincing to you.

You can miss the master very easily because he will seem a dangerous person to be around. A teacher seems to be very fulfilling; he enhances your ego. It is not accidental that the West has respected the teacher because the West has believed for thousands of years that the ego has to be strengthened, that a strong ego is needed; without a strong ego a man has no personality. It is true: without a strong ego a man has no personality; but ego is false, so is personality.

The word *personality* comes from a Greek word *persona*; *persona* means a mask. In ancient days Greek actors used masks. Those *personas*, masks, we are all carrying. A strong ego certainly gives you a strong personality in the original sense of the word, but the personality is not individuality and the ego is not your soul – just the contrary.

The master destroys your personality so that your individuality can be discovered. He dismantles your personality, he takes away all your masks, so that you can know your original face. His work is difficult and only very courageous people can be with him because it is surgical. Your mask has become almost part of your existence; to take it away now needs surgery. It is not easy to take it away, it is painful. Only a master is needed to take it away. Slowly, slowly, chunk by chunk, he goes on taking away your mask. Finally, when the mask has completely disappeared, you discover your reality, your original face.

The teacher gives you to think much; the master only gives

you a meditativeness. The teacher gives you much to dream about, to desire about; the master hammers on all your dreams and destroys them. The master is against your sleep; the teacher is a sedative, a tranquilizer. The master is not a solace, is not a consolation, is not a tranquilizer. The master hurts, wounds, but he transforms.

A man finds himself in purgatory. The angel-in-charge welcomes him in.

"Not your turn today," says the angel. "You still have more time to pass on earth. Come with me."

The angel takes him to a huge room full of small bottles full of oil. "These show how much life you have left," says the angel. His bottle is almost empty.

"Can I see my wife's and children's bottles?" he asks.

"Sure," says the angel, pointing to the three bottles next to his. The man cannot believe his eyes. For the children, the quantity seems normal, but his wife seems to have an extraordinary large quantity in her bottle.

Left alone and thinking, as the angel is working with newcomers, he delicately sticks his finger in his wife's bottle, takes a little oil and puts it in his own one. He keeps on doing this until the two bottles are more or less even. He wants to go on, but is suddenly awakened by a big slap and his wife's voice saying, "You dirty old man, always wandering fingers, even when I sleep!"

Man is deep asleep, dreaming, desiring, of hell, of heaven, of thousand-and-one things. The function of the master is to hit you so hard that you cannot avoid waking up.

Ko Hsuan says:

The Venerable Master said:
When he has clearly thought about these three he perceives
only a void, but when he contemplates the void, he realizes
that the void is also void and has become nothingness.

This is a very significant sutra, but first few words have to be put right. The translation is done by a scholar and that too by a Western scholar. He says:

When he has clearly thought...

TRANSCENDING THE TRANSCENDENTAL

Now the original cannot mean that he has "clearly thought" – because clarity and thought cannot exist together. That's impossible; their coexistence is impossible. If there is clarity there is no thought; if there is thinking there is no clarity. It is like saying, "The sky was full of clouds and very clear. The sky was full of clouds and it was very sunny." It is impossible. Either it is sunny and the sky is clear, then there are no clouds...If there are clouds, and many clouds, then the sun will be hiding behind the clouds and there can be no clear sky. You cannot see the sky because of the clouds.

Clarity is a byproduct of meditativeness, not of thought. But this is what is going to happen when scholars do these things. In their own way they are doing a great service, without knowing real differences. And one cannot expect that they will be able to know – they have not experienced clarity. They have thought about it, but to think about clarity is one thing; to know clarity is a totally different thing.

I know clarity, but in clarity there is no thought at all. And I have known thoughts: when there are thoughts there is no clarity. Hence, read this sentence in a little different way:

When he has clearly meditated these three things he perceives only a void...

In the last sutra we talked about the three things: sexuality...In India it is called *kama*; it is the source of all desires. Remember it: sexuality is not only the source of sex, it is the source of *all* desires. Hence you can change your desires, you can forget about sex completely, but if desires persist it is still sexuality. And you can watch it...

There are people who are obsessed with money. You can see one thing: they are no more interested in sex; their whole interest has moved into money. But now money has become their sex object. When they touch money they touch as if they are touching their beloved. I have seen people touching hundred-rupee notes with such tenderness – unbelievable.

I used to know one person whose only joy was money, even somebody else's money. Just if you are interested in beautiful women it does not matter whose wife it is. If a beautiful woman passes by you become immediately interested; a great desire arises in you. Civilization prevents you; the police is there, the law is there, so you don't do anything, you don't act – that is one thing – but the thought starts fantasizing. The mind starts spinning, weaving dreams.

The same was true about this man. He was a relative of mine. Somebody else's money...if he will see that you have many notes in your pocket he will just take the money out, will count it, with such tenderness – and it is not his money either! He will give it back to you, but when he will give you can see the sadness arising in his eyes, you can see the unwillingness.

He was always asking for money, and he had enough money. He was always borrowing money from others.

I used to ask him, "You have money – why you go on borrowing?"

And slowly, slowly he became very honest with me and he said, "I cannot use my own money in any way. It hurts to bring the money out of my own pocket – it hurts. I feel almost paralyzed! I can borrow it from somebody?"

And he never used to give back. He was well known all over the city, that once he takes money from you he will never give back – he cannot. Everybody used to feel pity for him. He had ten bungalows, but he himself used to live in a very small room, in one of his bungalows' servant quarters. He could have afforded a beautiful car, but he used to move on a bicycle so ancient and old that I have never seen anything older than that bicycle.

And I told him, "At least you can purchase a new bicycle!"

He said, "But this bicycle has served me for so long. Moreover, it is a gift from my father. Now my father is dead and this reminds me of my father always. And one thing is very good about this bicycle – nobody else can ride on it!"

It was really difficult to ride on it; only he was expert on riding on it. It had only the very absolutely essential things in it – no chain cover, no mudguards, no horn, nothing, no brakes – and it used to make noise at least from half a mile away. And he will put it anywhere. He said, "Nobody ever steals it. Who will steal it?" – the whole city knew whose bicycle it is – "You will be caught immediately. And wherever you will move the whole neighborhood will know that whose bicycle it is."

He will go into the movie house, but he will not put the bicycle on the stand because there you have to pay ten paise or twenty paise or something. He will put it anywhere outside the movie house and he will always find his bicycle in its place, he never lost it. To the very last day of his life he was using his bicycle.

He lived a poor man's life, a very poor man's life – the life of a beggar. And he collected so much money...He had no son, no daughter.

It almost always happens that miserly people don't have children; there must be some psychological reason in it. In India the very miserly people have always to adopt children – rich people they are. Poor people have many children, too many, in fact; they need birth control And the rich people, the very rich, the miserly people, don't have children. They are so miserly that something deep happens even to their chemistry. Their whole sexuality becomes obsessed with money.

Hence, remember, the first poison Ko Hsuan calls sexuality. It does not mean only sex, it means all desires.

A Scotsman arrives at the toll gate of a bridge, gives a penny to the attendant, and walks on.

"Hey, young man!" shouts the attendant. "The toll is two pennies!"

"I know, I know," replies the young man in a tired voice, "but I will only go half way and then I will jump!"

Coroner: "What were your husband's last words, Mrs. Boccafucci?"

Mrs. Boccafucci: "Emilio said, 'I don't see how they can make a profit on this Chianti at a dollar a gallon.'"

Last words! Last words are always very important; they are the essence of your whole life. There are people who even at the very end of their life are thinking of money.

When God created Switzerland he asked a Swiss, "What do you want?"

Without hesitation the Swiss replied, "I want a lot of milk!"

And so it was.

After a few days god, curious, asked the Swiss, "Is your milk good?"

The best, my Lord," replied the Swiss. "Try some!"

God tasted it and found it really good. then he asked the Swiss, "Do you want something else?"

Again, without hesitation, the Swiss replied, "Yes, my Lord. Four francs for the milk you drank!"

Even if you come across God, if you are obsessed with money you won't see God at all; you will do the thing that you have been doing your whole life. You will not change just by seeing God – nothing can change you unless you drop the poison yourself. And this happens only when a person becomes really meditative, when all thoughts disappear and he has a clarity to see, when he becomes a seer.

The first poison is sexuality. And when you are thinking in terms of sexuality, whatsoever form your sexuality has taken – it may have become money obsession, it may have become power obsession, it does not matter – when you are thinking in terms of sexuality, everything deep inside you becomes sexual. Your whole life functions as a transforming mechanism for everything, to create more and more sexuality. Whatsoever you see, you see your own sexuality projected – you can't see anything else. You lose all clarity. You become surrounded by your own inner poison; it goes on rising like smoke around you and you can see only through the smoke, and the smoke distorts everything that you see.

A black private and a white sergeant were getting ready to go on leave, when, at the last minute, orders came that the private's leave was canceled. The black man said to the white, "Sergeant, would you please tell my girlfriend what happened so she won't think I ran off with another lady? She will believe you because you are my sergeant."

The sergeant agreed and took the address. When he arrived in town he looked up the house number and it turned out to be a whorehouse in the red light district of town. He went up to the house and knocked on the door.

A large, black madam opened the door. She looked at the sergeant and said, "I am awfully sorry, sergeant, but we do not serve white men here, only black men."

The sergeant answered, "You don't understand, madam! You see, I have got this black private..."

The madam smiled and said, "Well, ain't you the fancy one"

The second poison, anger, arises whenever your sexuality is prevented. Anything that comes as an obstruction to your desires creates anger. You cannot drop anger unless desires disappear.

Many people have asked me how to drop anger, and they don't understand that they are talking of dropping a symptom. Anger is only a symptom. It simply says somewhere your desire has been obstructed: something is coming between you, your desire, and the object of your desire – hence the anger. Anger means, "I will destroy the obstruction!" You cannot drop anger unless your sexuality disappears.

It is not accidental that husbands and wives continuously quarrel and are angry with each other, for the simple reason...the sexuality. They are each other's sexual object, and wherever there is sexuality there is anger. Anger is like smoke. Logicians say, "Wherever there is smoke there is fire." You can say, "Wherever there is anger there is sexuality." When anger disappears, that means sexuality has disappeared.

The disappearance of anger happens only, is possible only, when the root is no more there. You cannot drop your anger; you will have to go to the very roots. Trying to drop your anger will only create new kinds of anger: you will repress it from one side, it will come from another side.

It is because of this well known fact that for centuries no country has allowed its army people to have free sexuality, because if soldiers are allowed to have freedom about their sexuality, if their sex is not obstructed, then they lose destructiveness, then they lose anger, then they are no more angry.

Their sex has to be obstructed in many ways. They have to be deprived of their wives, they have to be kept away from their wives. Not only that: they have to he allowed to see all kinds of pornographic films, all kinds of pornographic magazines; they have to he allowed to come in contact with actresses. When two countries are at war, actresses go to meet and visit the soldiers to encourage them. And what is their encouragement? The encouragement is this: that when an actress comes, a Sophia Loren comes, all the soldiers become sexually aroused. Of course, they cannot do anything about it; that aroused energy turns into anger, it becomes rage. Then they start destroying the enemy, then they are madly in destruction. If they are allowed to have their wives with them on the front, their girlfriends, then they will lose interest in war.

That is one of the reasons why Americans go on losing all wars: their soldiers are the least sexually repressed people; they are not going to win any war. Sexual repression is a must – it creates anger. And when there is so much anger and there is no other outlet, then the only possible outlet is destroy the enemy.

And have you watched? Always it happens whenever an army conquers a country: the first victims are the women of that country; they are raped immediately. Cannot you see the relationship? Were the soldiers fighting for the women? Why immediately, the moment the soldiers enter a city as conquerors, they start raping around as if they were just waiting for the opportunity? There was no opportunity available; now it is available. The first thing is: rape the women. And the second thing is: rob people of their money. The first comes out of anger and the second comes out of greed, but the cause of both lies in the first. Repressed sex will create anger and greed.

You will be surprised to know that any religion that has been teaching to its followers some kind of repression has always helped its followers to become rich. In India, Jainas have become very rich; they are the most repressive people. And something of significance has to he understood about their psychology. Their religion says: Repress sex; *brahmacharya*, celibacy is their goal. And second thing: Don't he violent; so anger is not allowed. Sex is not allowed, anger is not allowed. Now where the energy is to go? Now only the third possibility is left – greed. So all the Jainas have become the greediest persons in this country. They are a small community, very small community – in such a big, vast country they are nothing – but still they are very powerful because they have all the money.

TRANSCENDING THE TRANSCENDENTAL

You will not come across a single Jaina beggar; nothing like it exists. They are not poor people – they cannot be poor; their religion has made it absolutely certain for them that they will he rich. Sex has to he repressed and anger has to he repressed. Now only one outlet is left – greed. Become greedy.

Do you know? The English word "love" comes from a Sanskrit root *lobh*. *Lobh* means greed; it is greed for the other's body. So whenever a person looks sexually at somebody else you can see the greed in his eyes: he wants to possess the other's body. That's why every civilization allows only a certain time limit to see; more than that is thought to be offensive. Somehow a subtle agreement has happened, a deep contract: three seconds are allowed. If you watch at a woman for three seconds, no offense will be taken; it will be thought just casual. But if you watch more, then she will become annoyed. If you go on looking at her, then she will be angry; then you are behaving in an uncivilized way. You are looking at her body with greed to possess, to exploit, to use as a means. And. of course, nobody wants to be reduced into a means, into a thing, into a possession.

The English word "greed" also comes from a Sanskrit word, *griddha*; *griddha* means the vulture. The greedy person has a vulture-like quality, as if he wants to eat the other. And that kind of expression has come into many languages, particularly in French.

I have heard:

A ship wrecked, and a Frenchwoman swam to an island. She was absolutely naked; all her clothes had gone into the sea. But the beach was beautiful, and she was lying on the beach naked, taking a sunbath, thinking "What to do next?" – whether anybody lives on this island or not. There seemed to be no sign of anybody living...

And then suddenly she heard a noise; somebody was coming, a very big man, almost like a huge gorilla. A very small tribe lived there. The tribe was of cannibals, hence very small, because cannibals cannot grow – they start eating each other. And the cannibal was very happy seeing a new food – so delicious she was looking!

He came, looked at her and said, "I would like to eat you!"

And the Frenchwoman said, "Then what you are waiting for?"

The cannibal was puzzled. This was for the first time that somebody has said, "Why you are waiting? For what? Start!" – because in French "to eat" means "I want to make love to you."

Language gives great indications. In fact, when you look at a woman with greedy eyes you want to eat her – or a woman looks at a man...Ordinarily they don't look because they have been taught for centuries not to look at the man; that has become their feminine grace. When somebody says to a woman, "I love you," she looks downward – just to be certain whether he really means it or is just talking nonsense! She does not believe in words, she believes in the body, she believes in the physiology – and the body never lies.

When one has come to deep meditation there is a clarity. In this clarity all the three poisons disappear without leaving a trace behind. And then he perceives only a void.

The first experience of meditation is that of a void, but remember it is a first experience, the first *satori*: one experiences void. But remember, the experience is still there; that's why it is still the beginning, not the end. You experience the void, but the void *experienced* itself becomes something; it is not nothing.

That's why you will come across many Zen stories...

The disciple comes to the master and says, "I have experienced nothing," and the master hits him and says, "Go back and meditate again! You missed!"

"But," he says, "I have experienced nothing! And that's what you were saying – that to experience nothing is what meditation is all about. And I have experienced it!"

But the master still persists: "You go and meditate again – you missed." Because if nothingness becomes also an experience, then it is something. You can experience only something. You have experienced nothingness, but once experienced it becomes an object, and there is a division: the knower and the known. Hence it is the first *satori*.

Ko Hsuan's sutra is tremendously beautiful. He says:

> ...he perceives only a void, but when be contemplates the void...

but when he goes deeper into meditation

> ...he realizes that the void is also void and has become a nothingness.

As he goes deeper, the second satori opens up. Going deeper, he disappears as an experiencer. First the object disappeared, the void was there; but because of the old habit the void became the object. Now the experiencer has also gone. Now there is only nothingness – nobody to experience, nothing to be experienced. This is the second *satori*.

> The void having vanished into nothingness, he realizes that this nothingness of nothing is also nothing...

This is the last possibility of still getting hooked into an experience. You can start rejoicing, that "I have experienced nothing;" then you remain hooked with the first *satori*. You can start rejoicing, that "I have experienced that there is no experience and no experiencer. I have experienced that both are void." It is better than the first, deeper than the first, but somehow the experiencer has still saved itself in a subtle way. It has moved a little deeper – now it says, "I have experienced that there is no experience and no experiencer." You will be hooked in the second satori.

The third *satori* happens when:

> ...he realizes that the nothingness of nothing is also nothing, and when the nethermost nothingness is reached...

And this is the ultimate nothingness; then he does not claim at all. Now if you ask him, "What have you experienced?" he will smile. He cannot say, "I have experienced nothingness." This is *samadhi* – the third *satori*, the ultimate flowering. Now there is nothing left, neither as an object nor as a subject nor as a transcendental subject which transcends both. Nothing is left. Buddha has called it *anatta*, no-self – a state of total nothingness, absolute nothingness. Hence, what can be said about it?

Whenever anybody asked Buddha about his ultimate experience he will say, "Don't ask absurd questions, ask practical questions. Ask how to reach it, don't ask what has happened. It cannot he conveyed."

Lao Tzu says: Truth said becomes a falsehood Truth unsaid remains true: uttered, becomes false.

The Upanishads say: Those who say that "We know," know not.

Socrates in his last stage of life said. "I know only one thing, that I know nothing." But Ko Hsuan will say even that is not right: that is second satori, because he is still saying, "I know only one thing. that I know nothing." Still the statement is there, still the knower is there. According to Ko Hsuan, at least, the statement is wrong. Socrates attained the ultimate *samadhi*, but Socrates is a Greek, he is not a Chinese – he speaks the way Greeks could have understood. He cannot speak in paradoxes, he speaks logically. Hence he says, I know only one thing, that I know nothing."

Ko Hsuan will not even say that; Buddha will not say even that: Lao Tzu will not even say that.

> *...when this nethermost nothingness is reached, there is most truly to be found a deep and unchanging stillness.*

Now for the first time a deep, unchanging stillness prevails. Eternity has opened its doors to you. Now there is no more falling back. You have gone beyond the beyond. You have transcended even the transcendental.

> *In this profound stillness how can desires be begotten? When desires are no longer begotten, then there is essential and unchanging stillness.*
> *Truth is essentially unchanging.*
> *All things in heaven and earth are in essence unchanging.*

So whatsoever changes is only the appearance, what in India the mystics have called *maya*. It is only appearance.

Forms change; the essential truth remains the same. Waves change; the ocean remains the same forever. Once you have

TRANSCENDING THE TRANSCENDENTAL

seen this you are no more in any misery because you are no more in any desire, no more in any dreams. Once you have experienced this you have become part of the organic whole. You have disappeared; you have become the very ocean. You are no more a wave, you are no more a dewdrop, you are oceanic.

To experience this oceanic vastness is the experience of Tao. And the secret is in meditation. And one has to pass through three stages: first satori, the experience of the void; second *satori*, the experience that the void is void; and the third *satori*...now nothing can be said anymore. Now all is silent and still, absolutely silent and still.

The master is one who has reached to this third, one who has transcended the transcendental, one who has gone beyond the beyond Then he has the being of the whole. To be in tune with him is to be in tune with God, with Tao, with truth. To be in tune with him is to be in tune with bliss, with beauty, with benediction.

Just Joking Around

The first question:

Osho,
Could you say something about innocence and ignorance?

The difference between the two is immense; it is as vast as possible. It is the difference between darkness and light, the difference between death and life, the difference between unconsciousness and consciousness, the difference between hell and heaven.

Ignorance is darkness. It is a state of total negativity; it is a state of knowledge – the lowest state of knowledge, the zero state of knowledge. But it is not different from the knowledgeable mind; they belong to the same category. The ignorant person and the knowledgeable person, they are not qualitatively different, only quantitatively different. The difference is that of degrees: the knowledgeable person knows more, the ignorant person knows less. And you can be knowledgeable in comparison to one person and ignorant in comparison to another. Hence it is a question of relativity. Even the most ignorant person may be knowledgeable in comparison to somebody else, or even the most knowledgeable person may be ignorant except his own expertise. The mathematician is ignorant as far as physics is concerned, the physicist is ignorant as far as chemistry is concerned, the chemist is ignorant as far as mathematics is concerned and so on, so forth. All experts are knowledgeable only in one direction and in all other directions they are utterly ignorant.

That's why a very strange phenomenon is well known that the people who are very logical, very argumentative, rational in their particular field prove to be very gullible in other fields. You may find a great scientist believing in Satya Sai Baba. It looks absurd, but it is not so absurd. Deep down that great scientist knows nothing of religion. He is as ignorant or even more ignorant than an ordinary person. The ordinary person knows much more about religion than the great scientist. The great scientist has poured his whole energy into one concentrated field, excluding everything else.

You can deceive a scientist very easily; it will not be so easy to deceive a farmer. The farmer is not a great logician but he knows many things. He is not an expert in any specialized field, but his general knowledge is far more bigger, vaster than the expert. Many great scientists fall victim to all kinds of superstitions.

I have heard the story of a Nobel prize winner scientist. He was hanging behind his chair in his study a horseshoe. Another scientist had come to visit him; he could not believe his eyes, because it is believed by the ignorant masses that keeping a horseshoe hanging in your room is very good. It protects you; it is a kind of supernatural protection. The visiting friend asked the scientist, "I cannot believe my eyes! That you are a Nobel prize-winner scientist...Do you still believe in this nonsense, in this superstition that a horseshoe is protective?"

The Nobel laureate laughed. He said, "No, not at all – this is all nonsense. I never believe in such stupidity!"

The friend was even more puzzled. "Then why you are hanging this ugly horseshoe behind your chair?"

The scientist said, "But the person who has given it to me said whether you believe in it or not, it protects you all the same!"

It is defined that science is an effort to know more and more about less and less. That's exactly what specialization is. If you follow this logic, then the ultimate science will be to know all about nothing; that will be the logical conclusion. If science is knowing more and more about less and less, then where it will end? It will end in knowing all about nothing.

Scientists are very gullible people, and the priests and the so-called saints exploit this opportunity very much. And then they brag about that, "Look, such a great scientist is my follower!" In fact, it is not the scientist who is his follower, it is the remaining part in him which is not a scientist, and which is far bigger than the scientist. Only a small fragment of his being has become scientific – maybe just one per cent of his being – ninety-nine per cent is as stupid or even more than the ordinary people, because the ordinary people don't know more and more about less and less; they know something about everything. You cannot exploit them so easily.

Ignorance simply means you are missing knowlegeability. A little education, and your ignorance can become knowledge. Just a little conditioning, schooling, and your ignorance can be changed into knowledge. There is no difference between ignorance and knowledge; they are interchangeable.

But innocence is a totally different phenomenon. It has nothing to do with knowledge and nothing to do with ignorance either. It is a state of total freedom – from ignorance and knowledge both. It is a state of wonder. It is a very positive state of tremendous awe. When you are full of wonder and awe; when your heart starts throbbing with each beautiful moment that passes by – with the roses, with the marigolds, with the lotuses, with the stars, with the sun, with the moon, with people, with rivers, mountains; when you can experience and feel the mystery of life; when you are so sensitive, so vulnerable, so open that the miraculous can penetrate to the very core of your being, then you are innocent.

The knowledgeable cannot be innocent. It is because of his idea that he knows, his wonder dies. All his answers are borrowed. All that he knows he really does not know, but he carries all kinds of answers, ready-made answers. Because of those ready-made answers nothing surprises him, nothing at all. He can go on amidst this beautiful existence without feeling any joy, any surprise, any wonder, any thrill. Any excitement, any ecstasy. He is almost deaf. He cannot hear the music of the birds singing in the morning, he cannot hear the music of the wind passing through the pine trees. He cannot see the life of the trees, of the grass. He cannot see the beauty of a bird on the wing in the silent infinite sky. He walks without ever experiencing the splendor of the stars. He remains blind. He knows no poetry. His approach towards life is completely blocked by his acquired knowledge, by his accumulated answers. He has a ready-made answer for everything. Before a question arises, the answer is already there; even before the question, the answer is already there. The knowledgeable person never listens to the question. He never tries to go deep into the question itself He hears the question and a process of many answers is triggered in him and he starts answering.

But the man of innocence has no answers. He listens to life in silence. He listens, he sees, he tastes, he smells, he touches. He is very alive. The knowledgeable person is dead, completely closed. He lives in his own grave, that's why he drags. He has to carry such a burden.

The man of innocence dances; he does not even walk. He is very light. And each small thing fills him with the presence of the mysterious. A butterfly and all its colors, a rainbow in the sky, is enough to throw him into deep meditativeness. He knows no answer, he can only *watch* the rainbow. He has nothing to say, he can only see – his seeing is clear – he can only hear.

I used to know a very knowledgeable man when I was a child. He used to stay with my family once in a while. He was a great scholar. He was very much interested in all kinds of details. For example he knew the names of all the trees possible. He used to take me for a morning walk and he will tell me the name of each tree. I have never come across a man who knows the names of all the trees, small shrubs, bushes, all kinds of plants; not only the names – their history, from where they come, what country is their original place.

But one thing I became aware: that he never looked at the trees; he could not. Seeing a rose he will immediately say that, "This rose has come from Iran. The Indian word for rose is *gulab*; the word comes from Persian. That means the flower has come from Persia; it is not of Indian origin. There is no Sanskrit word for *gulab* – naturally, the flower never existed in

India in the Vedic age; it must have come later on. Who brought it first? How it came?" And he will go on and on; he won't look at the rose. And he was thinking that he was teaching me.

I told him that "You are destroying something tremendously beautiful in me. You please stop all this nonsense!"

He said, "What do you mean? Is this nonsense? I have acquired it through my whole life!"

I said, "You have wasted your life, because you don't allow me to see any tree, any plant any flower. If this is going to be so then I am not coming from tomorrow with you. You go alone, and you can say to yourself whatsoever you want to say. I am not going to be a part of this stupid dialogue. I am perfectly happy with the rose, I don't want to know from where it has come. Who cares? I am not interested in its origins. I am not interested in the word. What does it matter whether it has come from Persia or not? The rose is enjoying the morning sun, the morning breeze; it is dancing – and you are talking about Persia and language and grammar and how the word has come into use and when it started for the first time in Indian literature, when it entered Indian books for the first time. Either you have to keep completely silent if you want me to accompany you..."

And he certainly wanted me to accompany him because he was not acquainted with the territory of my town and the roads and the streets and the ways that lead you out of the town. And he wanted to go every day towards a new direction.

I said, "If you want to keep my company then you have to be silent; if you don't want my company then you can keep your knowledge. Then whatsoever you want to do you can do – neither I care about it nor the roses care about it."

He was very shocked. He told my father that, "Your son seems to be against knowledge and this is not a good sign. He should be interested in knowledge. This is the time when one should learn."

My father said that, "He is a little difficult child and I knew it before, that you are taking him for a morning walk – some difficulty will arise."

And he said, "He has given me an ultimatum: either I have

to keep quiet or he is not going to come with me."

My father told him that, "When he says something he means it! You decide."

He knew all the names of all the birds and he was trying to show his knowledge. I said, "You stop all this exhibitionism!"

But he said, "Whenever I go to other places and I talk to other people, they all appreciate that how much I know."

I said "They are just as stupid as you are! But I am not stupid. I am not interested in the names of the birds. I want to enjoy their beauty, of course. I want to see them on the wing, in the wind, moving towards the sun. What tremendous joy! What freedom! If I had wings I would have followed them. But I cannot follow you – you will destroy me."

It was very difficult for him to keep silent, but he had to keep silent because there was nobody else to take him, nobody else who was so acquainted with the territory around the town. I was acquainted with each inch of the whole territory because I always was roaming around, missing from the school. I knew all the hillocks and I had followed the river as far away as possible. I had gone to all the mountains surrounding. I was the best guide for him. Even in the night I could have taken to any direction, to anywhere. But I said that, "You have to fulfill the promise: you keep completely silent."

After two days he said, "This is too much! Many times I want to say something to you because you are ignorant!"

I said, "You leave me as I am. I may look ignorant to you; I am not ignorant because I am not hankering for knowledge. If I am hankering for knowledge then I am ignorant. I am not hankering for knowledge; I don't care a bit about knowledge. I am perfectly happy with my innocence and I want it to leave intact."

Innocence is a positive state of wonder, of awe. No society allows innocence because the society needs knowledge, it depends on knowledge. And I can understand that knowledgeable people will be needed; the whole technology, science, everything depends on them. So it is okay to be knowledgeable when you are working, but leave it there. Don't carry it around twenty-four hours. People are carrying twenty-four hours things which should not be carried twenty-four hours.

When you are a doctor, be a doctor But when you leave your hospital, forget all about medicine, forget all about what you know, forget all about your MDs and FRCS and everything. Just be innocent so that you can again be in that tremendously beautiful state of childlikeness.

Jesus says: Blessed are those who are like small children for theirs is the kingdom of God.

Never for a moment get confused between innocence and ignorance. Many times they appear to be the same but they are not same; they can never be the same. Innocence is a state of meditativeness. When you are silent, aware, open, in contact with the whole, in tune with Tao, then you are innocent.

Lao Tzu is innocent, Buddha is innocent, Krishna is innocent, Jesus is innocent. These are not knowledgeable people. Of course what they have said out of their knowing we have changed it into knowledge; what they have said out of their wonder, we have reduced it into philosophy, theology. That is our work; we have destroyed all that was beautiful in it. We have given it a certain shape, a certain pattern and structure. We have interpreted it, commented upon it, dropped many things out of it. And this happens always.

Just the other day I received a note from Arup, that Sarjano is translating your book into Italian; but he changes many things. He drops few things, he adds few things from his own knowledge."

Of course he is trying to do some good work, his intention is good! He wants to make it more logical, more intellectual, more sophisticated. And I am a little wild type of man! He wants to trim me here and there. You look at my beard! If Sarjano is allowed he will trim it like Nikolai Lenin, but then it will not be *my* beard. He is trying to make it more appealing. There is no doubt about his intentions, but these are the intentions which have always destroyed.

When he was told my message that he has to do exactly as it is: "Don't try to improve upon it. Leave it as it is. Raw, wild, illogical, paradoxical, contradictory, repetitive, whatsoever it is, leave it as it is!" It is so difficult for him. He said, "Then I will not translate. I would rather like cleaning work."

JUST JOKING AROUND

You see how the mind works? He is not ready to listen to me, he would rather like to do cleaning work. Otherwise he has to be allowed to interpolate, to change, to color things according to *his* idea.

Now, whatsoever you will do you will do wrong, because what I am saying is from a totally different plane and what you will be doing will be a totally different effort – it won't belong to *my* plane, it won't belong to *my* dimension. It may be scholarly, but I am not a scholar. It may be knowledgeable, but I am not a knowledgeable person.

Knowledgeable people have their own ways. Just small things they will do...

For example, I had said that Saraha is the founder of Tibetan Buddhism. Now, no scholar will say so decisively. Only a madman can say so decisively because you have to give proofs, you have to give footnotes and you have to make a big appendix in which you have to give proofs. I never give any proofs, I never give any footnotes, I never give you any sources from where...I know only one source – the Akashic records!

So just to make it more appealing, more digestible, he had changed it just a little, not much: that "Saraha can be said to be the founder of Tibetan Tantra, Tibetan Buddhism, *can be said.* Now this is a scholarly way, a legal way, but it destroys the whole beauty of it. It destroys its whole certainty, its decisiveness, its hammer-like quality. And hammers are not supposed to be digestible!

Sarjano, it is not a spaghetti! He is a good cook and makes beautiful spaghetti. I don't know anything about spaghetti, but I know Saraha is the founder of Tibetan Buddhism. And I will not give any proof about it – I don't believe in proofs, I simply *know*. I know Saraha; it is a personal friendship with Saraha. Even if the historians prove something else, I won't listen. I won't pay any attention to them, because I know Saraha.

Just the other day I was reading a beautiful report of the Protestant Church in Germany – again they have published a report! Now, it seems the man who has written a report on me and my work has become very confused, has also fallen in some kind of love with me. Now he is wavering. He cannot refute me totally – seems to be a man of some sensibility – he cannot say that I am utterly wrong, so he has found a middle way. He supports me on everything except Jesus. And he says about Jesus: Whatsoever I am saying *looks* appealing, but it does not come from Christian sources.

Who cares about Christian sources? Burn them all! I am interested in Christ, I am not interested in Christian sources. And I know Christ directly. And when I say I know Christ or Buddha or Saraha directly, I simply mean that I know that state of being. I know Christ can only say this because from such a state of *samadhi* no other statement is possible. This is something inner which needs no proof; it is intuitive. My certainty arises within me. Whether Jesus said it or not is not the question at all. When I quote Jesus...He says I quote Jesus and I interpret Jesus beautifully but my interpretations are very alien to Christian theology. They are bound to be: Christ himself is very alien to Christian theology – what can I do about it?

If Christ comes back he will not be able to recognize Christian theologians. He will not be able at all to understand what this fuss is all about. He was a simple man making simple statements, very direct, immediate. And these people are creating great sophistication around it. For two thousand years they have been going round and round.

But the man who has written it – he is a PhD, a DD, and the most important expert in the whole of Germany about Protestant theology, but the way he has written the report...He has fallen in love with me! Although he is supposed to refute me, but he goes on supporting me in many ways. Of course one thing he has to do to keep his salary intact and his profession, otherwise he will be thrown out of the church immediately, so he says everything is okay except what I say about Jesus. And the reason he gives is that it does not seem to come from Christian sources.

But Jesus never came from Christian sources! There were no Christian sources when Jesus was here. He was in contact with strange people; those people were not Christians. He was in contact with Essenes; those were great mystics. He traveled all over Asia, he traveled to India, to Tibet, to become acquainted with the eastern approach.

Buddha was still very much alive in the air – just five

hundred years before Buddha had died. And Buddha had said that, "My religion will remain alive for five hundred years." It was still alive; the last flames were dying. He must have felt the warmth. He must have contacted Buddhist mystics.

He went to Egypt in search of secret mysteries. That's why Christian sources miss completely many years about his life. They talk about him when he was twelve years old and then suddenly they start talking about when he was thirty years old. And what happened in between? Between age twelve and age thirty there is a long distance, and in a life which lasted only thirty-three years it is almost the whole life. Christian sources have no reference about it, but there are other sources.

In Ladakh there are Buddhist scriptures two thousand years old which say and talk about the visit of Jesus Christ. And they describe the man far more accurately because the people who wrote those things were mystics themselves.

But this has always happened. Innocence will always be interpreted by knowledgeable people and will be destroyed – and with all good wishes, with all good intentions they will do a great harm. They have always done that.

Remember, I am not telling you to remain ignorant; I am telling you to get rid of ignorance *and* knowledge both. They are not different – two sides of the same coin. Throw the whole coin, and then you are innocent.

The second question:

Osho,
What is ambition? To live without ambition seems frightening, like starting a new life up from the beginning.

Ambition is the greatest poison there is. It brings all other poisons in: greed, violence, competitiveness, struggle, a constant state of war with everybody else. It does not allow you any space for love to grow, and your real being flowers only with love. Ambition is against love. Anything that is against love is against you and your real life, your real destiny. And nothing kills love more than ambitiousness.

Ambition means you want to be ahead of others. Ambition

depends on creating an inferiority complex in you. It creates an ill state of affairs; it depends on that. Unless inferiority complex starts existing in you, unless you are full of it, ambition cannot function.

So each child has to be wounded in such a way that he starts feeling a deep inferiority: that others are superior and he has to surpass them, otherwise he is nobody Each child is taught to create a name in the world, fame in the world. Each child is told, "The way you are is not right. You have to prove your mettle, you have to become "somebody" – as if you are not anybody yet!

You are born with a certain flavor of your own, with a uniqueness, with an individuality. Nobody else is like you – nobody else has ever been like you – and nobody else will ever be like you. But this truth is never told to you. You are told, "Become somebody; as if you are nothing. So you have to become, you have to compete to become. And of course then struggle starts, because everybody is told to become somebody, everybody is told to become the president or the prime minister. Now how many people can be presidents and prime ministers? Then naturally there arises a cut-throat competition. Everybody is against everybody else. Life becomes a war, a constant war. In this state there is no possibility of peace, love, silence, joy, celebration. All is lost.

John Lennon, in one of his creative moods, was sitting alone in his room strumming his guitar. While doing this he saw a beetle scuttle across the floor.

"Hello, little beetle," said John, "I named my group after you."

The beetle stopped, turned around and said, "You called your group Eric?"

That was his name. You think only man is competitive? Even beetles are!

This competitiveness in the individuals becomes competitiveness on many planes, on many levels. Societies compete with each other, nations compete with each other. Everybody is trying that "I am superior to you" and naturally nobody will allow that "You are superior to me" – it hurts.

Hence so many wars. In three thousand years there have been five thousand wars. If somebody comes from some other planet and looks at us and our history he will think that this earth is a madhouse. Five thousand wars in three thousand years! What we have been doing except fighting? Our seventy per cent energies go into war; we could have transformed the whole earth into a paradise and we have made a hell of it.

But about everything there is competitiveness.

The NATO forces were on maneuvers in Europe and each country had a separate camp in close proximity to each other.

One day the British camp received a message from the American camp which read: "Please send three dozen condoms, as we have run out of stock. Size: twelve inches long by three inches thick."

The message was taken to the Commanding Officer who did not know what to do with it, so he sent for the Intelligence Officer. "Matter of prestige, old man," said the Commanding officer. "Have to do something!"

The Intelligence Officer returned within the hour. "All taken care of, sir. The motor workshop is making something out of old inner tubes and the silk-screen department is going to do the final touches."

"What are the final touches?" asked the Commanding officer.

"Well, sir," said the Intelligence officer, "on the package will be printed: 'Condoms, Made in England, Size – Medium.'"

This stupidity, about everything! But we are brought up in this way; our whole educational system depends on this foundation – and we think we are creating intelligence. If this stupidity is the foundation of our educational system, how can we create intelligence out of it? We can destroy intelligence, but we cannot create intelligence out of it.

An intelligent person is one who comes to see that there is no need to compete at all. "I am myself, you are yourself I need not be you, you need not be me." A rose is a rose is a rose; it need not be a lotus. The lotus need not become anxious, worried about becoming a roseflower.

The whole nature is in deep peace for the simple reason that competition has not poisoned it. There is no competition at all. The biggest cedar of Lebanon has no ego about it, that "I am bigger than others." Just a small rosebush has no inferiority complex that, "I am so small." Nothing of superiority, nothing of inferiority, but each is unique. This stupidity has entered only human consciousness – human consciousness is being conditioned for it.

You ask me: *"What is ambition?"* It is a feverish state, it is an insane state. It is not healthy. You say: *"To live without ambition seems frightening..."* Of course, because you have lived with ambition for so long, it has become your very lifestyle. You have become identified with it; you don't know any other way of living. To drop it means as if you are dying.

And in fact that's what has to be done by a sannyasin: he has to die in many ways before he can be reborn. And this is a must: that you should die as an ambitious person, you should die as an ambitious mind completely, totally. Not even a trace of ambition should be left in you because even if a small trace is there it will start growing again. It is like a root: it will again sprout, again leaves will grow, again there will be foliage. It has to be completely thrown out of your being.

Yes, it feels difficult, very arduous, almost impossible in the beginning, because we don't know any other way how to live.

People ask me, "If we drop competitiveness, if we drop ambitiousness, then how we will grow?" and trees are growing and animals are growing, and the whole existence is moving and growing – just *you* cannot grow without ambitiousness...

And with ambitiousness what has happened? Have you grown? Something wrong has grown in you; something like cancer in your being has grown. Yes, that cancer will not grow anymore. If you drop all ambition, then a totally new process sets in: your natural growth takes over. Then you are not competing with others; you are simply evolving each moment within yourself, not comparing. If you are playing music and it is beautiful this moment, next moment it will be more beautiful, because out of this moment the next moment it will be more beautiful, because out of this moment the next moment is going to be born – from where else it will come? – next moment you will have a deeper music arising, and so on, so forth. You need not be competitive with other musicians; in fact, if you are competitive with other musicians your inner music will never grow. You may learn more tricks, strategies, techniques how to defeat them, how to go ahead of them by right or wrong means – because competitiveness is so blind it does not bother at all what is right and what is wrong.

Competitiveness believes that whatsoever succeeds is right and whatsoever fails is wrong. That is the only criterion for an ambitious mind: the end makes the means right. For a non-competitive mind there is no question of thinking of others; you simply go on growing on your own. Your roots go deeper into Tao, into nature. Not that other trees have reached deeper so you have to reach – you reach deeper for your own nourishment, you reach deeper for your own enrichment, you reach deeper because your branches can go higher. Only the deeper the roots go, higher the branches reach – but it has nothing to do with others; others are accepted as they are. Nobody takes any note of others.

It is certainly starting a new life up from the very beginning. That's why Christ says: Unless you are born again you shall not enter into my kingdom of God. A rebirth is needed.

A championship competition is held to see who has the largest prick in the world. The theater is filled with people and the gays are screaming with excitement. Up in front sit the judges.

First a Russian comes on stage. He is enormous and the applause is loud. The judges measure him and there is more applause.

Next a black man comes on stage. He is huge and loud applause sounds through the theater.

Then an Italian and a Japanese come forward. Both are measured and receive standing ovations.

The excitement of the crowd is mounting when a dwarf suddenly appears on stage. Everyone whistles and yells for him to leave. But the dwarf raises one arm in the air and asks for silence. Then when all is quiet, he opens his fly and takes out a turtle, shouting, "Just a minute folks...this is just a crab!"

The third question:

Osho,
What do you mean by "live in danger"? Shouldn't man be careful for the future? Please explain it.

To live in danger simply means not to cling to the past, because the past gives you a certain kind of security – because it is familiar, well-known. Maybe it is all misery, all anguish, but still, because it is known and you have lived through it for long, you are well-acquainted with it. You know the ups and downs and you have become accustomed to it. In fact, you have become adjusted to it; now there are no more surprises in it. It gives you a certain comfortable, convenient, cozy feeling. It may be dirty, it may be enclosed like a prison, but still it feels like your home because you have lived so long in it. Even prison cells become people's homes.

I used to visit prisons, one of the governors of one of the states in India was my friend so he allowed me to visit all the prisons in that state. I used to go to the prisons. I was surprised to see that people were perfectly happy. In fact, they started becoming worried when their time for release was coming closer because the outside world looked so alien. Somebody has lived for fifteen years in the prison; now for fifteen years no worry about food, shelter, no problems of any kind. He has been taken care of; now he will have to look again for a job, whether he will get it or not. The unknown is outside the gate. Once he is outside the gate he will be thrown into an unknown world. Fifteen years is a long time.

I asked many prisoners that, "Why you come back again and again? Have you not learned the lesson that you should not do such things again?"

They said, "In fact, we have learned the lesson. Inside is so much security and outside so much insecurity – unemployment, poverty, starvation and all kinds of problems. And once you have been in the prison, problems increase because nobody wants a thief to keep as a servant. People ask, 'Why you have been sent to jail?' People ask, 'Bring certificates, character certificates.' From where we can get character certificates? Fifteen years we have been in the jail! We can get a character certificate from the jailer that, 'This man behaved well, did nothing wrong,' but that will be from the jailer and that is enough proof that nobody is going to give us employment, nobody is going to trust us. A vast unknown faces, outside, so the only thing left for us is to do something again so we are sent back to the jail."

Our whole system of punishment is stupid; it is utterly anti-psychological. Any person who goes to the prison once is bound to come back again and again and again. He creates friendship there, his friends are there, his room is there, his place is there. Even in prisoners a certain hierarchy arises: there are people who are important and there are people who are not so important and there are people who are just nobodies. And it is a small compact world. There are heroes people talk about that "This man has murdered seven people, and you have murdered only one, just one? And you brag so much? And somebody has been stealing for years, and you did your first stealing and ere caught? What kind of thief you are?" There are master thieves; and people start learning from the knowledgeable people, and when they come out they use their knowledge...

When I say live in danger, I mean always remain prepared to move into the unknown. It does not mean that you should not be careful for the future, but the best care that you can take about the future is: first get rid of the past. It is the past that does not allow you to take care of the future. It is the past that goes on repeating itself mechanically and you cannot improve upon your future. If you drop the past completely your future will be totally different and you will start growing. That is the first care you should take.

The second care that can be taken is to live in the present as totally as possible, because it is out of the present that future grows. And you never bother about the present; you think only of the future. You constantly think of the future. Either you think of the past or you think of the future, and both are foolish. Live in the present. That's what I mean when I say live dangerously.

I have come across a story. Somebody like you must have invented it because there is no reference about it anywhere – neither in Christian sources nor in non-Christian sources.

Two women are crying and weeping under Jesus' cross. One says to the other, "I would give everything to be able to take the nail out of his hand!"

After a few minutes, the other replies, "Yes, me too! I would give everything to be able to take the nail out of his hand!"

Jesus looks down and mumbles to himself, "Damn! Those two bitches want me to fall off the cross!"

You become even adjusted to your cross. You don't want even to fall off your cross. Even cross becomes cozy, comfortable – it is your *cross*. You start worshipping it, you start bragging about it.

Just watch people, listen to their stories. They are all bragging about their miseries. They go on magnifying their miseries, exaggerating their miseries, as if they are not satisfied with the small miseries that they are suffering; they want bigger ones. They have become adjusted to their cross.

I am telling you: Leave your cross behind. Jesus says: Carry your cross on your own shoulders. I say drop it, why carry? Forget all about it! And how can you dance if you carry your cross on your own shoulders? No wonder Christians say Jesus never laughed. How can you laugh when you are carrying your cross on your own shoulders? You can only weep, you cannot laugh.

When I say live dangerously, I say don't become adjusted to that which is dead, because if you become adjusted to that which is dead you will be dead. Remain alive, moving, growing, flowing, going into the unknown every moment, facing the unknown whatsoever it brings. There is no other way to grow, and even if sometimes it is painful – and it is painful sometimes, it is rough sometimes, it is very rough sometimes – but out of this pain is born great ecstasy. That is the price we pay for the ecstasy.

The fourth question:

Osho,
After yesterday's discourse a couple of women came up to me and asked if we could get together and tell jokes. I had to say no, that I only joke with one person and that I am not joking around. What to do?

That's a beautiful use of the word *joke*; it reminded me of a joke.

A young man is driving with his girlfriend and on a lonely road one tire gets punctured. So they jacked and jacked and jacked – and then went out to change the tire.

You are using "joke" in the same sense as "they jacked and jacked and jacked"...inside the car! It is good finding new meanings to old words, but you seem to be a little old-fashioned
If you joke only with one person, how long you will joke? You will get bored. And think of the other person too: he will also, or she will also, get bored. A little bit of joking around is not bad! It keeps waters flowing. And joking is not a one-way affair. When you joke with somebody, somebody jokes with you; you can't go on joking alone. Or do you think you can do that? – that you simply lie down and "I will joke alone." You will look very silly. The other has to joke also. So listening to each other's old jokes...it is better to joke around a little so you will learn few new jokes! Then come to the old person and joke in a new way, and she will be thrilled! And by that time she must have joked somewhere else, so she will bring some new jokes. And remember, each person jokes in his own way.
Don't be so old-fashioned – and not in my commune!

It was Easter time and the rooster was curious, hearing all the people talking about Easter eggs.
When the day came he walked into the house to take a look at the famous eggs. To his shock, he saw blue eggs, yellow eggs, green eggs, and a red egg.
Without stopping to think, he went back outside and beat up the peacock!

Now don't be that kind of traditional rooster! It is good to have all kinds of eggs, all colors, multicolors. Then life is more like a rainbow. Otherwise it becomes a drag and dull.

And joking with one person has created monotony – people call it "monogamy." And then slowly, slowly they stop joking because what is the point? – the same jokes again and again...And the women are very sensitive; the moment you want to joke with them they say they have a headache, or the child is growing teeth and the whole day they have been tired, or the cook has left, or the servant has not turned up, or there has been no electricity in the house the whole day. There are thousand-and-one problems. Simply the woman is saying, "Please, no more these jokes. Enough is enough!" She knows you, that you will again joke the same old joke.

A stranger walks into the local pub. The bartender welcomes him and says, "Well, sir, a pint of beer? Or do you prefer a whisky? You are my guest – it is on the house."

"No, thank you," replies the stranger. "I don't drink alcohol. I tried it once and it makes me feel dizzy."

"Well then, I am sure you will enjoy one of my best cigars," the cheerful bartender says, offering him the cigar.

"No, thank you. I don't smoke. I tried it once and it makes me feel sick."

The bartender, still smiling, continues, "Well, come on then, let us play some poker!"

"No, thank you. I don't play poker. I tried it once and lost my money," is the stranger's dry reply.

At this moment a young man walks into the bar and sits next to the stranger. The stranger turns to the bartender and says, "May I introduce you to my son?"

"Hello," says the bartender, "I presume you are his only child aren't you?"

Become a little more contemporary. You are living at least two thousand years back. And don't think this is the way you will ever get into paradise – the paradise has completely changed meanwhile; it is utterly modern. You will look like a fool there, you will look so out-of-date. You will not fit. If you cannot fit here with my commune, which is simply representative of paradise on the earth...We are just trying to rehearsal for paradise!

Four women arrive in paradise; three of them are English and one is Italian. Saint Peter asks the first one, "Have you been an honest woman?"

"Oh yes, sir," she replies. "I have been honest all my life."

So Saint Peter tells an angel, "Take this woman into the pink room!"

The same thing happens to the other two women: they are both sent to the pink room.

Then Saint Peter asks the Italian one, "And you, have you been honest?"

"I never did-a any harm-a to anyone, Peter!" she replies. "I could-a say I was-a honest. I loved love, I loved love more than anything-a else!"

Says Saint Peter to the angel, "Take this one to my room!"

This Moment Is All

The first question:

Osho,
So many times I want to say thank you, but somehow the silence says it so much better than the words.

The really significant things in life can never be said through words; only silence is capable of communion. Words are utilitarian, they belong to the marketplace; hence, when you really want to say something of the heart, you will always find it unsayable. Love cannot be uttered, gratitude cannot be spoken of; prayer is bound to be a deep silence inside you. And this is of fundamental importance to understand, because we are brought up through words with the idea as if everything can be said – and we try to say it. And by saying those things which are not sayable, we falsify them.

Lao Tzu says: Tao cannot be said; the moment you say it you have already falsified it. Truth cannot be communicated, no word is adequate enough, big enough to contain it. It is so vast, vaster than the sky, and words are so tiny. They are good for day-to-day things, utilitarian ends. As you start moving towards the non-utilitarian you start moving beyond words. That's what religion exactly is: transcendence of words and transcendence of the world that belongs to words.

The mind consists of words; the heart consists only of silence, profound silence, virgin silence, unbroken silence. Not even once anything has stirred there, in the very center of your being.

Feel blessed that something arises in you for which words seem to be irrelevant. This is prayer. The prayers that people do in churches, in temples, are not prayers; they are simply expressing their desires. And unless they stop this stupid kind of praying, they will never taste the real nectar of prayer. They will remain absolutely unaware of the transcendental.

Words can be Christian, Hindu, Mohammedan, Buddhist; silence is simply silence. You cannot call silence Christian or Hindu or Mohammedan. It is indefinable. No adjective can be put before it.

Silence is religious. Your so-called prayers are nothing but asking God to fulfill your desires. It is not thankfulness for all that has been already given to you; it is really a complaint. It is a complaint: why more has not been given to you? Desire means complaint, desire means hankering for more – that this is not enough, that you have not been fair to me, that this is unfair; others are having more. Prayer in its truest sense is thankfulness, gratitude, but there is no way to say it. There is no need to say it.

One of the greatest philosophers of this age, Ludwig Wittgenstein, used to say that that which cannot be said should not be said, because to say it is to profane it. To say it is to do violence to it. Saying it is destructive of it. Wittgenstein is not only a philosopher, he is just on the boundary line where philosophy disappears and mysticism begins. Hence, he is one of the most misunderstood philosophers of this age – one of the most profound and the most misunderstood. That is the fate of people who are really deep in their experiencing. Now, what he is saying goes beyond philosophy, it touches something of religiousness.

You say: "So many times I want to say thank you..."

There is no need to say. Whenever it arises in you, it is heard. By saying it you will destroy the beauty of it. Let it remain a communion of the heart to the heart. There is no need to make it a communication from one head to another head. Communication is between two heads; communion is between two hearts. Communion is love; communication is *about* love. And remember, talking about God is not at all concerned with

God. Talking about fire is not fire. Fire need not be talked; it has to be seen, experienced. Thank you, thankfulness, gratitude, love – these belong to a totally different plane of your being. They have nothing to do with the head, they have everything to do with the heart. And there is still a deeper layer than the heart.

There are three planes. First, and the most superficial, is the head. The second, deeper than the head but not the deepest in you, is the heart. You feel like saying, but at the same time you feel that it cannot be said. And the third is the plane of your being. You don't even feel like saying; you become it. Your very being becomes a thankfulness. There is no question of saying or not saying. Feeling that you want to say and cannot say – that too has been left far behind. You are simply thankfulness, now there is no need to say.

When the rosebush is full of flowers it need not utter to the world, need not declare to the world that, "I am beautiful." It is beautiful.

People live in the head. The first jump is from the head to the heart. It is a great jump; it is the beginning of a great pilgrimage. It will prepare you for the second jump and the last jump – from the heart to the being. The heart is just in between. That's why you will feel both a desire to say and also the incapacity to say it. The desire to say comes from the head part of the heart, and the incapacity to say it comes from the being part of the heart. Heart is a bridge between the two: half belongs to the head, half belongs to the being. Hence, the dilemma, hence the dichotomy. From here move towards being, then the whole dilemma disappears, you become a thankfulness. You bloom as gratitude. It is all over you: in your eyes, in your face, in your walk – just the way you breathe, it is there; in the very heartbeat it is there. Now there is no desire to say and no feeling of incapacity to say it.

The journey towards God has only two steps. In two steps only the whole journey is completed. You have taken the first step, now take the second too.

The second question:

Osho,
So many dull and crazy religions once started with a wonderful and enlightened person. Please tell me, will your sannyasins become as dull and crazy as all the other stupid religions? I am afraid to fall into another institution.

It is a significant question. There are many implications in it. Each implication has to be deeply pondered over.

First, have you ever loved a woman? Have you ever fallen in love with a woman? If you have ever fallen in love with a woman, have you thought before falling in love that every woman dies one day? All the women have died before; this woman will also die. Why are you falling in love with a person who is going to die? Prevent yourself. Stop yourself. In fact, have you ever thought that you yourself will be dying one day? Then why go on living? When one has to die, what is the point of living at all? Die right now. Why go on living in a corpse? Because this body will become a corpse one day. It may be sooner or later burned or buried, so why take care of it? Why look in the mirror in the morning? Why clean it? Why feed it? Why you are serving a corpse? But you have not asked these questions. In fact, these questions will make you very uneasy.

Making love to a woman is making love to a future corpse. Even the thought of it will be enough to put you off. But before taking sannyas, all these great philosophical questions arise in you. If they are authentic, then they will arise in other directions also; they will arise everywhere.

Yes, every religion sooner or later will die – that is the nature of things. That is simply the way of Tao, nothing is wrong about it. When your wife dies, it is not that you did something wrong by loving her while she was alive; it was perfectly right to love her while she was alive. And now it is perfectly right not to go on keeping her dead body in the house, otherwise it will stink. It won't allow you to live, it won't allow you...even your neighbors to live. It will become impossible to love this woman now. It was perfectly good to make love to her while she was alive, but you need not be any more concerned with the past. The past is over, now there is nobody inside the body, the soul has left. It is better to bury or burn it, and the sooner you do the better. And you are not doing any betrayal. It is perfectly right. Just as we accept life, we should accept death. Anything that is born is bound to die.

We accept it about people, but we don't accept it about religions – that's where we go wrong. When there is a Jesus walking, alive, a religion grows around him like a foliage growing around a tree – green leaves, flowers, fruits – because the tree has roots. Jesus is rooted in God, hence the tree is alive. Enjoy the beauty of the tree, enjoy the fragrance of the tree. Lie down in its shade while it is hot. Eat its juicy fruits. Don't be worried that one day this tree will die and there will be no more green leaves, no more flowers will come, spring will not have any meaning to it – don't be bothered with that! That is natural.

But about religions we have been doing just the opposite: Jesus disappears, but the corpse – the words, the formalities are carried on. Krishna disappears, the man who danced is no more there; the man who played on his flute is no more there, but we go on worshipping the flute. Nobody knows how to play on it, nobody knows what to do with this flute; because to play on this flute you have to become as empty as the flute so that God can flow through you. This flute had given beautiful songs to the world, because Krishna was simply a vehicle. He had disappeared as an ego, he was totally available to God, he had no will of his own. God was flowing through him. It was God's song.

The words of Krishna are called *Shrimad Bhagavadgita*. Literally it means the song of the God. Krishna is just a singer; the song is of God. He is just a medium. But when Krishna is gone you will go on worshipping those dead words. They are dead! They were alive on the lips of Krishna, they were very alive, very vibrant. They touched thousands of people's hearts. His dance made thousands dance, and blessed were those people who participated in that dance.

But if you had been there you would have stood by the side thinking that, "What is the point of joining into the dance? Sooner or later this man will die, this dance will die. Sooner or later there will be only a silly institution, a crazy ideology, a fanatic religion. Why participate in it?"

You would have been wrong. In fact, we have to learn how to live religions while there is a Jesus, a Buddha, a Krishna, a Zarathustra. And we have also to learn when Zarathustra is gone, how to burn the dead body of that religion, how to bury the dead body – of course, with celebration; of course, with great gratitude. Man has not learned that yet.

He goes on carrying dead corpses for centuries, that's why all religions stink. Only when there is an enlightened master alive, something alive starts happening around him. But when the master is gone, all is gone – the tree is dead. Then there are two kinds of fools. The first fool will be one who does not participate while the dance is happening. The second kind of fool is one who goes on carrying the dead body for centuries. He himself becomes dead under the burden of the past. And the dead body goes on gathering weight, because as centuries pass it collects dust, it collects theology; more and more books are added to it, interpretations are added to it.

Now Gita has one thousand commentaries – these are the very well-known commentaries; I am not counting the commentaries that are not so well-known – just the very famous commentaries, one thousand commentaries. Now the dead word goes on and on accumulating junk around itself, it becomes heavier and heavier. It kills people.

There is a beautiful story in the Indian scriptures. Shiva, one of the Indian gods...He is one of the Indian trinity; just like the Christian trinity there is a Hindu trinity, and the Hindu trinity is far more sophisticated, far more significant than the Christian trinity. The Christian trinity consists of God the father, and Christ the son, and Holy Ghost. And nobody exactly knows who is this Holy Ghost, whether man or woman, homo or hetero – or maybe bisexual. Because if the father is there and the son is there, where is the mother? It looks very childish.

But the Hindu trinity is far more sophisticated. The Hindu trinity consists of three faces of God. The God is one but he has three faces, hence the Hindu trinity is called *trimurti* – three faces of God. One is Brahma, the creator; the second is Vishnu, the maintainer; and the third is Shiva, the destroyer. These are the three aspects of existence: things are created, maintained for a while and then destroyed. And all processes of creation maintenance and destruction are divine; these are the three faces of God.

Nothing is wrong about destruction. Destruction follows creation out of necessity, just as day follows night, night follows day. No other religion of the world has the idea that one day the whole existence will disappear, except the Hindu vision. Hindu vision has this idea that one day the world was created, and anything that is created has to disappear one day. So creation and dissolution: sooner or later, the whole universe will be dissolved back into nothingness. Just as a child is born and then one day he dies, the whole creation will disappear one day.

Now physicists will agree more with the Hindu idea than with the Christian trinity. They have discovered black holes, and black holes are nothing but the possibility from where things disappear into nothingness. And now they are discovering white holes – the other aspect of the black hole – from where things appear out of nothing.

Shiva is the god of destruction, god of death, but even a god of death is created, projected by human mind, and human mind is after all human. You can create beautiful philosophy but something of you is bound to be projected in it.

Shiva's wife, Parvati, died. Now he is the god of destruction, death, but he could not accept the death of Parvati. You see the human element? He took the dead body of his wife, carried her on his shoulders for twelve years around the country in search of a physician. There may be someone – who knows? – a magician, a physician, a miracle man who will revive her. He loved her so much...

Now you cannot carry a dead body for twelve years. The body became rotten, it started falling into pieces. Somewhere the hand fell, somewhere the leg fell – that's how the Hindu sacred places were born. Wherever any part of Parvati fell, one sacred place was born. So there are twelve most sacred places in India. Those places are just graveyards of parts of

Parvati. Unless the whole dead body disappeared...Shiva carried her in search of somebody who can do a miracle and revive her.

Man does not want to believe in death, hence he creates all kinds of stories about miracles. When Buddha dies his religion dies; it is bound to be so. He was the soul of it. Now you can carry the ritual. And remember always, it is the *man* that matters, not the method – never the method, but the man – as far as religion is concerned.

In science it is totally different: the method matters, not the man. Edison may die, that does not matter, but whatsoever methods he has discovered will go on working. They are still working. Einstein has died, but his methods will work; as long as better methods are not found his methods will remain valid. And better can be found only on the foundation of his methods. Without his methods, the better methods cannot be found.

But in religion it is totally different; it is just the opposite. Man matters, not methods. With a buddha his methods are alive. It is his human touch; it is the magic of the man, it is his golden touch. It is his presence that works; but when that presence has left, you can go on carrying the method for centuries – nothing will happen out of it. And you will be very much puzzled, and naturally you will have to find many rationalizations why it is not working; hence the idea of karma. If some method is not working, you have to find some explanation why it is not working. It is not working because of your past karma, because you have done some wrong deeds in the past lives – that's why it is not working. That's all bullshit. The method is not working because the man is not present whose presence is essential for the method to function.

These methods of religion function only when the master is alive. Then *anything* will do. With Patanjali, standing on your head you may become enlightened. Without Patanjali you can go on standing on your head your whole life, you will not become enlightened. In fact, if you had been enlightened before, you will become unenlightened! With Jalaluddin Rumi, dancing works. It is his presence, it is his energy field. The moment you enter his energy field, you have entered into a magnetic world.

And you can see it in many ways in life too.

With a famous doctor, even water given to you may become medicinal – just the presence of the man, the trust in the man works, and can work miracles. But the same will not happen with anybody else. Somebody may imitate him exactly, but imitators won't do.

We have to learn one thing: not to institutionalize religions. When the master goes, let the religion also go. The really religious person will always find living masters. Yes, it can happen. For example, Buddha said, "My religion will live for five hundred years." Why he said that? He said it because he has created few living masters, and he could work it out that how many living masters these living masters will be able to create. It is not very mathematical, just a little guesswork. He could say that, "I can see that at least for five hundred years the chain will continue, but after that there will be only ritual."

Now Buddhists have not heard it. They have not listened to the master. He himself has said that, "After five hundred years there will be only ritual. Only for five hundred years it will be possible. I am creating few living masters who will live after me, and they will give the magic touch to my methods. They will be able to create few living masters, and so on, so forth – but not more than five hundred years. Then slowly, slowly the number of living masters will disappear."

But Buddhism is still alive. Those five hundred years have passed long before. For two thousand years Buddhism has been a ritual: you can go and worship; you can repeat the same formulas, mantras, prayers, meditations, and nothing will happen. Naturally, you will find faults somewhere within you – Buddha cannot be wrong. How can Buddha be wrong? And he was not wrong; you are wrong, but you are not wrong because you have committed some wrong deeds in the past life. You are wrong because you are still carrying something which is dead.

The Pope dies and goes to paradise. At the gates Saint Peter asks him, "Who are you?"

"I am the Pope."

"Never heard of you," replies Saint Peter and locks the gates.

"But I am the Pope," shouts the Pope. "Don't you know me? Ask God and you will see. He knows me well."

Saint Peter goes and tells God: "God, there is a guy here who wants to come in; he says he is the Pope."

"The Pope? The Pope? Ah, yes, now I remember. Call my son Jesus."

Saint Peter calls Jesus and when he arrives God tells him, "Hey Jesus, do you remember that club we created in Rome? – yes, that club we thought about in Jerusalem. Well, do you know? It still exists! Its president is outside the gates."

All the religions become just institutions, and if you fit in these religions then something is wrong with you. No alive person can fit with a dead ritual.

The supply sergeant handed the new army recruit a pair of trousers, and the soldier put them on. They fit perfectly. Then the sergeant handed him a shirt and cap. They too fit perfectly.

"We have a problem here," the sergeant finally said. "You must be deformed."

Otherwise, who has ever heard army dresses fitting somebody perfectly? Unless somebody is really deformed it is impossible. Army dresses are made for the average person, and the average person does not exist. The average person is only a mathematical entity. Have you ever come across an average person? All persons are unique.

The first man who had found the theory of averages was Herodotus. And naturally, when somebody finds something new he becomes absolutely infatuated with it. He was so infatuated with his theory – he was the first man to come across the theory of averages – that one day when he went for a picnic with his family, the wife and six children, the wife said that, "we have to cross the river. You hold one child and take him to the other shore and then come back."

He said, "Don't worry. I will find out the average height of the children and the average depth of the river."

The wife had no idea...the theory was very new. Just on the sand of the river he calculated, he went, he measured the depth of the river few places, he measured the length of every child, and he said, "Don't be worried. Average is perfectly right. No child can be drowned."

He was so confident, he went ahead, child followed, and the wife was at the back. And then one child started drowning, and the wife said, "Look! The child is drowning! What happened to your theory of averages?"

And Herodotus, rather than trying to save the child, ran back to the shore. He said, "Then there must have been something wrong with my calculation; otherwise it is impossible."

Now the river was somewhere deeper and somewhere not so deep, and somewhere it was very shallow. And one child was longer, another was smaller, and the last one was very small. There was no average child, no average height; and there was no average depth in the river either. Rivers and children don't know anything about theory of averages! But the man was mad – mad with his theory of averages.

Army dresses are made for the average person which exists nowhere. It is really very difficult to find the person to whom the army dress will fit perfectly. The sergeant is perfectly right in saying, "We have a problem here. You must be deformed." He had never come in his whole life across such a person. The trousers fit him, the shirt fits him – even the cap. Everything fits him perfectly, as if they are made for him!

In these dead rituals you call religions – Christianity, Hinduism, Jainism, Judaism – only dead people can fit, deformed people can fit, neurotics can fit. And these are the people who would not have fitted with Jesus, Buddha, Mohammed, Moses, no. A totally different kind of people would have fitted with Jesus, Buddha and Moses – the alive people. You have to understand this.

With a Buddha, you can fall into a synchronicity only if you are very alive and courageous, very intelligent, rebellious. But with Buddhism, when Buddha is gone, all kinds of fools will fit, all kinds of dead people will fit.

It is really strange: the same people who would have crucified Jesus are Christians now, and the same people who tortured Mohammed all his life are Mohammedans now. They are not different people. From where you can get different people? From where all these Christians have come? With Jesus there were only very few people, they could have been counted on fingers. What is wrong with humanity? When the man was alive here, when you could have seen him with your own eyes, felt with your own heart, then you turned your back towards him, you killed him; and when he is no more there you worship him. Almost half of humanity is now Christian.

Jesus must be wondering what has happened.

I have heard a story:

In Dostoyevski's *Brothers Karamazov* the story happens. Jesus was very much interested – naturally – that half of humanity has become Christian. He started to think that, "I reached the earth a little earlier...Now is the time! If I had gone a little later, just eighteen hundred years later, I would not have been crucified. People would have worshipped me. They are worshipping the cross, they are worshipping my statues, they are worshipping in my churches all over the earth. Millions of Christians, thousands of priests, monks, nuns, all praying – this is the right time for me. I reached a little earlier. That was not the right time."

So he came back. He was utterly disillusioned. He appeared one Sunday morning...Of course he had chosen Sunday because on other days people are engaged in other things. Sunday they are all Christians – it is a Sunday religion; at least for one hour everybody pretends to be a Christian.

He appeared before the church in Bethlehem. People were coming out of the church, and he thought, "This is the right moment. They will immediately recognize me!"

And yes, they crowded around him, and they started laughing, and they said, "You did well. You managed well."

He asked, "What do you mean?"

They said, "You seem to be a perfect actor. You have done so perfectly your makeup that you look just like Jesus."

Jesus said, "You fools! I am Jesus, I am not acting."

They said, "Don't try to befool us. And if you listen to us, escape before the archbishop comes out; otherwise you will be in trouble. Escape as fast as you can."

Jesus could not believe that these are the people who were

kneeling down and praying to him and calling him Lord, and now he is standing before them and they cannot even recognize him. And they are thinking that he is an actor or trying to befool them. He said, "Maybe these are uneducated people, but my archbishop – he is a great theologian, he MUST recognize me!"

And then the archbishop came, and everybody fell on his knees in respect for the archbishop. Jesus was puzzled. Nobody had fallen on his knees to honor him, and his servant is being worshipped like a god.

And they said, "Look at this man. This is very wrong on his part to pretend to be Jesus Christ. This is irreligious. He should be punished!"

Archbishop looked at him with very stern eyes, and he said, "Young man, come down and follow me. You come inside the church."

Jesus could not believe his eyes. He went in, the doors were closed and he was locked into a small room. The whole day he was there, and he was wondering, "What is going to happen now? Am I going to be crucified again? That time I thought it was because they were not Christians, they were Jews; but now these are Christians behaving in the same way."

In the middle of the night with a candle in his hand, the archbishop came, opened the door, fell on his knees before Jesus and said, "Lord, I recognized you immediately. But I cannot recognize you before others. You are an old disturber, you will create again chaos. Somehow we have managed everything perfectly well. You are no more needed. We are doing everything as you wanted it to be done. You remain in heaven, we represent you here – you are not needed. This is not your work now anymore. We have taken over the work. And if you insist, then I am sorry, we will have to crucify you again.

"So better you escape, because in the morning there will be trouble. I have just come to inform you. I recognize you, and I don't want to crucify you again; but I cannot recognize you before the crowd. You leave right now and never come back again; even though you have promised to come back again, don't come back again. What *we* are supposed to do here? We are your representatives, we are doing your work. You will create chaos, disorder. That's what you did the last time you were here, and again you will do the same. You will disturb our whole profession, our whole business."

This is just a fictitious story invented by Fyodor Dostoyevski, but has tremendous significance. Yes, the same will happen to Buddha, to Zarathustra, to Krishna, to Mohammed, to everybody.

You ask me: *"So many dull and crazy religions once started with a wonderful and enlightened person."*

Yes, that is true, they started always with somebody wonderful, an enlightened person. But when the enlightened person goes, the wonder goes. Then there is only a dead carcass left, skeletons.

You need not remain encased in any old religion. When I am dead, when the people that will become enlightened with me are dead, then it will be of no use. Bury it, burn it, but right now, don't be afraid of the future. That is the work your children may have to do, or maybe children's children. Right now you can drink out of this living water. Right now you can become transformed.

You say: *"Please tell me will your sannyasins become as dull and crazy as all the other stupid religions?"*

Nobody can be an exception. Life lives according to a fundamental law, it follows Tao: nothing is an exception.

So sooner or later the same is going to happen to my sannyasins. But before it happens take the jump. Because it is going to happen one day, you need not prevent yourself from taking the jump into this whirlpool of inner transformation.

You say: *"I am afraid to fall into another institution."*

You must be part of some institution – Christian, Jew, Hindu, Mohammedan, communist, theist, atheist – some kind of philosophy, some kind of religion, some kind of ideology. It is impossible to find a person who has no ideology, no religion, no philosophy. You must be part of some stupid institution already. Becoming a sannyasin will take you out of that stupid institution.

It is not yet an institution. Before it becomes an institution, don't miss the opportunity. Sooner or later it will become, so I will make my sannyasins aware that whenever it becomes an institution...And it can become an institution only when all light goes out. It will not go out with me; I will leave few candles burning. They will again create few more candles.

If Buddha could create a religion that lasted for five hundred years and did not become an institution, naturally I have far more experience. Buddha was born twenty-five centuries before, twenty-five centuries have passed. Since then many religions have been born. Christianity has come into existence, Mohammedanism has come into existence, Sikhism has come into existence, and many small religions have come into existence. I have all that experience. With all that experience I can predict very easily that at least for one thousand years my people will remain alive. But when it becomes an institution, immediately, with no second thought, burn it. Say good-bye to it.

But before that, don't try to find rationalizations for your cowardice. Don't be a coward. Cowards are always finding great rationalizations.

Two friends were talking:
"Your girlfriend, wow! Everyday I see her with a different guy."
"It is not true. Come to The Platter and I will show you."
So the two friends went and saw the girl wrapped around another man.
"So," said one, "are not you going over there to beat that guy up to show her your strength?"
"Wait a while," replied the second; "maybe she will come up with someone else more skinny."

A tavern in Mexico was crowded with Mexicans drinking tequila and eating guacamole, when a big guy in the front punched the counter and screamed, "Is there any brave man who wants to fight with another brave man?"
At first there was a gap of silence, and then a big guy from the back screamed, "Si! Yo! – Yes! Me!"
So the first guy continued, "All right, we have one, and now is there another brave man who wants to fight with this brave man?"

Please try to understand me. Don't wrap yourself into rationalizations, don't try to put meanings into my words which are not my own.

From the outside this place may also look like an institution; that is out of sheer necessity. But it is not an institution at all. To have the experience what exactly it is, the only way is to be an insider. From the outside it has to be an institution, otherwise it cannot function.

I am not an old-fashioned person at all; I belong to the twentieth century. I am absolutely a contemporary. I don't work like Jesus – traveling with few disciples from one place to another, staying under trees, talking to the people in the marketplace. I have learned some lesson, what happened to Jesus. I am not in any way interested to be a martyr, I am not at all suicidal. I am not saying that Jesus was; he was simply not aware. He could not have been aware, because nothing like that has happened before. It had not happened in the whole Jewish history before Jesus, for the simple reason that in the whole history of Judaic religion and tradition, there has never been a man like Jesus. He was the very climax of Jewish intelligence, of Jewish genius. He could not have thought that he will be crucified and within three years his ministry will be finished.

From the outside I don't function like a Jesus, I have my own ways of working. I have learned few lessons from Jesus, Socrates, from Mansoor, from others, and I don't want to repeat the same. My whole interest is to create as many enlightened people as possible, and for that I have to hang around here a little while more. So from the outside you will find it absolutely an institution; but it is not – not at all. That is a facade, it keeps us separate from the stupid people. It keeps us separate from the crowd, so that we can function and work whole-heartedly with those who really want to be transformed.

So don't misunderstand. Anybody who looks at my work from the outside is bound to misunderstand. You can experience it only from the inside, and then you will be surprised that it is a totally different phenomenon. I am not at all interested in creating any institution; I am against all institutions. I have never gone to the office of this commune, never, even for a single visit – and I am not going ever. I have not visited the whole place either. I don't know who are the people who live here, I don't know who lives where. All that I know is my room and the way from the room to Buddha Hall. Except that I know nothing. I don't know anything about the economy of the commune, I don't have a single paise with me. Even if I had, I don't have any pockets to keep it!

It is not an institution at all, and the people who are working here are working out of love for me. They are not paid. They are living in all kinds of difficulties. We don't have space enough – not even space enough to breathe. People are living in very crowded situations, but their love for me is such that they are ready to go with me even if they have to go to hell. In fact, they are in hell – we don't say anything about it; what is the point? Everybody knows – but you will not find a happier bunch of people anywhere in the world, for the simple reason they are here, that they love me – for no other reason, because there is no other reason at all.

They have come from far better societies, more cultured families, more educated backgrounds, richer affluent societies. They have left their beautiful jobs, highly paid jobs just to be here with me. And I am not giving them anything, except my love. It may be the only place in the whole world which is run only through the power of love.

But you can experience it only when you are part of it, when you are a participant; otherwise there is bound to be great misunderstanding. And many people misunderstand, for the simple reason that they come as observers, outsiders, onlookers, watchers. This is not a place to be understood that way; it is a mystery to be experienced.

Majewski was standing in the entrance of a hotel lobby without any clothes on. A policeman grabbed him. "Okay, buddy,' said the cop. "Let us get something to cover you up and go to the station."

"Wait a minute," cried Majewski.

"You can't stand here stark naked!"

"But officer, I am waiting for my girlfriend," pleaded the Polack. "We were up in the room and she said, 'Let us get

THIS MOMENT IS ALL

undressed and go to town.' I guess I beat her down."

You have to learn the language that is spoken here. Don't be a Polack. And the language can be learned only if you dissolve yourself into this tidal wave of sannyasins.

Don't bother about the future. Who cares about the future? This moment is *all*. Live this moment here with me. Taste the joy of it, the celebration of it.

And as long as this place remains a living force, go on inviting people. The moment it dies – and everything dies, remember, sooner or later – the moment it dies accept the death. Then don't try to hide it then don't try to keep the dead body, then don't try to worship it. Then free the people and tell them to go and find living masters somewhere else. Because the earth is never without few living masters. God's compassion is such that somewhere or other there is always a living master, and if you are real seeker you will find him.

But you are trying to simply convince yourself that, what is the point? Sooner or later it will become an institution as if you are going to live forever. What I am creating will die, and you will live forever...You will also die; and one thing I can tell you: this phenomenon that is being created here is certainly going to live longer than you, so why you should miss the opportunity?

Two hippies are sitting on a beach. It is a beautiful night, a warm soft breeze coming from the ocean, palm trees swaying. they are getting stoned on some very good grass; the stars are twinkling, a full moon is shining bright.

Says one to the other, "Ah, that beautiful moon. I must have it. Whatever it costs me, I will buy it."

Says the other hippie, "No you won't. I am not selling it."

Don't go on arguing with yourself. Come out of your sleep, come out of your dreams. See the truth that is alive here, and while it is alive take something out of it, imbibe it, digest it so that you can also become part of a living truth.

And don't wait for tomorrow – only fools wait for tomorrow – because we can be certain only of this moment. It is always now or never.

The last question:

Osho,
Why am I always living in a kind of hell?

It is always your own creation. Whether you live in heaven or hell, you live in your own creation. Nobody else is responsible. Don't throw the responsibility onto God, fate, *kismet*, society, economic structure. Don't throw the responsibility on your past lives, on others. Take the whole responsibility on yourself, because that is the only way to move, to change, to go beyond.

The only cause of hell, the only cause of misery is you and nothing else. Except you, nobody can cause it. And it is not the past; you are creating it each moment.

A construction worker is sitting astride a beam on the twenty-fifth storey of a New York skyscraper which is being built. The lunch hour bell rings and he takes out a box of sandwiches from his lunch pack. He bites into the first sandwich, then grimaces.

"Shit! Peanut butter again!" And he throws it away. He takes a second sandwich and takes a mouthful, then spits it out. "Shit! More peanut butter!" He takes out a third sandwich, and this time eats it with pleasure. Then he digs back into his box and takes out a fourth sandwich. "Shit! Peanut butter!" he exclaims.

One of his work-mates has been watching him and finally says, "How long have you been married now, Mike?"

"Ten years," says Mike, looking up.

"And your wife still does not know that you don't like peanut butter?"

"Don't bring her into this. I made these sandwiches myself."

One goes on creating the hell, and then hates it, and then wants to get rid of it. And even while you are trying to get rid of it you are still creating it. Man is so unconscious.

Two drunkards are talking to each other in a pub.

"My name is Smith," says one.

"That's strange," replies the other. "My name is Smith too. Where do you live?"
"Just across the street."
"Ahh? Me too! What floor?"
"Third."
"Blimey! That's where...where I live too."
At this point the bartender turns to another client, and shaking his head says, "Every Saturday night it is the same thing. They are father and son."

A woman committed suicide by jumping off a ten storey roof onto the sidewalk. She was lying naked on her back when a priest came up and put his hat over the woman's vagina.

A drunk passing by seeing the woman and the hat exclaimed, "The first thing we have got to do is to get that guy out of there!"

Be a little more conscious. Watch how you create your hell. Watch carefully each step, and you will be able to find how you create it.

People only reap the crop they have sown themselves. To become aware of it is the greatest moment in one's life, because from there transformation begins, from there a new life starts.

Take the whole responsibility of whatsoever you are, and wherever you are. This is the first principle of my sannyas: The whole responsibility is yours, don't blame anybody, and don't try to find causes somewhere else. It is easy, and it is the strategy of the ego always to find causes somewhere else, because then there is no need to change. What can you do? The society is wrong, the social structure is wrong, the political ideology is wrong, the government is wrong, the economic structure is wrong – everything is wrong except you. You are a beautiful person fallen into everything wrong. What can you do? Then you have to suffer, and then you have to learn how to tolerate.

That's what people have been doing for centuries – learning tolerance. I don't teach you tolerance; I teach you transformation. Enough of tolerance! Tolerance means you have misunderstood the whole thing. Transformation means you have started to begin – at least the first ray of understanding has entered in you. Now whatsoever it is, watch each step how it comes. If it is anger watch; if it is sexuality, watch; if it is greed, watch – the three poisons of Ko Hsuan. And through watchfulness you will be able to get rid of them. In fact, through watchfulness they simply start disappearing.

I Really Mean Business

The first question:

Osho,
Tao is greater than mind. Then why do we keep choosing the mind instead of flowing with the Tao?

It is precisely because of that. Tao is so vast that one is afraid to lose one's identity in it. We are like dewdrops and Tao is like an ocean. The dewdrop is afraid, very much frightened to get closer to the ocean – one step in the ocean and he will be lost forever. He wants to cling to his identity; howsoever small, howsoever tiny, howsoever mediocre, but it is *his* identity, it is *his* personality. He is only because he is separate from the ocean.

That's the way of the ego: the ego can exist only in separation. Separation creates misery because you become uprooted from the whole, but one is ready to suffer misery rather than to die and disappear into absolute bliss. People only talk about bliss, nobody really wants to be blissful. They talk about bliss as if they can remain the same and bliss can be added to them as they are. They want bliss also to be a kind of new possession so that their ego can feel more enhanced, more defined, more precious, more enriched.

But as the ego becomes more defined you become smaller. As you become smaller you become miserable because you start feeling suffocated, you start feeling closed from all the sides. Your prison cell becomes smaller and smaller – even to exist in it becomes impossible. But people are ready to suffer all kinds of misery, they are ready to sacrifice everything for the ego.

That's why we cling to the mind. Mind is nothing but the process of the ego, the functioning of the ego. Mind is the boundary between you and the whole. It is a wall, not a bridge – no-mind is the bridge. Hence the emphasis of all the awakened ones to move from mind to no-mind. The ego can exist only if you remain in constant fight; a continuous struggle is needed, because it is a false entity. You have to maintain it; it is not something spontaneous, it is not something natural that can exist on its own. It needs competitiveness, it needs conflict; it needs all kinds of jealousies, possessiveness, hatred, war. It can exist only with all that is wrong.

Ego represents the unhealthy state of our being. It is assertive. To relax is against the ego, to be non-ambitious is against the ego. Just a moment of relaxation is enough and you will have the taste of Tao, because it is always there, it is never lost. You go on creating the walls, but all walls crumble in a split second. Hence, wherever it happens, in whatsoever situation it happens, you become frightened of that situation.

People have become afraid of love for the simple reason because love is the most potential force in existence – when the window in Tao opens on its own accord. Love means the wall disappears, the wall is no more, and the bridge arises. Of course it happens only between two persons, but even to let it happen between two persons gives you such joy, such orgasmic glow, such tremendous experience of the splendor of life that the ego is afraid.

The ego has created false substitutes for love. The ego is perfectly ready for marriage, but not for love. Marriage is a legal institution, a social institution produced by the cunning mind, by the cunning priests, by the vested interests. Love is natural. Love is dangerous for the ego. If love is allowed you will start tasting little bits of Tao, but that taste will create in you a longing to have more of it. It is so sweet, it is so exquisite, it is so beautiful! Then you will be ready to sacrifice all nonsense that goes with the ego. You will be ready to disappear into the whole.

It is love that will give you the courage to take the ultimate jump – first with a single person...But once the experience is there you cannot step back, you will have to go ahead; you cannot go back. First it is with a single person, but you cannot stop the process now. It is so ecstatic that if it is so beautiful with one single person, how much it will be with the whole...!

A Buddha is one who is in an orgasmic relationship with the whole. Tao is the ultimate orgasm, not between two individuals but between the part and the whole, between the dewdrop and the ocean. But the dewdrop has to disappear, but it loses nothing.

Our all fears are unfounded; they are rooted in ignorance, but ego exploits the ignorance. Hence all societies have distorted the natural flow of love, because it can open the floodgates and then it will be uncontrollable. It is better to give people a false substitute. Marriage is that substitute. Hitherto, for five thousand years, man has lived with marriage *and* misery.

You are not allowed to experience beauty. Your minds are from the very beginning distorted, channelized towards utilitarian ends. You are taught mathematics, you are taught geography, history. Now history is all bunk, utterly useless. Why go on reading about the ancient idiots? For what purpose? It is better to forget all about them. Why bother about Genghis Khan, Tamerlane, Nadir Shah, Alexander, Napoleon? For what? What these people have given to human consciousness? They are like poisons; they have stopped in every possible way human progress, human evolution.

And in your history books you will not find names of Lao Tzu, Chuang Tzu, Lieh Tzu, Ko Hsuan – not even in the footnotes. And these are the people who are the real foundations of human consciousness, these are the people who are the real hope. But you will not find their names even mentioned; on the contrary, historians will always create doubt in you whether Jesus ever existed, whether Krishna is a historical person or just a myth, whether Mahavira was a reality or just a fiction; did Buddha really walk on the earth or has been a projection of our dreams, of our desires?

Sigmund Freud says that these people are wish-fulfillments. We want that there should be people like these, but they have not really existed and even if they have existed they have not existed the way we have described them. That was the cause of the rift between Freud and his disciple Carl Gustav Jung; the rift was of tremendous significance. Freud is very pragmatic; Jung is far more poetic. Jung has tremendous trust in mythology and has no trust in history. And I absolutely agree with Jung about this.

All the mythologies of the world are closer to truth than your so-called histories. But we teach our children history, not mythology. We teach them arithmetic, not poetry. And the way we teach a little bit of poetry – we teach it in such a way that they become so fed up and bored with it that once the student leaves the university he will never read Shakespeare again, he will never look at Milton's works again. The very names of Shakespeare, Milton, Kalidas, Bhavbhuti will create a kind of nausea in him. The professors have tortured him so much behind these names that he is finished forever. His interest has not been encouraged, he has not become more poetic; he has lost all interest in poetry. He has not been supported to be creative, he has not been helped to learn how to poetize.

The scholars are so clever in destroying all that is beautiful by their commentaries, interpretations, by their so-called learning. They make everything so heavy that even poetry with them becomes non-poetic.

I myself never attended any poetry class in the university. I was called again and again by the head of the department, that 'you attend other classes, why you don't come to the poetry classes?"

I said, "Because I want to keep my interest in poetry alive. I love poetry, that's why. And I know perfectly well that your professors are absolutely unpoetic; they have never known any poetry in their life. I know them perfectly well. The man who teaches poetry in the university goes for a morning walk with me every day. I have never seen him looking at the trees, listening to the birds, seeing the beautiful sunrise."

And in the university where I was, the sunrise and the sunset were something tremendously beautiful. The university was on a small hillock surrounded by small hills all around. I have never come across... I have traveled all over this country; I have never seen more beautiful sunsets and sunrises anywhere. For some unknown mysterious reason Sagar University seems to have a certain situation where clouds become so colorful at the time of sunrise and sunset that even a blind man will become aware that something tremendously beautiful is happening.

But I have never seen the professor who teaches poetry in the university to look at the sunset, to stop even for a single moment. And whenever he sees me watching the sunset or the sunrise or the trees or the birds, he asks me, "Why you are sitting here? You have come for a morning walk – do your exercise!"

I told him that, "This is not exercise for me. You are doing exercise; with me it is a love affair."

And when it rains he never comes. And whenever it rains I will go and knock at his door and tell him, "Come on!"

He will say, "But it is raining!"

I said, "That's the most beautiful time to go for a walk, because the streets are absolutely empty. And to go for a walk without any umbrella while it is raining is so beautiful, is so poetic!"

He thinks I am mad, but a man who has never gone in the rains under the trees cannot understand poetry. I told to the head of the department that, "This man is not poetic; he destroys everything. He is so scholarly and poetry is such an unscholarly phenomenon that there is no meeting ground between the two."

Universities destroy people's interest and love for poetry. They destroy your whole idea of how a life should be; they make it more and more a commodity. They teach you how to earn more, but they don't teach you how to live deeply, how to live totally. And these are the ways from where you can get glimpses of Tao. These are the ways from where small doors and windows open into the ultimate. You are told the value of money but not the value of a roseflower. You are told the value of being a prime minister or a president but not the value of being a poet, a painter, a singer, a dancer. Those things are thought to be for crazy people. And they are the ways from where one slips slowly into Tao.

Tao is certainly greater than mind – Tao is greater than

everything. Tao is God, Tao is the whole. But we are very much afraid of losing ourselves, and we keep on feeding our egos in thousand-and-one ways.

We are doing two things in our life: closing all windows and doors to the sun, to the moon, to the stars, to the wind, to the rain, to the birds, to the trees, to love, to beauty, to truth. We are closing all the windows, we are creating a grave around ourselves with no doors and no windows. We are becoming Leibniz monads, windowless capsules. Our life is encapsulated. That is one part that we go on doing. And the second part is to go on making the walls thicker and thicker. That is done by competition, ambition: have more and more; whether you need or not, that is not the point at all. Do you think the richest people in the world need more money now? They have more than they can use, far more. But the desire for more does not stop, because it is not a question that they need money; the question is to go on making the walls of the ego thicker and thicker. They are continuously in competition with each other. Competition creates conflict. Conflict keeps your ego alive.

A beatnik was boppin' down the sidewalk just a-poppin' his fingers and feeling good, when a Jaguar pulled up at the intersection.

"Hey, daddy cool, wanna drag?" said the beatnik.

"Sure," laughed the sports car driver, amused.

The light turned green and off they shot, the beatnik in the lead, running like hell. The driver was amazed! He looked at his speedometer: twenty, thirty, not until forty miles per hour did he finally overtake the beatnik.

Then he looked in his rearview mirror and noticed that the beatnik had suddenly disappeared. Concerned, he went back to find him lying in the ditch all bruised and battered.

"Hey," said the man, "you were doing great: I could not believe it – what happened?"

"Like man," groaned the beatnik, "I mean, you ever had a sneaker blow out on you at forty-five miles an hour?"

One has to decide one thing once forever: whether one wants to live the life of the ego, which is more like death than like life, or one wants to live the life of Tao, which is death in a sense and resurrection in another sense. It is both a crucifixion and a resurrection. The dewdrop disappears, but it becomes the ocean. It loses nothing, it only gains.

Sannyas means that you have decided to live the life of Tao, that you will not cling to the mind, that you will let it go, that you will not nourish it anymore, that you will not support it in any possible way, that you will go on finding how you have been supporting it and withdrawing your support. When all supports are withdrawn it falls on its own accord. And the moment the ego falls and disappears is the greatest moment in life. That's the moment of enlightenment, the moment of awakening, the moment when you become a Christ or a Buddha or a Krishna.

The second question:

Osho,
Are you absolutely against intellect? Should one never use one's head at all?

I am not absolutely against intellect. It has its uses but they are very limited, and you have to understand their limitations. If you are working as a scientist you will have to use your intellect. It is a beautiful mechanism, but it is beautiful only if it remains a slave and does not become the master. If it becomes the master and overpowers you then it is dangerous. Mind as a slave to consciousness is a beautiful servant. Mind as a master of consciousness is a very dangerous master.

The whole question is of emphasis. I am not absolutely against intellect – I use intellect myself, how I can be against it? Right now, talking to you, I am using it. But I am the master; it is not my master. If I want to use it I use it. If I don't want to use it, it has no power over me. But your intellect, your mind, your thinking process continues whether you want or not. It does not bother about you – as if you are nobody at all – it goes on and on; even when you are asleep it goes on working. It does not listen to you at all. It has remained in power for so long that it has forgotten completely that it is only a servant.

When you go for a walk you use your legs. But when you are sitting there is no need to go on moving your legs. People ask me, "Osho, for continuously two hours you go on sitting in the same posture. You don't even move your legs once." Why should I move? I am not walking! I know you, because even if you are sitting on your chair you are not really sitting. You are moving your legs, changing your positions, postures, doing thousand-and-one things, tossing and turning – a great restlessness.

The same is true about your mind. If I am talking to you I am using the mind. The moment I stop talking my mind stops too, immediately! If I am not talking to you my mind has no need to go on working, it simply goes into silence. That's how it should be. It should be natural. While asleep I don't dream; there is no need. You dream only because so much work has been left undone in the day that the mind has to do it. It is overtime work – you have not been able to finish in the day.

And how can you finish anything? You are doing thousand-and-one things simultaneously. Nothing is ever finished; everything remains incomplete – and remains incomplete forever. You will die, but nothing will be complete. Not even in a single direction your work will be complete, because you are running in all the directions, you have become many fragments, you are not integrated. The mind is dragging you into one thing, the heart is dragging you into another, the body wants you to go somewhere else, and you are always at a loss whom to listen. And the mind is also not one, you have many minds – you are multipsychic. There is a crowd of minds in you. There is no unity, no harmony. You are not an orchestra – nothing is in tune; everything is going on its own; nobody listens to anybody else – you simply create noise not music.

Intellect is good if it functions as a servant of the whole. Nothing is bad if it is in its right place and everything is wrong if it is in the wrong place. Your head is perfectly good if it is on your shoulders. If it is somewhere else then it is wrong.

Working as a scientist, intellect is needed. Working in the marketplace, the intellect is needed. Communicating with words, talking to people, the intellect is needed. But it is a very limited use. There are far greater things where intellect is not needed at all. And where it is not needed it goes on functioning there, too; that's the problem. You should be capable...a meditator becomes capable, he becomes very fluid, flexible, he does not become idiotic. He uses his intellect, but he uses his intuition too – he knows that their functions are different. He uses his head he uses his heart too.

I used to stay in Calcutta in the house of a High Court judge. His wife told me that, "You are the only person my husband has any respect for. If you say something he will listen, otherwise he won't listen to anybody. I have tried my best but I have failed. That's why I am telling it to you."

I said, "What is the problem?"

She said, "The problem is becoming bigger and bigger every day. He remains a judge twenty-four hours. Even in the bed with me he is a judge – as if he expects me also to say 'Your Honor'. With children also he behaves as if they are criminals. With everybody! We are tired. He never gets down! He carries this role continuously; he never forgets. It has gone into his head."

And she was right – I knew her husband.

It is good to be a judge when you are in the court, but by the time you leave the court...It is only a function to be a judge, you are a functionary; you don't become a judge – that is not your being! But we get confused; it becomes your being.

He carries it home, then he starts behaving the same way with the wife, with the children, with everybody. The wife was afraid of him, the children were afraid of him. The moment he entered the house there was fear everywhere. Just a moment before, the children were happily playing, enjoying. They will suddenly stop, the wife will become serious. The house will immediately turn into a court.

This is the state of millions of people: they remain the same, they carry their office home.

Your intellect is needed, your head has its own function. God never gives you anything without any reason. Head has its own beauty, but it should be in its place. There are far greater things which are beyond the reach of the head, and when you are moving into those realms you should put the head aside. You should be capable of that. That's flexibility, that is intelligence. And remember never to get confused between intellect and intelligence.

Intellect is only a part of intelligence. Intelligence is a far bigger phenomenon, it contains much more than intellect, because life is not only intellectual, life is intuitive, too. Intelligence contains intuition.

You will be surprised to know that many great discoveries have been done not by intellect but by intuition. In fact, all the great discoveries have been done by the intuition.

Something far more deeper exists in you. You should not forget it. Intellect is only the periphery, the circumference, it is not the center of your being; the center of your being is intuition.

The word *intuition* is worth understanding. Intellect needs tuition, it has to be taught. Hence the schools, colleges, universities, they all give you tuition. Intuition needs no tuition, it is your inner world; it is something given by God as a gift – you bring it with yourself.

When you put your intellect aside, your head aside, then something deeper inside you starts functioning which is incomprehensible from the periphery. Your center starts functioning, and your center is always in tune with Tao. Your circumference is your ego, your center is in tune with Tao. Your center is not yours, it is not mine; the center is universal. Circumferences are personal – your circumference is your circumference, my circumference is my circumference – but my center and your center are not two things; at the center we all meet and are one.

That's why religion comes to realize about the oneness of existence – because it depends on intuition. Science goes on dividing, splitting. It reaches to the minutest particle, called it the electron. The world becomes a multiplicity, it is no more a universe. In fact, scientists should stop using the word *universe*, they should start using a new word, *multiverse*. "Universe" has a religious tone – "universe" means one. Religion reaches to one; that is the experience of the center. But the center can function only when you move from the circumference to the center. It needs a quantum leap.

You say: "Should one never use one's head at all?"

I have not said that. I am talking against the head only because my work is religious.

There was a nymphomaniac whom nobody could satisfy. Men from all over the world did their best, yet failed. When Machista came, the two went into a room for five hours...but when he finally came out he was totally exhausted, an absolute wreck. He had to admit failure.

Tarzan too made an attempt. He was brought all the way from the jungle to try. Lots of people waited outside for hours, thinking that he would surely make it, but when he came out he just muttered: "That woman is a wonder! Nobody can do it!" and disappeared.

More and more ambitious men came with high hopes – still, it did not happen. Then one day this little Jewish tailor, whose shop was on the street corner, passed by. He was curious to know what it was all about, and even though most of the crowd thought such matters were not for him, they told him. To their great surprise he said immediately, "I will do it!" So just for a laugh, they let him go in.

Fifteen minutes later he and the lady came out, hand in hand, beaming, smiling from ear to ear. There was no need to say anything. It was a success.

"What's the trick, how did you do it?" everyone wanted to know.

"Well, there are situations when you have got to use your head," he said nonchalantly.

Get it?

The third question:

Osho,
Is Tao a synthesis of the paths of love and awareness?

Tao is not a synthesis in the sense we understand the word. It is not synthesis in the sense Assagioli uses the word *psychosynthesis.*

The ordinary meaning of the word *synthesis* is making two

opposites meet, creating a certain meeting ground between the two opposites. It is not synthesis in that sense. It makes no effort to create that kind of unity. But it is a synthesis in a very different meaning, in a very higher sense, in a totally different dimension. It is transcendence of the paths of love and awareness, it is transcendence of the opposites. And whenever the opposites are transcended synthesis happens on its own accord. But you have to understand the difference.

Assagioli's synthesis is very poor; it has no depth, it cannot have – it is mind effort. It is far poorer than Sigmund Freud's analysis for the simple reason because mind is very efficient in analyzing things; mind is incapable of synthesizing things. That's why, although Assagioli is trying to do something far more important than Sigmund Freud...but he fails. If you study both, Sigmund Freud looks like a genius. Assagioli looks just a pigmy by his side.

And, let me emphasize again, he is trying to do something far bigger, far more important than Sigmund Freud, but Freud succeeds because he is doing the right kind of work that the mind is capable of doing. Assagioli is trying to do the same thing as Tao but through the mind. Mind is *not* capable of synthesizing. Tao does it from a totally different dimension: it goes beyond mind, it goes into no-mind. And when you reach into no-mind synthesis happens – not that you have to do anything about it.

Assagioli's synthesis is man-made, man-manufactured. Hence it is more like a hotchpotch, somehow trying to make two opposites meet, but they are unwilling to meet; forcing them to meet, but basically, because they are opposites, they cannot meet. And he is using the mind which cannot create synthesis, which is capable only of analysis.

Tao uses meditation, not mind. It is not interested in synthesis at all. It simply moves beyond the mind, and then synthesis comes like a shadow. You can see it happening here.

For example...Take a more contemporary example. Just few years before Mahatma Gandhi tried a great experiment of synthesizing all the religions. He utterly failed. It was bound to happen because he was trying to manufacture synthesis, and synthesis cannot be manufactured. He was trying to do it through the mind. He knew nothing of meditation, he never tried meditation. In the name of religion, all that he knew was prayer – and prayer is of the mind; it is not meditation, it is talking to God. Just as you talk with others you can talk to a God, who may be just imaginary, who is in fact imaginary, because there is no person there.

Prayer is a dialogue, dialogue between you and an imaginary God. Meditation is silence – no dialogue, no monologue either.

Gandhi knew nothing of meditation, but he tried hard to create a certain facade of synthesis. What you can do through the intellect?

Basically he was a Hindu and he remained a Hindu all his life, to the very end. He calls Bhagavadgita his mother, but he never calls Koran his father – not even an uncle. Although he talks about that the teaching is the same, but the way he manages is absolutely political – clever, cunning, but not authentic. It is a mind effort, it cannot be authentic. He does it well. What he does is: whatsoever he finds in Koran, in Bible, in Dhammapada, which is in agreement with Gita, he immediately picks it up, and he says, "Look! All the religions teach the same thing."

But there are many things which go against Gita in the Bible, which go against Gita in the Koran, in the Dhammapada. He does not take any note of them, he ignores them; he knows he will not be able to manage, to cope with them, so his synthesis is bogus. In fact, he reads Gita everywhere; wherever he can find Gita echoed, he immediately says, "Look! They are talking the same thing."

But what about the differences? What about the totally opposite standpoints? For example, Koran does not believe in non-violence. Mohammed never believed in non-violence; he himself carried a sword always, he fought many wars. And Gandhi believes in non-violence But Koran is a big book; you can find few pieces from here, from there which can support love, compassion, kindness, sympathy, and you can use them as if Mohammed is supporting non-violence.

Mahavira supports non-violence, Buddha supports non-violence; even Krishna in Gita does not support non-violence. Then Gandhi does a political trick again. He says the war in which Gita was spoken for the first time, the great war called Mahabharata, in which Arjuna became aware of the fact that millions of people will die and the whole thing seems to be useless – just for the power, for treasures, for kingdom, to kill so many people...A great desire to renounce the world arose in him. And he wanted to renounce, and he said, "It is better I should go to the mountains, become a sannyasin," and Krishna persuades him to fight because "That is your duty. God wants you to fight. Surrender to God's will; don't bring your own will in, don't bring your mind in. You be in a let-go and let God function through you."

Arjuna argues in many ways, but finally Krishna wins him over, convinces him of the necessity of war, because, he says, "This is the war of right against wrong, of religion against irreligion, of light against darkness, of divine forces against evil forces."

Now Gandhi played a trick. He said that this war is only a metaphor, it never happened in reality, it is not historical. It is really the inner war in man between the forces of evil and the forces of God, it is the inner war between darkness and light. And Krishna is saying to Arjuna, "Don't escape from the inner war – fight it and win over the darkness."

Now this is a very cunning strategy. Nobody before Gandhi has ever said that the war between the Pandavas and the Kauravas was just a metaphor. For five thousand years, thousands of commentaries have been written on Gita; nobody has said that it is a metaphor, it has always been known as a reality. But Gandhi has to call it a metaphor, otherwise he will not be able to synthesize religions. And Jainism and Buddhism are two of the most important religions – they have to be incorporated.

And Jesus also creates many troubles, because Jesus goes into the temple of Jerusalem, becomes very angry, takes a whip, hits the money-changers, turns their boards, throws them out of the temple. Now, a non-violent person cannot be so angry. If Gandhi was asked, he will say, "Go for a fast. Sit in front of the money-changers and do a fast unto death unless they stop money-changing in the temple. That will be the non-violent way to transform their hearts." But taking a whip in your hand and hitting them and turning their boards and throwing them out of the temple does not seem to be very non-violent.

He never talks about it. He drops the whole matter. He only talks about Beatitudes: "Blessed are the meek for theirs is the kingdom of God." But Jesus does not seem to be so meek. This man is meek who is turning money-changers' boards and throwing them out of the temple? Is he meek? Can you call him meek? He is a warrior. He cannot tolerate such nonsense in the temple. He said, "You have polluted the house of my father. Get out from here!"

Gandhi chooses only pieces and then makes a hotchpotch which he calls synthesis of all religions. It never happened. Neither the Mohammedans were convinced with him, nor the Hindus. He could not even convince Hindus – he was a Hindu – and he was murdered by a Hindu. He could not convince Hindus. He could not convince Jainas either, because they continuously believed that Krishna is not a good man.

In Jaina mythology Krishna is thrown into seventh hell for the simple reason because he distracted Arjuna, who was going to renounce war. He forced him, persuaded him, convinced him, seduced him by beautiful logic – silenced him somehow – to fight. And millions of people died. Who is responsible for all this violence, for all this blood? He is responsible – more responsible than Arjuna. Jainas have never forgiven him; not even after Gandhi a single Jaina has written a book in which Krishna is forgiven or accepted. What to say of Krishna? Jainas don't even agree with Buddhists and their nonviolence, Buddhists don't agree with the nonviolence of the Jainas. They both are non-violent, but their nonviolences are different.

Jainas say, "Don't kill. Don't eat meat." Buddha has said, "Don't kill, but meat you can eat if the animal has died on his own accord – then what is wrong in eating the meat of the animal?"

Now that is a big problem between Jainas and the Buddhists. And I think that Jainas are right in a way. Logically Buddha is right, that killing is bad – "Don't kill animals. They have life, as much life as you have, and they want to live as long as you want to live. Don't kill them. But when an animal has died, why waste his meat? It can be used as food. Its skin can be used, its meat can be used, its bones can be used. They should be used. Why waste them?" He seems to be very pragmatic; he was a pragmatic man.

But Jainas are also right. They say that once you allow that meat-eating is not bad, then who is going to decide whether the animal has died on his own or not?

And that's exactly what has happened: in China, in Japan, in Korea, in Burma, in the whole of Asia, Buddhists eat meat. So many animals don't die every day on their own accord! All the five-star hotels in the whole of Asia, from where they get the meat? And if this meat comes from natural death of the animals, then why so many butchers exist in Buddhist countries and so many butcheries? – for what reason? Every hotel in Buddhist country keeps a signboard that, "Here only that meat is served which comes from a naturally dead animal – one who has died a natural death."

Man is so tricky that he will find a way; if you give him just a little loophole he will find a way out. No loophole should be given, that was Mahavira's emphasis.

Gandhi could not convince anybody, but here you are seeing a synthesis happening on its own accord. And I am not interested in synthesizing anything. I never talk about synthesizing religions – but it is happening. Here you will find all religions, people belonging to different religions. Nobody bothers who is a Jew, who is a Mohammedan, who is a Hindu, who is a Jaina, who is a Buddhist, who is a Parsi; nobody takes any note of it.

A synthesis is happening. It is not being manufactured; it is happening through meditation not through mentation. This is true synthesis. It is happening through transcendence. When you meditate you go beyond the mind. When you go beyond the mind you are no more a Christian, no more a Hindu, no more a Jaina, no more a Jew. You are simply a consciousness, a pure consciousness, a mirror-like clarity. That clarity is true synthesis.

You ask: "Is Tao a synthesis of the paths of love and awareness?"

In a sense, no; in a sense, yes.

The fourth question:

Osho,
I am deeply interested in your works, but still I am afraid of taking sannyas — why?

Bavasimhan,
Sir you have never been here — the question has come by post — what do you know about my works? You have never participated in what is going on here; you don't have any direct experience. And what is happening here is not an abstract philosophy, it is a very concrete experience. Hence you must be interested in my *words*, not in my works. You must be reading my words — and my words don't contain me, or my work. They only contain invitation to come here, to be here. They are just invitations, nothing else. They cannot carry my truth to you. You have to be here to be with me, to live with me. And you have not come here yet.

I have received many questions from Bavasimhan, many times. This is for the first time I am answering him. But all his questions have come by the post — he lives somewhere in Madras; it is not that far away. But it must be fear that is preventing you — the fear of being here, the fear that if you are here there is every possibility that you may take the jump into sannyas. It is almost impossible to be here and not to become a sannyasin, unless you are absolutely dead, insensitive, dull; unless you have such a mediocre mind that you cannot understand; unless you are so much prejudiced already that you have arrived at all the conclusions; unless you are so much knowledgeable that you think there is nothing more left to know and learn, sannyas is bound to happen. That fear is preventing you from coming here.

·And in this question the fear has come up. It is good that you have recognized it, because in other questions you have been trying to avoid it — not only trying to avoid it, you have been trying to rationalize it. In one question you wrote: "What is the need of an outer sannyas? I am already an inner sannyasin." Then what is the need of writing an outer letter to me? Just go on writing inner letters, that's enough. Then what is the need of reading my books? They are very outer things. These are cunning rationalizations.

In another question, Bavasimhan, you had written that you want to take sannyas, but from my own hands. And you wrote that, "I have heard that now Indians are being given sannyas by some of your disciples. I can take sannyas only from you."

I have been giving sannyas for ten years. You never wrote that before. Now, hearing that now Indians are getting sannyas from some disciples, you must have thought, "This is a good strategy, a good protection – to make a condition." Come here. I will give you sannyas! Don't be worried about that.

Now you ask...and this is more authentic, that's why I'm answering:

"I am deeply interested in your works," – read "words" "but still I am afraid of taking sannyas – why?"

Because words are words, and sannyas means a real transformation. And you must be clever with words. Seeing your so many letters and questions, it is very apparent that you are well acquainted with philosophical terminology, with abstract ideas, with esoteric jargon.

Angelo and his buddy Frank were strolling along a Pittsburgh street. After a long silence Angelo said, "Eh, what is eatin' you?"

"Aah, somethin' has been botherin' me for days," said Frank. "Maybe it ain't none of my business, but you and me have been buddies for years and I just gotta tell ya."

"Go 'head, spill it!" said Angelo.

"Last Saturday night I was in a whorehouse and who do I see there but your wife, Betty. I hate to say it, Angelo, but Betty is a prostitute!"

"Nah! Betty ain't no prostitute!" answered Angelo. "She's just a substitute. She's only there on weekends!"

People who are clever with words get lost into a jungle of words. You seem to be very clever with words.

That's why people go on reading the Gita, the Vedas, the Bible, the Koran – because now Mohammed is not there so there is no danger; Jesus is not there, so there is no danger of meeting him; Krishna is not there, so you can play around with words at your ease, to your heart's content – you can manage to put any meaning in them that you want. But I am still here. You cannot go on playing with my words. If you become interested in my words, a desire is bound to arise to come here. And then the fear – the fear that if you are really getting interested into words, who knows? – you may get interested into the person himself. And then there is no going back.

It is easy to play with words; it does not disturb your sleep, it does not disturb your unconsciousness, it does not disturb your dreams. But being with a master is a disturbance, a great disturbance.

A drunk staggered into a fairground, went to the rifle range. "Give me ten shots," he belched.

"That will be twenty pence," said the attendant, smirking.

The drunk fired and each shot was a perfect bull's-eye.

The attendant was amazed and gave the man his prize – a large tortoise.

Some time later the drunk returned again, fired ten shots, each one a bull's-eye.

"You can have any prize you choose," said the surprised attendant.

"I will have another one of those crunchy meat pies!" said the drunk.

It is very easy with the words – you can befool yourself But here I am going to hit you hard, I am going to break your skull. And then, naturally, dreams escape. I make windows in people's skulls, and all dreams escape.

All the inmates of an asylum are going for a swim in their new swimming pool.

"Okay," says the nurse, "enough for today! Tomorrow we meet again, same time, same place, and then we will do it again with water in the swimming pool!"

You are afraid of the water. In the empty swimming pool, with the words alone, you can enjoy.

Come to your senses! Everybody feels afraid of sannyas,

because sannyas means commitment, sannyas means a love affair. Sannyas is not of the head, it is of the heart. It is getting into deep waters, and you have become accustomed of sitting on the shore dreaming, thinking, brooding.

Two drunkards are driving along a road at high speed, when suddenly one shouts to the other, "Careful, there is a dangerous curve ahead."

"Why are you shouting at me?" the other replies. "I thought you were driving!"

I mean business. I am not a philosopher – just the opposite – I am absolutely existential; hence my emphasis on sannyas, because I know unless you are committed, unless you are involved, unless you risk something, you cannot grow.

Words you can accumulate – as many as you like; it is very easy to have great words. And you live, Bavasimhan, in Madras. Adyar is very close by – just few minutes drive on the outskirts of Madras. You can go there. Adyar has the most beautiful esoteric library in the whole world because it is the headquarters of the Theosophists – world headquarters. It contains all kinds of nonsense. You will never find anywhere else so much nonsense accumulated together in one place.

When I was in Madras the Adyar people invited me to come, at least for few minutes. I said, "I will come."

I went there. They showed me around – it is a beautiful place – they showed their beautiful library. And they asked me, "What do you think of our library?"

I said, "This is rare. I have seen many libraries, but no library contains so much nonsense."

They were shocked. They said, "What...?"

I said, "Yes. Theosophy is the most stupid thing that has happened in this century."

Bavasimhan, you can go to Adyar – in fact, you must be going – you can find all old scriptures collected there, you can read beautiful things and you can remain the same. No change is expected of you. But coming here is a totally different thing. I am a no-nonsense man.

The little boy was pissing in the middle of the plaza when a good-humored guard passed by and said, "Don't pee there, little boy, or I will come by and cut your willie off!"

The little boy ran very fast, and when he got to the other side of the plaza, he saw a little girl his age, also pissing. He looked at the girl and exclaimed, "Oh my God! This guard really means business!"

That's why you are afraid – I *really* mean business. Come and see, come and have a taste of it. Don't miss this opportunity. Words will always be available to you, but to be in communion with a living master is a rare opportunity; it happens only once in a while. Don't just go on writing stupid questions from Madras, come here. When people can come from Mexico...Madras is not very far off, not more than one hour's flight.

The fear is because you have become aware through the words that there is something more to words which is happening here. You are not afraid of me, you are not afraid of sannyas, you are afraid of your own longing – that you may take the jump. You are afraid of your own potential which is hankering to grow, which needs a certain opportunity, which needs a certain climate, which needs a certain energy field. That field is ready now, here. Come, drink out of it, and your thirst will be quenched forever. But you will have to pay the price.

Sannyas is simply the price. I know just by wearing orange clothes you cannot become enlightened, but it is a device. Just wearing orange clothes you will be known as a madman. That's what I want you all to be known all over the world: my mad people.

God is only for those who are mad enough, only for those who are mad for God. Just as people are mad for money and mad for power, unless you are mad for God there is no hope for you. You are afraid because here something *can* happen. And you know that there is a great desire and longing in you for that happening. The seed is there, and you know it needs only a right climate and right soil. And once you have the right soil the seed will start growing.

You are afraid of the unknown. Sannyas is a pilgrimage

towards the unknown. It is a voyage into the uncharted. God is the unknown – not only the unknown but the unknowable.

Come! Jalaluddin Rumi says, "Come, come, come..." Again and again I say, "Come," because I may not be here for long.

The fifth question:

Osho,
Do you always tell the truth?

Reverend Banana,
Yes sir, I always tell the truth, even if I have to lie a little.

The sixth question:

Osho,
I would like to meet a woman and marry her, who does not flirt, giggle, gossip, smoke, drink, pet or kiss. Is this possible?

Michael Potato-Singh,
Sir, just one question: Why? For what?

The seventh and the last question:

Osho,
Have you really been waiting for me? I have come now. I want to ask you: Can your hugging, kissing sannyasins ever enter heaven?

Michael Tomato,
I am happy that you have come. Welcome home. So now the whole trinity is here: Banana, Potato, Tomato. This looks far more delicious than God the father, and Jesus the son, and holy ghost. The writings of all the three persons is exactly the same. So it is more like trimurti, three faces of one God, rather than trinity, rather than three persons. It is not three persons but one person with three faces. Moreover, the writing is not that of a man but that of a woman, which makes it even more

mysterious.

Just this morning I asked Vivek to bring one banana, one tomato, one potato, so I can determine the sex – whether they are men or women. I tried every possible way: Patanjali Yoga, all kinds of yoga postures, standing on my head – which I have not done for twenty-five years; I looked from every possible angle – I even tried a little whirling. But when I started whirling I became even more confused: the banana started looking like a potato, the potato started looking like a tomato, the tomato started looking like a banana...Then I remembered, maybe it is a hangover. Last night Arup's boyfriend, Niranjan, has come back with good beer for me, so I had taken too much.

When nothing worked and I could not manage what these people are, men or women, I became so tired with all this great spiritual effort that I told them to fuck off. At that very moment Vivek came out from the bathroom, shocked. She said to me, "Osho, that is no way to talk to such innocent people like bananas, potatoes and tomatoes. Just tell them to scat and they will fuck off!"

You are asking, Michael Tomato, that "Can your kissing and hugging sannyasins ever enter heaven?"

I think you don't know anything up-to-date about heaven. You must be having very old ideas. Yes, in the old days it was difficult, but God always remains up-to-date. He is always contemporary. Who else can be more contemporary than God? In fact, now your so-called saints cannot enter into heaven, only my sannyasins.

The Pope arrives in New York and wants to meet the Archbishop. He is told that the Archbishop is spending the day at the beach, so the Pope, curious, decides to go and meet him there.

He is met by an extremely handsome, muscular man with a beautiful tan, wearing a red bathing suit, who, with a big smile, asks the Pope, "What is the news from Rome?"

While the Pope is too astonished to reply, the Archbishop turns to a beautiful young lady wearing a white bikini, and calls to her, "Mary, come to see who's here!"

The Pope, in consternation, asks, "Who...who...who is that lady?"

"Oh," replied the Archbishop, "she is the Mother Superior of the Sacred Heart Convent!"

Things are changing, Mr. Tomato. Your old idea of heaven just exists in your scriptures, in your head. It has disappeared from existence. I am preparing my people in the latest possible way. They will be the first to enter.

Three nuns die and they meet at the main gate of heaven.

Saint Peter comes out and says, "So girls! Before you come in I must ask you one question: What did you use your pussy for when you were in the world?"

"Only for pissing!" answers the first one.

"Good, and what about you?" he asks the second one.

"Just for pissing," answers the second nun.

"Good," he says and he turns to the third one.

"Well..." she starts and then hesitates. "Ahem...well...you know...I met this nice young priest and...he was so nice that...well, I couldn't resist, so I gave him my pussy!"

"Okay," says Saint Peter to the last one, "you can come in. But you two, I'm sorry, you're not allowed!"

The two nuns, very offended, ask, "Why?" and Saint Peter answers, "Heaven is not a piss house!"

I Have Heard

The Venerable Master said:
The unfoldment of man's mind leads him to this unchanging truth.
In unchanging stillness, unchanging purity and rest are found.
He who attains purity and stillness enters into the immutable Tao.
Having entered into the immutable Tao he is named the possessor of Tao.
Although he is named the possessor of Tao he knows that he does not possess it.
Only when he can transmute all living things can he be truly named the possessor of Tao.
He who is able to understand this can lead others to sacred Tao.

Ko Hsuan's sutras always begin with this immensely significant statement:

The Venerable Master said...

But it seems that the translation is literally true, but not true to the spirit of the sutras. All the Buddhist sutras start in the same way – only with a little difference, but a difference that makes great difference. The Buddhist sutras begin: "I have heard the master say..." And you can see the difference. The master may have said it for a different reason, the master may have meant something totally different. The master exists on a different plane; he speaks from the peak, the ultimate peak of consciousness. And the disciple hears from the darkest valley of his existence. By the time the words reach to the disciple they are bound to be distorted, they are bound to take many colors which will be imposed and projected by the disciple.

Hence, my feeling is that Ko Hsuan cannot commit this mistake. It must be that the translator has missed the point; the point is very subtle. It seems simply to the ordinary mind to make no difference whether one says, "I have heard the master say," or "The venerable master said." But when you say, "The venerable master said," you are making an absolutely certain statement as if you can report it authentically. It is not possible: you can report only what you have heard.

Now, here you are listening to me, near about three thousand sannyasins. Each sannyasin will listen according to his own conditioning, according to his own state of mind, according to his own prejudices, concepts, ideologies, philosophies, according to his own background. If you don't have any background, if you have transcended all concepts, ideologies, philosophies, religions, if you are no more in the mind, then you can hear exactly that which is said. But then there is no need to hear it; then you yourself know it. Then Ko Hsuan will not say, "The venerable master said," he can simply state the sutras. Then it will be his own experience. He is very close to the peak and finally he reached to the peak, but these notes were made before he himself became an enlightened master. These notes are of a disciple, and you should remember it.

Whenever you report me, always remember that you have heard. You cannot be certain whether it was said exactly the way you have heard or not.

In Italy, on the bus next to the driver there is the following note: "Do not talk to the driver."

In Germany there is: "It is *forbidden* to talk to the driver."

In England: "It is not polite to talk to the driver."

In Scotland: "What will you gain in talking to the driver?"

The moment a master says something it comes from his innermost core. When you hear it, it is heard on your circumference. By the time it reaches to your innermost core – if it reaches at all, if you are fortunate enough to allow it to sink in to the very core of your being – then too the meaning will not remain the same. It cannot be; it is not in the nature of things. It would have changed: it may have become distorted, it may have lost something, your mind may have added something to it.

The scientists have very recently discovered...Up to now it was thought that our mind and our senses exist only to allow us to be bridged to the existence that surrounds us. But the latest research is that the senses and the mind have double functions. One function is to connect us with the existence, but even far more important than that is the second function: *not* to allow that which can disturb us. They function as screening agents of our mind, of our attitudes, of our life styles, of our conditionings. Only two per cent reality is allowed to enter in; ninety-eight per cent reality is prevented outside, on the gate, because if all that is available is allowed in you will go berserk, you will not be able to cope with it.

Only in absolute meditativeness one is capable to be able to relax totally, to allow everything in, to be vulnerable without any conditions, to be available to existence with no strings attached.

I would like to change this statement. I would like to make it exactly as Buddhist sutras begin. They are written by Buddha's closest disciple, Ananda. He lived with Buddha for forty-two years; not even for a single moment he left Buddha. Day in, day out, year in, year out he was with Buddha like a shadow. Even shadow sometimes leaves you, but he will not leave Buddha at all. He heard everything that Buddha had said and when he was asked to report it after Buddha's death he said, "I have heard the Buddha say." Each sutra starts with that "I have heard..." A great insight is there in it.

Ko Hsuan cannot do this: he cannot say, "The venerable master said;" he can only say, "I have heard..." The translator must have changed it to look it more certain, to make it more categorical, more emphatic, more clear-cut, more mathematical. But the enlightened masters are mysterious; their words are mysterious, not mathematical. They can have thousand-and-one meanings and everyone hears them according to his own capacity.

The egoist will hear the same words but will not hear the same meaning. The egoless person will also hear the same words, but those words will connote a totally different meaning; they will resound in him with a totally different melody. When it rains, it rains on the mountains, it rains in the valleys, it rains everywhere; but the mountains remain as dry as ever – they are already too full. But when it rains into the valleys, the valleys become lakes. They are empty: they can absorb, they can contain. The valleys are feminine; the mountains are too masculine. The mountains are too egoistic; the valleys are humble.

When the master speaks there are many categories of listeners. The first category is that of the curious person, who has just come out of curiosity; he will hear only something very ordinary, something very unessential, something even meaningless, and that will become most important for him. He is there for a wrong reason. He will collect all kinds of data, but they will all belong to the surface.

Then there is the student who has come to gather more knowledge, more information. He will hear a little better than the first one, the curious one, but still his interest is in information. He is not ready to be transformed, to be converted; he is not ready to go that far. He has a certain limit beyond which he won't move a single inch. He will go with a little knowledge, with a little more accumulation, thinking that now he knows more. He knows nothing; he has become simply more informed – and information is not knowledge. *Transformation* is only knowledge, real knowledge; information is pseudo.

Then there is the disciple who listens in a deeper way than the first two categories. He listens not to gather knowledge; he wants to be changed, but he has a certain idea of what change means. He wants to go into the beyond, but he has a certain direction, a conclusion which he has already decided. He comes with a decision, an *a prior* conclusion that this is what conversion is. He is not all open – open only on one side, open only in one direction.

There are people here who write to me that, "We would like you to speak more on great lovers of God like Meera, Chaitanya, Kabir, because when you speak on Kabir, Meera, Chaitanya, our hearts are moved, our eyes start showering tears of joy, of bliss; we are thrilled to the very core of our being. But when you talk about Buddhist sutras they look dry, logical, but seem to be more appealing to the intelligence than to the world of feelings." Now, they are open only on one side.

When I speak on Meera, Kabir, Rumi, then there are people who are lovers of Buddha and they start writing letters to me, that "These are beautiful words, but not so profound as the Buddhist sutras. Each sutra has such depth! You can go on digging it; you never come to the bottom rock." They are also open only on one side.

These are disciples. One is open to love, another is open to awareness, but they are not totally open. They will hear, but they will hear with this *a priori* conclusion. They will hear in a far better way than the student, they will learn deeply, but it will be a partial learning. They will know more than the student, but it cannot be a total knowing.

Then there is the fourth kind, the devotee, which is open from all the sides, which has come with no *a priori* conclusion, which has come just to be with the master in all the seasons, in all the climates. He makes no conditions, he has no conditions. He will hear more totally, his hearing will be multidimensional, but still he will not hear exactly what the master is saying. He will be the best hearer out of all others, but still he is not on the same plane as the master.

That is the fifth category, nameless category...Then there is no need to speak even, no need to hear. One sits with the master and that's enough. Whether he speaks or not is not the point, just *being* with the master is enough, just to be with him is enough. And there is some movement between the two centers – invisible, intangible. Something transpires which is unspeakable, inexpressible. Only this fifth type person is capable of reporting, but he will be very conscious in reporting. He will always say, "I have heard..."

And my feeling is Ko Hsuan cannot say, "The venerable master said;" he can only say, "I have heard the venerable master say."

A veterinarian came to a small Italian farm to give artificial insemination to some cows.

"Lady," he says, "have you everything ready? A towel, soap, a bucket of hot water?"

"Of course, everything is here, and on this hook you can hang your trousers," replied the woman.

The teacher asks the class to mention an object round and hairy. A boy raises his hand and says, "The coconut!"

"Very good!" says the teacher.

Then Pierino raises his hand and says, "Billiard's balls!"

"No, Pierino," replies the teacher. "Billiards balls are smooth not hairy."

"No, it is not true – I saw them!" cries Pierino. "Look!" and turning to the boy next to him says, "Billiard, show your balls to the teacher!"

Young officer joining his first regiment is being interviewed by the colonel. The usual conversation concerning family connections is in progress.

"So your name is Fortescue," says the colonel. "Tell me, young man, was your grandfather Fortescue of the 68th Leicestershire Rifles?"

"Yes, sir, actually," replies the young officer.

"Splendid! So your father's a Fortescue – might I guess Major Fortescue of the 9th Cumberland Infantry Regiment?"

"Why, yes, sir!"

Are you married?" asks the colonel.

"Yes, sir. But my wife is joining me later – she is in bed with cramps."

"Not Cramps of the 33rd?"

A little boy and his father are listening to a speaker.

"Comrades!" starts the speaker.

"What does 'comrade' mean, Daddy?" asks the little boy.

"'Comrade' indicates all those who think and act alike," answers the father.

"Our government..." continues the speaker, and again the little boy asks, "What is 'government', Daddy?"

"'Government' are those who are responsible for the well-being of everybody and make decisions accordingly. At home, for instance, your mum is the government."

"...and the people..." goes on the speaker.

"What is 'people'?" asks again the boy.

"The 'people' are we who are in need of organization and

defense. At home, your baby sister is the people."

That night the father is awakened by the little boy who whispers, "Listen, comrade, tell the government that the people are full of shit up to here!"

Man lives in a state of immaturity; he is childish. He goes on growing physiologically but not psychologically. What to say about his spiritual growth – even his psychological growth is retarded, very much retarded.

Only in the First World War, for the first time in human history, we became aware that the average man's mental age is not more than thirteen years, because for the first time in the army people were psychologically tested. It was a shock all the world over. People who think about humanity and its progress were really in a great shock: thirteen years is the only average psychological age...?

The person may be seventy years old or eighty years old and his age, psychological age, is only thirteen. What about his soul? Nothing can be said about his spiritual growth because only when the body and the mind grow together in synchronicity, when the chronological age and the psychological age go together simultaneously, *then only* there is a possibility of spiritual growth, never before it.

People are immature, people are childish. And they talk about God and they talk about *nirvana*, enlightenment, and they talk about Tao, Dharma, they talk about truth – they talk about great things without being at all aware that their psychological age is that of a child. All they need is toys to play with. And that's what they have done with their religion: their churches, their temples their mosques are nothing but big toys; their popes, their *shankaracharyas*, their *ayatollahs* are nothing but people who go on giving them new games to play with. All they need is some new game so that they can remain engaged and occupied.

The scientists also go on giving them new gadgets, sometimes absolutely useless gadgets, but people are ready to purchase anything to fill their inner emptiness. And there is great emptiness because of the gap. Thirteen years psychological age and seventy years physiological age – the gap is big. How to fill that gap? How to bridge that gap? On the surface they look very grown up, but just scratch them a little bit and you will find a child inside, and immediately they go through a tantrum.

You see people when they are in anger, and you will not see any difference between them and children. You see people when they are fighting – the husband fighting with the wife, the wife fighting with the husband, throwing pillows and things – you simply watch. You may be doing the same thing yourself, then watch. Once in a while just watch – what are you doing? Is this act that of a grown-up person? You may be growing old, but you are not growing up, and growing old has no value: growing old simply means you are coming closer to death.

Growing up is a totally different phenomenon: it means you are coming closer to immortality, to deathlessness. Growing old means coming closer to your grave and growing up means coming closer to God, to Tao, to eternity. They are not synonymous; not only that they are not synonymous, they are diametrically opposite to each other.

And when there is a deep rhythm between your body-mind complex, then your soul can start growing for the first time. Your body and mind being in tune become the soil in which your soul for the first time starts moving upwards. Otherwise you will hang around the body-mind phenomenon; you will never go beyond it.

It is not an accident that the psychologists don't believe in the soul – for the simple reason because they have no glimpse of the soul. Sigmund Freud himself was very childish in his behavior, utterly childish, very much afraid, just like a small child. He was afraid of ghosts, he was afraid of death, darkness – not even the word *death* was allowed to be uttered in his presence. Twice it had happened in his life that somebody started talking about death and he fainted. Just the talk about death and he fainted! Now, this man becomes a prophet of the twentieth century.

The twentieth century has been dominated by three prophets. One is Friedrich Nietzsche, who was utterly mad. Adolf Hitler and his Nazism and all the fascist ideologies in the world are offshoots of that madman.

The other prophet was Karl Marx, who was absolutely atheist. He never believed in any consciousness, he never believed in any possibility of the growth of consciousness, because he had no glimpse of it. He called it an epiphenomenon – it is nothing but a byproduct of matter. Just like a clock functions mechanically, the same is the way that man functions: he is only a machine. He reduced man into a machine.

He himself lived a very mechanical life, utterly mechanical life. There was no joy in his life, no laughter, no song in his heart. He never came to know any experience of meditativeness; he lived just on the periphery. But he became the prophet. Communism, Joseph Stalin and Mao Zedong, Tito and Fidel Castro – these are his byproducts. Joseph Stalin could kill millions of people for the simple reason because "Man is a machine. What is wrong...?" If you kill a bicycle or if you kill a clock or if you kill an electric fan there is no harm; nobody can blame you, that you are a murderer. He could kill millions of people think nobody before him has been able to kill so many people without even a prick of the conscience. There was no question of any conscience – there is no consciousness, there is no conscience either. Man is a byproduct of matter, so when you kill somebody, matter disappears into matter.

And the third prophet of this century is Sigmund Freud, who himself is pathological, and he has projected his pathology into his philosophy.

Now, these three people have become your background. You may be aware of it, you may not be aware of it, but behind you these three are always standing. These three persons are responsible in many ways for the deterioration of human consciousness in this age. Because of these three persons, Buddhas have almost disappeared. People like Lao Tzu are not possible anymore even in China; communism won't allow them. Taoist monasteries have been destroyed, converted into schools and hospitals. Taoist meditators have been forced to work in the fields or in the factories. Even old mystics, seventy years old, eighty years old mystics, have been forced to do ordinary work just because the government cannot allow anybody to live without work; you have the right to get bread only if you work. Buddhists have disappeared.

In Russia, Jesus is no more possible, and the same is going to happen almost everywhere sooner or later.

With this background whatsoever I say will be interpreted inside you without you ever becoming aware, because you are not that watchful; you are almost in a state of drunkenness. Each ideology intoxicates; and the really conscious person gets rid of all ideologies, then only he goes beyond intoxication.

One day a guy decided he was an alcoholic. So he went to the doctor and the doctor said to him, "The treatment has to be based on self-control. You go home and try not to drink. If by chance you cannot hold yourself, next day you come to my office and inform me. This is fundamental."

"Okay," said the guy.

After some days the guy comes to the doctor's office already very drunk.

"Doc, I came here to inform you that yesterday I got very drunk."

"But you are drunk now!" said the doctor.

"Yes," said the drunkard, "but this I will inform you of tomorrow!"

The drunkard has his own logic and to him it seems to be perfectly right.

Two drunks were walking along a railway line, one said to the other, "I hope these stairs come to an end soon!"

The other replied, "Ya! The height of the handrail is killing my back!"

A Texan travels to Las Vegas to let off some steam Texas style. He starts off at the flashiest casino he can find and soon starts winning at blackjack.

After a while he heads for the roulette table where he resumes his winning streak. Soon a crowd gathers to watch him rake it in while knocking back double bourbons.

Eventually he wins so much money that he and the crowd move off to a penthouse suite to continue the party.

The next day he wakes up with a splitting hangover, lying next to a gorgeous Negress who has a serene smile on her face.

"Holy cow!" he exclaims to himself. "That was some party!"
He gently tucks a couple of hundred dollar bills under the pillow and tiptoes out of the room. As he crosses the living room, he stops short as he sees two more gorgeous girls wearing little else than the same serene smile.

"Son of a gun!" he says as he drops a few more bills down beside them.

As one of the bills flutters down it brushes a cheek of the last girl. She slowly opens her eyes and says, "You don't have to tip the bridesmaids!"

You go on doing things...You will get married, you will move into a profession, you will become educated, you will become Christian, Hindu, Mohammedan – you will do thousand-and-one things absolutely in a state of unconsciousness. If by chance you come across a master you will hear him from your unconsciousness.

Hence, before I begin this last sutra I would like you to remember always: never say what the master has said; always say that this is what you have *heard* him say. And it is not only a mannerism; it has tremendous truth in it.

The unfoldment of man's mind leads him to this unchanging truth.

The translator goes on wrong on many points. And I can understand why he goes on wrong, particularly on points which are of very great significance. He can't help; he has no understanding of meditation. He says:

The unfoldment of man's mind...

Ko Hsuan must have said: *The unfoldment of man's consciousness*, not man's mind. The mind has to be dropped, not unfolded. In fact, the moment you drop the mind, the unfoldment of your consciousness begins. But we believe in mind – we don't know anything else than the mind – we are addicted with the mind.

In western languages there are not many words for the mind, but in eastern languages there are many words for the mind, for different purposes, because mind can function in many ways. And the East has gone very deep into the phenomenon of the mind, and beyond it.

It is just like if you look into the language of the Eskimos you will be surprised: there are one dozen words for ice; no other language has one dozen words for ice. Only Eskimos have one dozen words for ice, because they have lived with ice for thousands of years and they have known all its possibilities; and they know that there are differences, minute differences which are not visible to those who have not lived in the world of an Eskimo. No other language has so many words.

Sanskrit has at least one dozen words for mind, because as you go deeper into mind you come upon different layers. They are so different that it is not possible to call them all with the same name; they are qualitatively different. And as you go on moving deeper and deeper, a point comes when mind is left behind and pure consciousness remains. That consciousness knows unfoldment. Mind cannot unfold; it can only close. The more you become addicted with the mind, the more closed you become. Mind in fact is a prison, and the stronger the mind, more unfortunate the person, because then it will be very difficult for him to get out of it. And our whole educational system enforces the mind, strengthens the mind.

Hence I can understand the difficulty of the translator. But you have to remember, because you are working on meditation here you can understand in a far better way.

The unfoldment of man's consciousness leads him to this unchanging truth.

Everything is changing in the world; you cannot find anything in the world which is unchanging unless you go deep within yourself and reach to the very center of your being. There only you will find the center, the center of the cyclone, which remains absolutely unchanging. It is on that very center that the whole change depends, the whole wheel of life and death moves. Without that center, the world will disappear. That center, that unchanging truth is the very foundation of this changing world; it is rooted there. Not to know it is to live a lie which is not worth calling life. Not to know it you will have to go on doing foolish things all your life in order to give a certain fallacy to yourself of the unchanging truth.

For example, why people are so much interested in money rather than friendship? If it is a question of choice you will choose money more than friendship; why? Because money seems to be more unchanging. You can depend on it, it is more reliable. If you have a good bank balance it is far more reliable. Who knows about the friend? Today he is a friend, tomorrow he may become the enemy.

Machiavelli, in his great book, *The Prince*, writes: Don't say anything, even to your friend, which you would not like to be known by your enemy. Why? Because your friend can become enemy any day. And he also says: Don't say anything against your enemy either which you would not like to say against your friend, because the enemy can become your friend any day. Things go on changing: the friend becomes the enemy, the enemy becomes the friend.

You can depend on money. People love money more than anything else; more than love, money seems to be significant. You can purchase love; if not love, at least sex you call purchase. But money, if you don't have you simply don't have: you are a beggar. With money everything comes. Money seems to have a certain permanence, a certain stability.

People are more interested in things than in people. People die; things don't die. People go on accumulating things for the simple reason that a good furniture, a good painting, a good house are far more lasting – they may last longer than you – but you cannot say the same about people. You love somebody, and tomorrow the person dies. Then you are left empty, with a great wound which will take years to heal or may not heal ever, and it will always hurt.

Hence people are afraid of love, people are afraid of people. People make friends with animals rather than with people. They would like to have a good dog – more predictable, more reliable. Whenever you come home he is there to welcome you, wagging his tail. You can hit him, you can shout at him, you can scream at him, you can scold him, but he never changes his loyalty to you, his obedience to you. You can't do the same with people – people are dangerous. Hence you see more and more persons becoming interested in birds, dogs, horses, for the simple reason that they give a certain feel of permanence.

Carlo and Elena are in love and want to spend a night together.

"Have you understood, my love?" says Elena. "When my parents are asleep I will throw down a cent and that will be the signal. I will leave the door open and you can come up."

Carlo waits under the window. Finally Elena throws the cent down, then eagerly lies down in the bed wearing a flimsy nightgown, and waits...and waits...and waits...

After about half an hour she goes to the window and exclaims impatiently, "But, Carlo, are you coming up or not?"

"Yes, my love," replies Carlo, "as soon as I find the cent."

On his tenth birthday, Abraham calls his son.

"Now, my son," he says, "it is time for me to explain the facts of life. We will start from the hands. Be very careful and don't forget.

"So, the thumb is used to show that a bargain is good. The index finger is used to show what is the best in a bargain. The medium finger is used to show power. The ring finger is just used for the wedding ring. The little finger is used to clean your ear. Have you understood?"

"Yes, Pa," replied the son, "but I would like to know the use of the medium – what you call the power finger."

Abraham leans over his son and whispers, "The power finger, son, you use it at night under the blankets...when you count the money!"

Why people are so much interested in money? For the simple reason they are in a great need to find something permanent in this life where everything goes on changing every moment; they want something to rely upon. Unless they find their own center they will go on finding these stupid things. These are poor substitutes.

The real thing is the unfoldment of consciousness, because that leads you to the unchanging truth.

In unchanging stillness, unchanging purity and rest are found.

And when you have found your innermost core, when your lotus of consciousness has blossomed – the Indian mystics have called it the one-thousand-petaled lotus – when all the petals have opened and you have found the center of the lotus, there is great stillness, a stillness which is unchanging, there is great purity, great innocence and deep rest. You have come home. The pilgrimage is over. In finding yourself you have found God. In reaching to your own center you have reached the center of the whole universe. Now there is no need to go anywhere; you have found the infinite treasure – what Jesus calls the kingdom of God.

People have tried to create substitutes. You can create a certain stillness by learning some yoga posture. If your body is still you will feel a certain stillness, but that is not the real stillness; it will be disturbed. It can be disturbed very easily by anything – just an ant crawling up your body is enough to disturb it. Anything can distract it: just a bird calling and you will be distracted. A child starts crying, a small girl starts giggling, a dog starts barking, and that's enough. And the world is full of so many things continuously happening. You cannot remain still for long; sooner or later it will be disturbed. Because of this, people have moved to the monasteries, people have escaped to the mountains, to the caves. But there too something or other will disturb you.

Rather than escaping from the world, escape into yourself: Remain in the world because the world is a great opportunity; it is a constant testing ground. It gives you thousand-and-one opportunities to see whether you have attained the real stillness or it is just an imposed phenomenon, only skin-deep and can be disturbed by anything.

Your so-called religious people are only superficially still; anything can disturb them. In fact, things disturb them more than other people. Even if one person in your house becomes religious he becomes a torture to the whole family – because children cannot play because he is doing Transcendental Meditation, he is "doing his TM." Children cannot play, the wife cannot work – everything has to stop for him. And even then he will be disturbed by any small thing. Just the clock ticking is enough, and the TM disappears, because what he is doing is just imposing a mantra, a constant repetition of a certain sound or word. Anything far more interesting is bound to attract him. If somebody puts on beautiful music or somebody starts playing guitar he will be disturbed, he will be immediately disturbed. The reason is not the guitar, the reason is what he is doing is boring and the guitar is far more attractive. Naturally the mind moves towards that which is more attractive. He is concentrating on Jesus Christ, and a beautiful woman passes by...Now, looking at a man crucified...Who wants to look at a man on the cross? One wants to avoid such things. And a beautiful woman passing by immediately attracts; that becomes a distraction.

That's why your so-called saints have always been against women; that simply shows the women have been disturbing their meditations. In fact, it simply shows their meditations were so boring that any woman could have disturbed it.

One person in the family becomes religious, starts praying or meditating or doing something stupid, and the whole family becomes afraid because he is doing something great. In fact, if he is really a meditator there is no question of getting distracted.

You cannot distract *my* meditators – they will distract you! The whole family will be distracted. Just start doing Dynamic Meditation or Kundalini, and not only the family but the whole neighborhood is distracted: they start phoning to the police. This is something! Rather than being distracted by any small thing, they are all distracted by your meditation.

Real rest – real relaxation, real purity and stillness – is not imposed by any artificial means; it is a spontaneous unfoldment. Then how it happens? It happens through understanding. Tao believes in understanding. Try to understand Nobody wants to understand – we want to avoid, we want somehow to bypass our problems. You have problems – you go to somebody like Maharishi Mahesh Yogi and you ask him that, "I am very much worried, anxious, tense. What should I do?"

And he says, "You do TM. You repeat this mantra: Coca Cola, Coca-Cola, Coca-Cola. Go on repeating fifteen minutes morning, fifteen minutes evening. It will help." It will help you to repress the problem, but only to repress; the problem is not solved. How the problem can be solved by repeating "Coca-Cola"? Or maybe "Aum," which is the same; it makes no difference. In fact, "Coca-Cola" seems to be far more sweeter, far more appealing! Both are the same – any word will do. How it is going to solve your problems? Your problems will remain there; you will have to solve them still. Sooner or later they will surface again. And repressing them is dangerous because they will gain more energy, and the time that is being lost meanwhile is wasted.

Tao depends on understanding. Now in the world there are only two things prevalent. One is analysis, Freudian analysis, and many offshoots of it: analyze the problem, go on analyzing it. It is like peeling an onion: one layer is removed, another layer is there, far more fresher. Remove it, another is there. And all the time tears will be coming from your eyes. Some bargain! And your problems are not so small as an onion, because sooner or later the onions will be finished, you will come to the very end the last layer, and then...emptiness in your hand. But your problems are not so easy. Hence psychoanalysis needs seven years, ten years; still it is never complete.

I have never come across a single person – and I have hundreds of my sannyasins who are psychoanalysts, therapists, well-known therapists – but I have never come across a single person whose analysis is complete. It cannot be complete; it is an unending process. You go on, go on, and each layer will reveal another layer.

Sigmund Freud used to reach to your childhood. At the age four or three you start collecting memories, so he will reach to that point. Then Arthur Janov found that that doesn't help, you have to go beyond that, so Primal Therapy came into existence. Now you have to go beyond that.

Naturally, a three-year-old child or two-year-old child cannot tell about his problems; he can only scream and kick and throw things. So the Primal Therapy is kicking, shouting, screaming. And Janov thought that there will be a final scream – the primal scream, the first scream.

When the child is born the first thing he does is scream; that is a physiological necessity. By screaming he cleans his whole breathing system; by screaming he throws his mucus out. That's why the children's noses go on flowing...because when he is in the mother's womb all his breathing system collects mucus – naturally, he is not breathing; he lives on mother's breathing. And when he comes out of the womb he has to breathe on his own, and, the system has never worked and the breathing mechanism is full of mucus; that mucus has to come out. Doctors hang the child upside down; they make him do *shirshasana*, headstand, so that the mucus starts flowing downwards because of gravitation. And naturally when you hang somebody upside down he screams, and that very scream helps: the mucus is thrown out and he starts breathing. That is the primal scream.

Janov thought, "If we can reach to the primal scream we have come to the very bottom of it; then, problems will be solved." But now there are other therapists who say, "That won't help, because there is still nine months' conditioning in mother's womb. Now we have to go into that – then, problems can be solved."

But I would like to tell you, problems will not be solved then too, because after those nine months you will come across another layer that will be of the previous life. Then start again Freudian psychoanalysis and then Primal Therapy, and so on, so forth.

Indian mystics who have tried to enter into the whole realm of consciousness say there have been at least eighty-four million lives before you became man. Now, if you somehow finish eighty-four million lives analyzed, then you will find you have to enter into the world of the monkeys...So monkey analysis! And then go on and on...Then finally you will find you have been a fish in the ocean; that is the beginning of life. Then fish and the problems of the fish...I don't think that there can be any end to psychoanalysis – it is an exercise in utter futility. That is one thing, the western thing.

And the eastern approach has been: Seeing that this thing is too long and will never end, bypass it. Just repeat a mantra and forget all about it. But by forgetting all about it you cannot solve anything.

Tao is absolutely right: neither analysis will help nor forgetting, but witnessing, understanding, seeing – seeing clearly. It is neither analysis nor a repetition of a mantra. Tao does not believe in either; its approach is totally new. And then only you will find, in that understanding a transformation happens. You will find stillness, purity and rest.

> *He who attains purity and stillness enters into the immutable Tao.*

And through that witnessing, through that understanding, awareness, you enter into the eternal Tao. Tao means the ultimate law of nature, what Buddha calls *aes dhammo sanantano*. This is the ultimate law of existence, Tao.

> *Having entered into the immutable Tao he is named the possessor of Tao.*

He is only *named*, Ko Hsuan says, remember. We have to say something, we have to give that experience a certain name But he immediately adds:

> *Although he is named the possessor of Tao he knows that he does not possess it.*

Because he is no more an ego, how can he possess anything? I here is nobody inside him, just a mirror, a pure mirror that reflects; the mirror cannot possess anything. Do you think the mirror can possess anything? You look in the mirror: it reflects your face, but it does not possess it. For the moment it appears it possesses, but that is only an appearance; it does not possess you. You move away, the reflection is gone and the mirror remains in its stillness, in its purity. Whether it reflects or not, its purity remains unaffected.

This mirrorlike duality of consciousness cannot be said to possess anything – there is no ego to possess in the first place. Secondly, there is nothing to possess – the very idea of possession divides existence into two: the possessor and the possessed, the subject and the object, the owner and the owned, the observer and the observed. But when you enter into ultimate rest, stillness, all duality is transcended; there is only one.

In fact, saying that one possesses Tao...it will be far better and far more true to say that one is possessed by Tao. Tao fills you, totally fills you; you become part of it. Not that Tao is in your hands, but that you are in the hands of Tao. But our language is such...our language is made by people who are interested in possessing things.

Just the other day somebody has asked that, "Osho, my whole mind always goes on thinking how to possess more, bigger things, how to have a big house, a palace, how to have a bigger bank balance, how to have a longer life."

If you ask Freud, if you ask the western approach they will say, "This is nothing. This is just the desire to have a bigger sexual organ, that's all." Freud reduces everything to sexuality; he seems to be obsessed with it. In fact, it is a revolt against the Christian obsession with sex. Two thousand years of Christianity made people so sex-repressive that somebody had to revolt against it, and Sigmund Freud revolted against it. But the revolt went to the other extreme; again everything is colored by sexuality. He thinks people like bigger things – a big house, a big name, fame, a taller body – but these are all just substitutes for having a bigger sexual organ. In a way it is true, but only in a way. It is true particularly to the eighteenth-century western man; the Victorian morality was rooted in it.

But the East has a different approach which is far more true. The East says people are interested in bigger things because they see such hollowness in themselves, such emptiness in themselves that they want to fill it somehow. And they go on putting things into it but they disappear – those things disappear and more and more things are needed. hence the desire comes to have such big things that somehow the inner emptiness can be filled.

But it cannot be filled: that inner emptiness is your nature. It has to be loved, lived, understood. Once understood, you will start rejoicing in it; there is no need to fill it. It is beautiful, it is tremendously beautiful; there is nothing more beautiful than that inner emptiness. You are just afraid of the word, of the idea of emptiness, and just because of the idea you go on asking for bigger things. in fact, the desire to have a bigger sexual organ may be nothing but to fill the inner emptiness!

Freud was so much obsessed with it that he started thinking that women suffer very much from phallic jealousy! That is utterly wrong. If they suffer from phallic jealousy then it should be stated, to keep the balance right, that man suffers from breast jealousy. But that Freud never said; he remains a male chauvinist pig. He would have loved this story:

The Danish king and the Swedish king and Prince Philip, Duke of Edinburgh, are sitting in a pub having a few beers together. Somehow they end up having a competition to see whose prick is the longest.

The Danish king puts his prick on the table. Twelve inches! Everyone applauds and vigorously sings the Danish national anthem.

Then the Swedish king puts his prick on the table. Sixteen inches! Everyone screams and shouts and jumps around and sings the Swedish national anthem.

Lastly, Prince Philip puts his prick on the table. Twenty-five inches long! And everyone starts singing:

"God save the Queen!"

Only when he can transmute all living things can he be truly named the possessor of Tao.

Who can be called a possessor of Tao? One who knows that he does not possess – that is the first condition to be fulfilled – one who knows that he is possessed by Tao, that he is no more, only Tao is. But what will be the indication? How we will recognize that he possesses the Tao? He gives a beautiful symbol to recognize the man of Tao. Ko Hsuan says:

Only when he can transmute all living things can he be truly named the possessor of Tao.

The translation is again a little wrong. Ko Hsuan must have meant all living beings, not living things. Things are not living, that's why they are called things. Living beings...But why call living beings? – because beings are naturally living. But things are complicated: all living beings are neither living nor beings. Many living beings are dead – apparently living, only apparently, not really living.

Mrs. Carrot had a very bad car accident and was hospitalized.

Her concerned husband, Mr. Carrot, asked the doctor what her fate would be.

The doctor reassuringly said, "Do not worry, she will live, but she will probably be a vegetable for the rest of her life!"

Many people are just vegetating...and you know three are here: Banana, Potato, Tomato! These people cannot be called living. And even if people are living they don't have beings. Being is only when you have reached the unfoldment of your consciousness. Being means when becoming is finished, when becoming is no more needed, when you have arrived home.

The man of Tao is one whose touch transmutes people into living, first, and then into being. That's the miracle of a master: If you allow him to touch you, if you become available to him, he can stir life in you and, finally, he can make you aware of your own being.

The only proof of somebody's being the man of Tao is that in his proximity people start living on a totally different plane, become more and more livelier, start attaining a certain crystallization of being. The man of Tao is one who can impart his Tao to others, who can function like a catalytic agent, that if you fall in tune with him you go through a transformation, a mutation.

He who is able to understand this can lead others to sacred Tao.

One who understands the alchemy of how to transform the dead into living and how to help the becoming into being, who knows this art of alchemy, can lead people to the sacred Tao.

The word *sacred* is used only in the last sutra. This is very significant because when you use the words *sacred Tao* it becomes synonymous to God. But he has not mentioned it before because to mention it before will make you worshippers. And all worshippers have gone wrong: they have become Christians, Hindus, Mohammedans; They are not transmuted. Hence he has kept this beautiful word *sacred* for the very end; this is his last word: "sacred Tao." This can be said only when you have understood all the sutras; now you will not become a worshipper.

Worshipping is not going to help, praying is not going to help – only meditation, only understanding, only awareness. And calling Tao sacred means everything is sacred, because Tao fills everything. The whole existence is the manifestation of Tao. There is no other God than the universe. There is no other God than this very life. There is no other God than this moment, this now, this here.

We Can Share

The first question:

Osho,
Please say a few words about Sanjay Gandhi and his death. He respected and loved you and had said to Laxmi just a week before his death that soon he will be coming here to visit and to see you.

Sanjay Gandhi was a beautiful person, a man of immense integrity, individuality, adventure. He lived adventurously and he died adventurously. In fact, that's how one should live and one should die. He lived dangerously, the only way to live is the way to live in danger, because it is only in moments of tremendous danger that one transcends lower planes of being.

It has been reported in the newspapers and when Vivek read she asked me how it was possible – because dying in a plane crash his whole body was just a mess. All his bones were broken, his skull was broken, his brain had come out of the skull – but on his face there was great peace. She was puzzled. After such a horrible death, how one's face can be peaceful?

But there is a secret in it worth understanding. When one dies on a deathbed after a prolonged disease, continuously thinking and worrying about death, the face cannot be calm and quiet; the worry, the tension, the clinging to life will be there. But when one dies suddenly, when death comes like a surprise, suddenly the mind stops.

I have been in many accidents myself and the people who have been with me in those accidents have all experienced that in the moment when the accident is actually happening the mind disappears, because the mind cannot *think* about it. There is nothing to think about it, there is no way to think about it. The mind stops because the mind can only move in the vicious circle of the known, and the unknown has entered so suddenly that the mind is absolutely incapable of figuring it out, what is happening. In a deep shock the mind stops; for a moment there is a glimpse of the no-mind.

Sanjay Gandhi died in a better death than millions of people who die in their beds after a long, long disease, because they cannot use the opportunity of death. He may not have experienced meditation while he was alive, but he must have tasted just a drop of the nectar of meditation while he was dying. Death came with such immediacy, giving no time for the mind to think about it. Such a death is a beautiful death.

Many questions have been asked to me for the past week, since he died. I had not answered them for the simple reason because people who have not meditated, people who have not been here, who have not been my sannyasins will not be able to understand what I am saying.

Vinoba Bhave said on Sanjay Gandhi's death that he died an immature death. That is absolutely wrong. He was far more mature than Morarji Desai. Chronologically he was very young, only thirty-three, but chronological age is not the real age. He had far more perceptiveness, he had far more intelligence, he had far more clarity. He lived totally, he lived each moment of his life. And it was a very natural death to him; it belonged to his very style of life.

That's why I have kept complete silence about it. Now all the people who had to say something have said, I can say my word, which is going to be absolutely different. I don't feel sad about his death. Yes, the country will miss him, but as far as he is concerned he died beautifully. The country has lost a great opportunity in him because he was a promise, a great hope, because he had the guts to go against the traditional, orthodox mind of this country. He was a man of steel – he could have fought against conventions, and he was learning how to fight. And he was succeeding. Slowly, slowly his grip on the events was growing better every day.

The country has certainly lost an immense opportunity of becoming contemporary. He was a contemporary man; he had no hangovers from the past, he did not believe in the past. But as far as he himself is concerned he could not have died in a better way. This death is a logical conclusion to his whole life.

If dying at the age of thirty-three inevitably means immature death, then Adi Shankaracharya also died an immature death – he was exactly thirty-three. Then Jesus also died an immature death; he was exactly thirty-three. Then Vivekananda also died an immature death; he was also exactly thirty-three. Just living long means nothing; length has no meaning. Meaning comes from intensity. It is not a question of quantity but of quality. How long you live makes no difference. *How* you live, how deeply, how totally, how intensely, how passionately – everything depends on that. And he certainly lived totally, intensely, passionately – and he risked everything for it; he was not in any way a coward.

People like Sanjay Gandhi are bound to die in some strange way. This country needs more people like Sanjay Gandhi. For centuries this country has been a coward country. The Himalayas belong to this country – the greatest mountains in the world – but for one hundred years continuously people have come from all over the world to climb the virgin peaks of the Himalayas. But no Indian has bothered: Indians believe in security, comfort – why take the risk? Many have died in trying to climb the Everest.

And when Edmund Hillary came he was asked "Are you people mad? Why do you bother? What are you going to gain out of it? Even if you reach at the top of the Everest there is nothing! Why so many people from all over the world have tried to climb the mountain?"

Hillary said, "Just because it is there. It is a great challenge. Standing there, unconquered, it is a challenge to human spirit. It has to be conquered – it is not a question of gaining anything. Just a challenge to the spirit of man..."

Indians can't understand this. That's why they have lived for two thousand years in slavery. They will not climb the mountains, they will not swim in the ocean they will not glide in the sky. They will move very mathematically, very calculatingly.

Sanjay Gandhi was a good beginning; he was a pioneer in this way. He was always interested in adventure. He could not fit in any school, he could not fit in any conventional pattern of life. I loved the man.

We need many more people who can die in adventures. Their death raises the spirit of the people. If they live they bring new quality, new perfume to people's life; if they die, their death also brings a new fragrance. Hence I am not sad about him. I am certainly sad about the country. It is really a misfortune for the country, a great calamity, far more greater than the death of Jawaharlal Nehru, Sanjay Gandhi's grandfather, because Jawaharlal had lived his life, he had done whatsoever he wanted to do. There was nothing else that he could have done even if he had lived ten years more; he had blossomed. He was a poet, not a politician; he was also adventurous. Something of him has entered into Indira Gandhi, his daughter, and something of him was very much in the bones and the blood and the marrow of Sanjay Gandhi.

Sanjay Gandhi's death is far bigger a calamity to the country because he had yet to contribute much. He had just begun to open his petals; he had yet to become a flower. He was still a potential. Certainly he would have been a great prime minister of the country if he had lived – he may have proved the greatest prime minister this country has known up to now – he was showing every indication of that.

Hence, as far as the country is concerned, it has been a calamity. But as far as he himself is concerned he lived beautifully, he died beautifully. And the peace that was on his face which must have looked miraculous to everybody – not only to Vivek but to everybody...Whosoever must have seen his face must have wondered why he looked so calm and quiet and serene.

You have to understand the psychology of such accidents. The mind is very clever about day-to-day affairs; it continues its chattering. It stops only when there is some shock, something which is not digestible, which the mind cannot take in. That's, in fact, the attraction of adventure. The people who go on mountain climbing know it, what really is the attraction. The attraction is not just climbing beautiful mountains with a scenic panorama surrounding it – that is not the point. Far deeper there is a psychology of it. When you are climbing a mountain there are thousand-and-one dangers. When you are surrounded in dangers your mind stops. You become suddenly aware. There is great alertness and a serenity. You have to take each step very carefully, consciously. That is really what meditation is all about.

In my childhood days I used to take my friends to the river. There was a small path by the side of the river. To walk on that edge was very dangerous; just one step taken in unconsciousness and you will fall into the river, and that was the place where the river was the deepest. Nobody used to go there, but that was my most loved spot. And I will take all my friends to come along with me to move on that narrow edge. Very few were ever ready to go along with me, but those few had really a beautiful experience. They will all report, "This is strange, how the mind stops!"

I will take my friends to the railway bridge to jump from the bridge into the river. It was dangerous, certainly dangerous; it was prohibited. There was always a policeman standing on the railway bridge because that was the place from where people used to commit suicide. We had to bribe the policeman, that "We are not committing suicide, we have just come to enjoy the jump!" And slowly, slowly he became aware that these are the same people – they don't die or anything, they come again, they come again and they are not interested in suicide. In fact, he started loving us and stopped taking bribes. He said, "You can jump – I will not look at that side. Whenever you want you can come."

It was dangerous. The bridge was very high and to jump from there...And before you will reach the river there was a time between – the gap between the bridge and the river – when the mind will suddenly stop.

Those were my first glimpses of meditation; that's how I became more and more interested in meditation. I started inquiring how these moments can be made available without going to the mountains, to the river, to the bridges; how one can allow oneself to move into these spaces without going anywhere, just by closing one's eyes. Once you have tasted, it is not difficult.

Sanjay Gandhi died beautifully. He will be born on a far higher plane because he died in a moment when the mind was no more functioning. He died the death of a meditator without knowing what is happening. Of course it was not a conscious meditation, but still there was something of meditativeness in it. His next life will be of a higher quality. Maybe his next life will become more concerned with the *inner* adventure; this life was more concerned with the outer adventure. He was an extrovert.

He wanted to come here. Many times I had been informed that he wants to come, and this time he had seen all the slides of this place. For two hours he was with Laxmi, with Indira, talking, inquiring, was very much interested and wanted to come.

But my feeling was that this life he was more of an extrovert. But this sudden death will bring a transformation into him: he will become an introvert in his next life, and that is something of immense value.

Indira Gandhi must be in great pain. She cannot understand how we celebrate death here. She also wants to come, has been thinking for many days to come. Now she has settled that in August she will be coming, but now the death of Sanjay may again postpone her coming. She is interested in meditation, but she is, obviously, too much occupied with the world, with the problems. And this country has so many problems, almost insoluble.

This country is in such a situation that if you solve one problem you create ten others immediately. It is a mess! If you really want to solve the problems, people go against you. She told Laxmi that, "I perfectly agree with Osho that population has to be reduced, and it can be reduced only forcibly. But we have tried and that does not work because the country is a democratic country: people become enemies, then you can't come back into power again." And whatsoever Indira and Sanjay together did in five years, Morarji Desai undid within three years. Now the problems are again the same – or even far more worse.

China now has the greatest population in the world, but by the end of this century India will have the greatest population, because China is not a democracy and they are using every possible way to prevent the growth of population. And they are succeeding.

By the end of this century India will be the greatest populated country in the world and, of course, it will have the greatest problems – almost impossible to solve. They can be solved right now, but to solve them means you have to fight with the people for their own sake. They will be against you. They are against me for the simple reason because whatsoever I say can be of help, but it goes against their traditions, against their conventions, against their orthodox mind.

Sanjay created more enemies in the country than friends for the simple reason that he *really* wanted to help the country. He was far more interested in the well-being of the country than becoming a popular leader. If you want to be a popular leader you have to be a follower of your followers; you have just to say what they want to listen. He created more enemies than friends, he was the most hated person, for the simple reason because he had great dreams to help the country. And he had a clear vision – and he was on the right track.

All the idiots of the country deep down will be feeling very happy, that "It is good that he is gone!" Now they can continue living their old stupidities and superstitions.

I was shocked to know that on his funeral they were chanting Vedic mantras; that is not right. He would not have liked that at all. He was not a believer of any religion. He certainly believed in service and he believed that to serve is the only way to come closer to God – and he was right! And they were doing all kinds of foolish things, and Indira was in such a shock that she simply looked dazed, didn't say anything. The Indian priests, the Indian priesthood, immediately took over the chants; in their hands...

And the people who were against him are now praising. People are so stupid, so unconscious, so mechanical; they don't know what they go on doing. If they had supported this young man he would have been a blessing to the country. But they tried in every possible way to prevent him. There were at least hundred cases against him in the courts. He was running from one court to another court, for last three years. He has been harassed as much as anybody can be harassed, but he faced all that harassment without any strain, without any tension; he accepted it as part of his life.

If you want to change people, if you want to bring a radical change in their life, if you want to bring a revolution, you have to accept all these things as your destiny; they are inevitable.

We need more people like him, particularly in this country. More young men should die climbing the mountains, flying in the sky, diving deep in the ocean, exploring the unknown – first outwardly and then inwardly too.

My work is totally different – it is inner – but on the fundamentals Sanjay Gandhi would have absolutely agreed with me. I believe in adventure. Of course I am not interested that my sannyasins should go climbing the mountains because I know of far bigger mountains that are waiting inside you. And I would not encourage you to fly in the sky because there is a far bigger sky within you, far more unknown, far more unexplored, unmapped, uncharted. But the fundamental is the same.

The quality of adventure to me is a religious quality, it is a spiritual quality. Whether you use it outwardly or inwardly, it doesn't matter. But I love all adventurous people, and I love all those who are courageous enough to live in insecurity – and he lived in insecurity – and of course, in insecurity you are always living with death. That's what insecurity means: that each moment of life is also a moment of death.

You ask me to say a few words on Sanjay Gandhi and his death.

Death is an illusion, death never happens – only the form changes. And because we become too much identified with the form, that's why we feel so miserable. To know that you are not the body, not the mind, is to know that there is no death, that you are eternal. Everybody is part of eternity.

There are only two illusions in the world, and they are not really two but two aspects of the same illusion. One is ego, which is false; it gives you the false idea that, "I am separate from existence." And out of this illusion arises the second illusion – the illusion of death. You are not separate from existence, hence how can you die? The wave is not separate from the ocean; it cannot die either. Yes, sometimes it manifests and sometimes it rests and goes into unmanifestation.

There is no death, remember it. But I am not saying to believe in me; I would like you to experience it. There is no death. There is only life and life eternal.

The second question:

Osho,

I was born a Christian but became convinced that Hinduism is the right religion, so I became a Hindu. I was initiated into Hinduism by the founder of Krishna Consciousness Movement himself and given a new name. But listening to you I have become very much confused. Please guide me as to what should I do now.

There are many things to be understood. The first thing: nobody is born as a Christian or a Hindu or a Mohammedan. You are simply born as a pure consciousness with no adjective attached to you. You are brought up as a Hindu, as a Christian, as a Mohammedan; that is another matter. That has nothing to do with your birth; that is conditioning by your parents.

And it always happens that whenever you are conditioned by others you feel a deep resistance against it. That is natural; nothing is wrong in it, not at all, because that child wants to remain free and by making him a Christian or a Jew or a Hindu the parents are drawing a small circle around him. They are making him defined; he was born undefined. He was born infinite; now they are making him finite. He was born open, open like a lotus flower; now the parents, the society, the educational system, the church, they are all trying to close him, to make him a prison cell. Nobody likes it – nobody can like it – it is against nature, against Tao.

Freedom is our natural love, hence the child starts resisting. He has to repress his resistance; he cannot assert it because he has to depend on the parents. He is utterly helpless; he cannot live without their support. It is a question of survival for him, hence he has to compromise; he compromises with the parents just to survive. By the time he is capable of standing on his own feet he is already conditioned. Now the walls are too thick around him, and living within those walls for twenty-five years, which is almost one-third of one's life, and the most important one-third, one becomes attached to the walls. One starts accepting them, one starts even becoming attached. But that resistance somewhere in the unconscious continues. If some opportunity arises to go against your condition you will not miss the opportunity.

That is what happened to you.

You say: *"I was born a Christian..."*

Nobody is born a Christian – you were brought up as a Christian and you must have carried a deep resistance against it. Coming in contact with Hinduism you became convinced of its rightness. What type of contact was this? It was only intellectual. And of course, the eastern religions are far more appealing intellectually than the western religions for the simple reason because the East has explored consciousness for a longer time than the West. Eastern science is childish, so is western religion. Eastern religion is very mature; western religion is very childish.

The greatest religions were born in India – Hinduism, Buddhism, Jainism; they contain the highest flights of human consciousness. Mohammedanism, Judaism, Christianity are far behind; intellectually they cannot be very much convincing. They will look very primitive compared to Buddhism, Hinduism, Jainism.

You must have become intellectually convinced. But intellectual conviction is not real conversion; it remains in the head. You simply change from one prison into another – maybe a little bigger, a little better, with more facilities – but the prison is still a prison. If you are really rebellious you will not change one prison for another, you will simply get out of all prisons.

That's why you are becoming very much confused here, because I am not here to convert you into another religion – for that, you will be very willing. My sannyasins don't belong to any religion at all; they have a kind of religiousness. They are religious without any religion.

Religion is for me a quality – not a philosophy, not a theology. I am against people moving from Christianity to Hinduism or from Hinduism to Christianity. I am against all these conversions; they are simply stupid.

A Polish captain called all his men to the barracks.

"Right, men! Today we are changing underwear. Kozlowski, you change with Zabriski! Pilsudski, you change...."

Now finally the Polacks have decided to change the underwear, but now they are changing amongst themselves, so what kind of change is this? It was far better to keep your own underwear – at least it had your own dirt! Now you will be carrying somebody else's dirt.

Are you a Polack?

A Polish man walks into a doctor's office with third degree burns on both sides of his face. The doctor, in amazement and concern, asks what happened. The Polack explains that he was at home ironing clothes when the telephone rang. Without thinking he put the iron to his ear instead of the phone.

"But how did the other side of your face get burned?" asked the doctor.

The Polack answered, "He called me back!"

It was enough that you were a Christian – only one side of the face was burned – now what kind of nonsense is this, that you became a Hindu?

And I know this man who initiated you, the founder of Krishna Consciousness Movement, Prabhupada. He certainly had some talent in attracting stupid people all over the world. He must have been a Polack himself for many lives! I have never come across any Hare Krishna Movement person who has any kind of intelligence. Now from Christianity you fell into another ditch.

Two Polacks arrived late at a concert where pianists of many nationalities are playing. Since they did not have a copy of the program they could not tell which pianist was from what country.

Suddenly one of the Polacks said, "That is the Polack pianist."

"How do you know?" asked the other.

"Simple. He does everything like the others, but instead of pushing the stool closer to the piano, he sits and pulls the piano closer to himself!"

And do you know what happened to the Polack parachutist? He missed the ground!

It is good that now you are feeling a little confused. That shows the beginning of intelligence, because unless you have some intelligence you cannot be confused. You cannot confuse a rock: confusion means some indication of intelligence. Don't be worried – you are still a little bit alive. A fragment of you is still intelligent, and that is enough. We will take hold of that fragment and from there we will start changing you – not converting you into another religion but simply making you aware that religion has nothing to do with beliefs, Hindu, Christian, Mohammedan.

Religion is a revolution – a revolution from mind to no-mind, from darkness to light, from death to immortality. Religion is a radical change of your inner gestalt. What you did was just substituting your old beliefs with new beliefs. But I don't think that makes any difference. You worshipped Jesus Christ, now you will be worshipping Krishna; but the worshipper is the same, the worship is the same. You have not changed – you cannot change this way. You can go to the church, you can go to the temple, but you are the same person. Just by changing from church to the temple, do you think there will be any transformation of your consciousness? It's not so cheap. It needs tremendous inner work, it needs great awareness. It is not a question of placing one belief instead of another, one image instead of another, finding substitutes.

The basic question is how to get unidentified with the body, with the mind, how to know that you are just a watcher, a watcher on the hills, above the clouds, unidentified with any cloud, totally beyond, beyond the beyond.

My sannyasins don't belong to any religion although all religions belong to them. They are vast enough: they can absorb whatsoever is beautiful in Jesus and they can absorb whatsoever is beautiful in Krishna. Why change Jesus with Krishna? – because Jesus has something beautiful which Krishna has not got, and Krishna has something else which is beautiful which is missing in Jesus. And you will be far more complete if Jesus, Krishna, Mohammed, Moses, Zarathustra, Lao Tzu, Ko Hsuan, Kabir, Bahauddin, all become part of your inner being. There is no need to be so miserly. Your consciousness is so vast it can contain the whole universe, it can contain the whole sky. Even the sky is not the limit!

That's my whole effort here: to make you more and more available to all aspects of religiousness. Krishna has something beautiful – the flute, the song, the celebration – which is missing in Jesus. But Jesus also has something immensely significant – the cross, the sacrifice, the readiness to die so willingly, with a prayer on his lips that, "Forgive, father, all these people, because they know not what they are doing," with such compassion, with such forgiveness. There is no need to drop Jesus. Why not make space enough that they all can be part of you? They are aspects. And you will be missing Buddha – the serenity, the calmness. And you will be missing Bodhidharma – the laughter. And you will be missing Meera – the dance.

Why choose? Why be this or that? Why not love all that is beautiful? You can love the roses, you can love the lotuses, you can love all kinds of flowers. These are all flowerings of God.

You will feel a little confused because you would like me to give you another substitute, and I don't give you another substitute. I make you spacious, I make you more open to *all* possibilities.

A religious consciousness can contain all that has happened up to now, that is happening now, and that will ever happen in the future. That vastness is the real change that brings you into the shrine of God. And God has many doors – Jesus says: My God's mansion has many rooms – he can contain contradictions.

You are worried because you will see many contradictions here. When I am speaking on Meera I will be speaking for love. When I am speaking on Buddha I will be speaking for meditation. When I am speaking on Tao I will be speaking on transcendence of love and meditation both. And you will be confused, you will think that I am contradictory. I am not contradictory, I am simply vast enough – I can contain contradictions. And my whole effort is to make you also capable of containing all contradictions in such a deep synchronicity that the opposites become complementaries. Then your inner noise disappears and a melody arises. That melody, that harmony is prayer.

The third question:

Osho,
What is the hardest work that you ever do?

I do my hardest work before breakfast. That is getting up!

Have you heard about the guy whose name was Will Knott, but who was so lazy he signed his name Won't?

I belong to the same category. I am a lazy man's guide to enlightenment!

The fourth question:

Osho,
Can't people learn by imitating others?

That's how people learn, but that's how people remain stupid, too. The only way practiced hitherto is that of imitating others. That makes you knowledgeable but it does not make you intelligent. It makes you more informed but it does not release your wisdom. It will make you efficient as far as outer world is concerned – you will become a better mechanic, a better technician – but as far as the inner dimension is concerned you will become more and more stupid if you imitate.

There are things which are learned by imitation: for example, language you have to learn by imitation, otherwise you won't know any language. Science has to be learned through others. But the inner world is totally different; it follows a totally different law. There imitation is a barrier not a bridge, a wall not a bridge. There you have to learn on your own.

But people go on doing the same kind of imitation in the inner world too, so they start imitating Buddha, they start imitating Jesus, they start imitating Mahavira, and they end up by being only carbon copies. They become more and more stupid. They cannot find their original face.

You can sit like a Buddha, you can close your eyes like a Buddha, you can use the same posture, you can sit under the same kind of tree, you can eat the same kind of food in the same quantity, you can sleep the way Buddha used to sleep, get up at the time Buddha used to get up – you can do everything in the minutest detail exactly like a Buddha, but it will be all acting; it won't make you an awakened one.

A little rabbit is ready to become an adult, so his daddy says, "Today I will show you how to behave with the ladies!" So they go and find in the garden six beautiful female rabbits.

"Look at me," says daddy rabbit. "Watch! Be aware!"

"Hello, madam," says daddy as he jumps on the first female. And then some time after his jerking is over he says, "Good-bye, madam!"

Then he jumps on the second one with a very polite, "Hello. madam," then "Good-bye madam!"

And so on and so forth, very very slowly...

When he is finished he goes to his son. The little rabbit seems very feverish. "Did you get it?" asks his father.

"Oh yes, yes, yes!" says the young one. And running at full speed without a single stop he goes on jumping, "Hello madam, good-bye madam, hello madam, good-bye madam, hello madam, good-bye madam, hello madam, good-bye madam... hello daddy, good-bye daddy!"

Imitation will make you very stupid, unintelligent. It is the way of the mediocre. Beware of it. In the inner world – and that is the world I am concerned with and that is the world you are here for – imitation won't help not at all. You have to drop imitating completely, totally entirely, because each individual is unique, so unique that if he imitates anybody else he will miss his uniqueness, and in that uniqueness is his spirit, is his very being. In his uniqueness is hidden his god.

Cannot you observe that Jesus happened only once? And for

two thousand years, how many people have tried to imitate him? Millions. And how many have become Jesus Christ? Not a single one. The same is true about Zarathustra, about Lao Tzu, about Buddha, about Mahavira, about Krishna. Not even a single person has been able to repeat, and it is not that people have not tried; people have tried in every possible way. Millions of people have tried to be like Buddha – who would not like to be like a Buddha? – but they have all failed, utterly failed. Is it not a great lesson to be learned?

Just open your eyes and see that God never creates two persons exactly similar; he does not repeat. He is really a creator.

It happened once:

A man purchased a Picasso painting. It was very costly, one million dollars, but he knew perfectly well that it is authentic – he knew it because he was an eye witness when Picasso was doing it. When he had purchased he was so happy – he was a friend to Picasso – he went to show him the painting and to tell him that, "I have purchased your painting. Of course it has cost me a fortune, but I am immensely happy that I have got one of your original paintings with me."

Picasso looked at the painting and said, "This is not original – this is a copy."

The man was shocked. Then he has been robbed of one million dollars! He said, "But what are you saying? – because I have seen with my own eyes! I was staying with you in those days when you were painting this!"

And the woman who used to live in those days with Picasso also said that, "You must be joking because I also remember. You have done this painting yourself and your friend was staying with us."

Picasso said, "I know perfectly well that I have painted it, but it is still not an original because I have painted the same painting before too. Whether I have made the copy or somebody else had made the copy, it makes no difference; it is a copy, it is not original. Yes, I have painted it, but it is a repetition. I will not call it original."

God is not repetitive; he is always original.

Rejoice in the fact that he has created you an original being. You are not supposed to be anybody else but yourself. It is disrespectful towards God, it is ungrateful towards God – even the effort, even the desire to be somebody else. Feel thankful and grateful that he has never created anybody like you and he will never create anybody like you. Don't miss this opportunity by imitating.

And why people imitate? – because they don't trust their own intelligence. They are afraid that if they move on their own they may commit some mistake, so it is better to follow somebody who knows. That is the greatest mistake in life, to follow somebody who knows, because then you will never mature. One grows by committing many mistakes.

Commit as many mistakes as possible. Commit new mistakes every day – be inventive, be creative about mistakes. Just remember one thing: don't create the same mistake again; that is not intelligent. But if you commit the mistake for the first time it is beautiful, it is great, because that will help you to grow; that will help you to find out who you are. Just following somebody, even if you reach heaven it will not be worth reaching. You will reach like a child; you will not be able to enjoy, and you will remain foolish even there, and you will go on doing your foolish things even in heaven. It is better to fall into hell but remain unique, remain yourself; then even hell can be transformed into a heaven.

After thirty years of happy marriage, Sadie was on her deathbed. The doctor had given up all hope.

Her loving husband, Saul, cried out tearfully, "Oh Sadie, oh Sadie, just tell me if there is anything I can do!"

From her deathbed Sadie whispered, "Oh Saul, oh Saul, I want you to do something for me you have never done in all these years."

"Oh yes, Sadie!" cried Saul. "I will do anything for you, my Sadie!"

"Saul, I want you to kiss me here between my legs."

"Oh Sadie, I can't do that!"

"Oh, but Saul, you said you would do anything!"

So bravely Saul said okay and proceeded to kiss her between

her legs.

All of a sudden a great rosy glow came over Sadie. She became completely well and jumped up out of bed crying, "Oh wonderful Saul!"

But Saul slumped back on the floor crying and beating his breast. Sadie asked, "What is wrong, Saul?"

Saul said through his tears, "Oh, but I could have saved my mother and my sister too!"

Be a little more intelligent. In the outer world, imitate, or whatsoever you want to, do. But in the inner remain original, remain authentically your own self

I would like to see each of my sannyasin a unique peak, incomparable to anybody else. That's why I don't give you any discipline: I want you to discover it. I will help you to become more conscious, but I will not tell you what to do; that has to come out of your own consciousness. I will not give you ten commandments, I will not make rules and regulations for you. You all hanker for rules and regulations because that is easy: I tell you, "Do this, don't do that," you need not use your own intelligence. It is perfectly good: you trust me and you go on doing whatsoever I say, but that will be only control, repression; it will not be freedom, it will not be consciousness.

And in the world of freedom the first step is the last step too. You have to begin from the first step: If the first step is taken in slavery, the last step will also be part of it. The first step has to be taken in tremendous freedom.

If you are here you are here on your own accord. If you are sannyasins it is your surrender, it is your own decision, it is your own commitment. I don't make any conditions on you and I don't want you to make any conditions on me from your side.

Just the other day I received a letter... The person asked for sannyas in such an aggressive way, as if he is doing some favor to me. And the way he writes the letter is not at all that of a man who wants to surrender, it is that of demand – each word is violent. He says, "Give me sannyas today. I cannot wait. Either say yes or no. I don't want to follow Arup's suggestions; I don't want to do anything told by somebody else. You simply tell me whether you are going to give me sannyas today or not.

This afternoon I want the answer!"

Now is this a way to be a sannyasin? This is for the first time in my life I have said no to any person – first time! I have given sannyas to one hundred fifty thousand people; for the first time I had to say no. Sadly I had to say no, because this is not the way. If you make conditions, if you demand...today it is sannyas, after sannyas there will be other things, that "Today I want enlightenment, this very afternoon!"

I don't make any demands on you; please remember not to make any demands on me. I am here just out of my joy; you are here out of your joy. We have met for no other reason. You are not here because of me, I am not here because of you. You are here because of you, I am here because of me. And it is beautiful that we have met – it is a coincidence that we have met.

We can share. I can share whatsoever I have, but it is not an imposition on you. You are not to follow it, you have only to understand it. And if out of your understanding something starts happening in you, then you are the source of that happening, I am not the source of that happening. You need not even be grateful to me.

The fifth question:

Osho,
The transcendental meditators have an advanced siddhi course where they learn to fly, as they call it. I have seen photographs of them hovering above the ground. How they do it?

Mandira,
You go to the photographic department here and learn a little bit about trick photography – and there is nothing more in it. Krishna Bharti, Champa, they will be of immense help to you. Or if you want really a crazy man then go to Sarjano; he will teach you trick photography. It is all trick photography, nothing else – no *siddhi*, no flying, nothing else.

But stupid people become very much interested in such sheer nonsense. If transcendental meditators can fly, what is the need for Maharishi Mahesh Yogi to have an airplane? There is no need at all! We have met – I have met Maharishi Mahesh Yogi just by accident. I was having a camp in Pahalgam in Kashmir and he was also having a camp in Pahalgam. His disciples became very much interested and they wanted me to come to them and to talk to them, so I went there. We met. The man is simply ordinary, nothing special. And what he is teaching in the West is a very traditional thing in India; any stupid person knows about it.

Just by repeating a mantra you can create a false sense of serenity. It is just autohypnosis and nothing else. You need not go to anybody, you need not learn any Sanskrit mantra, you can just repeat your own name. Your name is Mandira – you can simply go on repeating "Mandira, Mandira, Mandira, Mandira..." Go on repeating. If you repeat it for fifteen minutes you will feel a tranquilizing effect; it is a nonmedicinal tranquilizer. It is good as far as tranquilizers go, but it has nothing to do with meditation. Transcendental Meditation is neither meditation nor transcendental. But now it is flopping, and because it is flopping, something new has to be invented. Now they have invented *siddhis* and this is nothing but trick photography.

The last question:

Osho,
I am continuously worried what others are thinking about me, because I have a very long nose. How can I stop worrying about others' opinions?

I don't think anybody has taken any note about your nose – nobody has reported to me. In fact, when I gave you sannyas I didn't notice it either. I started thinking, reading your question, that "What nose she is talking about?" People are worried about themselves – why they should be worried about you?

Sant Maharaj has written to me that, "Osho, you are talking about that Prince Philip has a twenty-five-inch-long prick, and my prick is getting smaller every day, and I am worried! Am I becoming a child again?" Now, if Sant comes to see you will he be concerned about his own problem or about your nose?

Everybody has so many problems... Even a person like me who has no problems did not notice your nose then what to say about others? You simply forget!

In an old ladies' home things were pretty boring, so one of the inmates decided to create some interest by running naked through the common room. After she had done it one old lady looked up from her knitting and said, "Was that Millie?"

"Yes," said the old lady next to her. "What was she wearing?"

"I don't know," said the first, "but it really needs ironing!"

And you don't know about long noses...

The platoon is ready for inspection by the general. The captain walks up and down to check that everything is in order. Suddenly he turns to the corporal and says, "Could not that soldier with the long nose be put in the second row?"

"He is in the third row, captain!" replies the corporal.

Don't be worried about people. And a long nose has its own beauty! It shows intelligence! You see the Jews – from where their intelligence comes? Long noses and small pricks! Now Sant should be worried because as the prick will become smaller the nose will become longer – because somewhere it has to show! You being a woman, don't be worried at all. And be assertive as the liberated women all over the world say. Just exhibit your nose everywhere. Don't be worried. What is wrong in having a long nose? Just you can do better *pranyam*. You can have better and stronger lungs, you will live longer. Nothing is wrong in it.

A sex maniac walks up to the reception desk of a hotel. He is carrying a chicken under his arms.

"Do you have a room for the night?" he asks.

"Yes, sir," replies the clerk.

"Then make it a double, please!"

You missed it!

This is assertiveness. Why bother about people? If you love

the chicken, you love the chicken!

It is your nose and God has made it long. He must have some hidden purpose behind it. Enjoy it. Don't try to hide it. Exhibit it. And next time when you come, please inform me before you come so I can see also. I enjoy all kinds of unique things!

Mind Is the Only Problem

The first question:

Osho,
What is wrong with me that I cannot see what you are showing to me?

There is only one thing wrong with everybody, not only with you. That is a universal problem; it has nothing to do with individuals. It is the mind – the mind keeps your vision closed. Mind means your past, your memories, your prejudices, your conditionings; whatsoever you have been told, taught, educated – all that functions as a barrier. It does not allow you to see clearly, it does not allow you even to listen what is being said. The moment you hear something, immediately it turns into something else; passing through your mind it is distorted. Unless you put your mind aside you cannot see. And that is a universal problem: it cannot be avoided.

Each society has to give a certain mind to the children. The children cannot be left without minds, otherwise they will not be able to cope with life, they will not be able to survive. It is absolutely necessary that a certain kind of education should be given to them, but whatsoever education is given to them becomes a barrier to their inner vision. It is a necessary evil.

The function of religion is to undo what the society has to do out of sheer necessity.

I am not telling you not to use your mind. Use it when it is needed, but remain capable of putting it aside when it is not needed. Being here with me, being a sannyasin being in this

Buddhafield you can put the mind aside, you can face me in total nudity. And only then there is a possibility to hear that which is said and to see that which is shown to you.

It is difficult, arduous, because we have become so identified with the mind; we are so close to the mind that there seems to be no space between us and the mind. We don't know what is what, where our consciousness begins and the mind ends. They have got mixed into each other, intertwined, intermingled; their boundaries have become confused. There is no definite, clear-cut separation between consciousness and mind.

Learning to watch your thought processes will help you to create the space. Watching creates distance from your mind. The watcher becomes slowly, slowly distant from the watched; the observer and the observed start moving farther and farther away from each other. Soon the watcher is on the hilltop and the watched is in the dark valley far below, and the distinction is so clear, then there is no problem at all.

Education is a necessity, unavoidable; mind is a necessity, unavoidable. But there comes a moment in your life when something higher than the mind is needed, when you need to transcend the mind, when you go beyond it. That is the whole process of meditation.

Listening to me *through* the mind is bound to create more problems for you rather than solving them, because whatsoever I say will be heard with so many prejudices that by the time it reaches to you it is no more the thing that was said.

A little boy and his father are in front of the lion's cage at the zoo. Suddenly the little boy comes too close to the cage and the lion is almost on the boy.

A man standing by with a swift movement grabs the boy and saves him.

A journalist happens to be among the crowd, so he decides to write an article about it. Among other questions he asks the man, "What party do you belong to?"

"I am a Nazi," replies the man.

The next day the newspaper carries the following headline: "A dirty Nazi snatches the lunch of a hungry African immigrant."

That's the way how prejudices function. Prejudices create immediate interpretations in you, and they are so quick, they don't give you any time to ponder over. You understand only that which you *can* understand, but that is not understanding at all; you are moving in circles.

What I am saying to you is something that you have never known before, is something absolutely unknown to you. It is something mysterious; you cannot figure it out by your own calculations. You have to be more aware so that your prejudices don't interfere, so that your old ideas don't come in, otherwise you will immediately jump upon conclusions.

And mind is very stupid, it is never intelligent. Mind is never original – it cannot be by its very nature – it only goes on and on repeating the old junk that it knows already; it cannot see anything new. If you come across something absolutely new you will simply miss it; you will not be able to see it or you will see something which is not there at all.

Gilliardi arrived in the United States and after a few weeks found he had great need of a woman. He tried flirting with a few at a nearby bar but was unsuccessful because he spoke very little English. Finally one night he picked up a streetwalker and she took him to her apartment. They were in bed making violent love when suddenly Gilliardi realized that he had not spoken a single word to her.

"Miss-a," he said, "I come-a from-a the other side."

"Oh?" said the girl. "This I gotta see!"

You will have to forget your language if you want to understand my language. You will have to forget yourself if you want to be in tune with me. That much risk you will have to take.

That's why people who are very knowledgeable when they come here are absolutely incapable to understand anything, not because they are ignorant but because they are knowledgeable. The Hindu comes here to listen me quote the Vedas; instead I quote a joke. He is shocked. He wanted to hear *richas* to be repeated from the Vedas and the Upanishads: that's what he has been expecting. His expectation is so much that he cannot understand what is happening here. If I had quoted from the scriptures he would have relaxed, he would have felt that he has understood, simply because he would have thought that I am supporting his ideas. He comes here not to understand something new, he comes here to be strengthened, supported, nourished in his own beliefs. He will go very happy if I am supporting his ideas. And one thing is absolutely certain: his ideas have not helped him at all, otherwise there was no need to come here. To come here and still hanker to be supported simply shows the stupidity.

If your ideas are right you need not come here; you live your ideas, you practice them. You have lived according to your ideas and you have reached nowhere. Your Vedas have failed. Your Upanishads have become just a parrot-like phenomenon in you. You go on repeating beautiful words. If you have come here to get some support, some props for your falling ego, for your disintegrating ego, then you have come to a wrong place. Then listening to me he will be shocked; he will immediately close himself. He will become almost blind and deaf.

Jesus says again and again to his disciples, "If you have ears, listen. If you have eyes, see." Was he talking to blind people and deaf people? He was just talking to ordinary people like you who were able to see and hear perfectly well. Then what does he mean? He simply means your ears are so much full of noise and your eyes are already so full of ideas that it is impossible to reach you, to touch your heart, to move your heart.

Every day I receive many letters, many questions from Christians, from Mohammedans, from Hindus, from all kinds of people who have come with a certain idea. If by chance they feel that I am saying things according to them they are immensely happy and they write to me great letters of thankfulness, gratitude. And all that is nonsense; it is neither gratitude nor thankfulness, because in their letters it is very clear: they are not agreeing with me, they are happy that they are finding me agreeing with them. But that is just a coincidence. Now, here are three thousand people – I am bound to say something which will support somebody's idea.

And the next day the same person writes an angry letter –

because once I receive somebody's letter of gratitude I know what has been the cause; immediately the other day I am bound to say something specially for him. And without fail he writes an angry letter, that "I used to think that you are enlightened, but you are not! I am sorry to say, but I have to say the truth. "Just the other day the truth was totally different. Truth changes so easily; if it fits with you it is absolutely okay.

I am not here to support you, I am here to dismantle your mind. You need hammering in many ways.

A follower of Gurdjieff was here few months before Nirvana's father, old man, and he had come with great love and great respect – and he has been writing letters to me that "I want to come before I die, I want to see you. I could not see Gurdjieff; at least I don't want to miss this opportunity of seeing you." And then he found an opportunity – some money came by and he immediately rushed...And he was very happy because whatsoever I was saying was fulfilling his expectations.

And then Pradeepa disturbed him. She asked a question to me about him, that "Why he is not taking sannyas? When he is so much in tune with you, why he is not taking sannyas?" And just few words I told and all his joy disappeared. The next day in anger he left – immediately wrote a letter that, "I am very much disillusioned. I had never expected that you will say such things."

If I was saying nice things about Gurdjieff or things which were fitting with his idea of Gurdjieff – they may fit with Gurdjieff or not, that was not the point – if they were fitting with *his* idea of Gurdjieff...He had never been to Gurdjieff; if he had been to Gurdjieff the same would happen there – he would have gone angry. If he had not come here he would have remained loving and respectful towards me his whole life; he would have died with great love towards me. But what kind of love is this? This is not true love.

True love has courage enough. It is ready even to die, what to say about dropping few prejudices? But people cling to their prejudices as if they are carrying a great treasure.

Knowledgeable people are the most ignorant people in the world; the ignorant people are not so ignorant.

You must be carrying some knowledge within you – drop your knowledge. This is not a place to carry your knowledge. This is not a place where you can gather more information, where you can become more learned. This is a place to become more innocent, and then things will start happening very easily. If you are carrying some subtle ideas deep down in your unconscious, then you are always looking – maybe not consciously, maybe not very deliberately, but always looking – to be supported, nourished. And if something is not supporting, it hurts, it wounds, and immediately you shrink back, you withdraw from me.

And this thing goes on happening every day. People come close to me, they withdraw; they come close to me, they withdraw again. This game goes on happening until finally they realize the whole stupidity and wastage of time.

An aboriginal, working at a sheep station in the outback of Australia, rides into the homestead on his horse, obviously upset, dismounts and runs over to the boss. "Hey, boss, my wife – she just hadum one plenty white baby!"

"Hold on there, Jacky," replies the cocky, "these things happen. You know we have hundreds of white sheep and occasionally we get a black one...it's just one of those things."

Jacky considers thoughtfully for a moment and then says, "Okay, boss, I won't make trouble for you about the white picaninny and you don't say nothing about them black sheep!"

You ask me: "What's wrong with me that I cannot see what you are showing to me?"

Nothing specially wrong with you, just the same human problem: the problem of the mind. If you are intelligent you can put it aside immediately, right now. All that is needed is an intelligent grasp, just a single moment's glimpse, and you are out of it – because the mind is not holding you, you are holding the mind.

It happened:

A man came to Sheik Farid, a Sufi mystic, a great Sufi mystic and a very strange man. The man said, "How can I get out of my chains, my attachment, my ideas, my prejudices?"

Farid had his own way of answering things. Rather than answering to the person he simply ran to a pillar which was nearby, clung to the pillar and started shouting, "Save me from the pillar!"

The man could not believe what is happening – is he mad or something? And he was shouting so loudly that people started coming from the street in. A crowd gathered and they asked, "What is the matter with you? Have you gone crazy? You are holding the pillar, not the pillar holding you. You can leave it!"

And the man also said, "I had thought that this man is a man of great understanding and he seems to be just a madman! I had asked a very subtle question, a very spiritual question which has always been asked by seekers: how to get out of my attachments with ideas things people? And rather than answering me he simply jumped and clung to the pillar and started shouting, 'Save me from the pillar!'"

Farid looked at the man and he said, "If you can understand this, then you don't need any answer. Go home and ponder over it. If the pillar is not holding me, neither your chains are holding you – you are holding them. I can leave the pillar – look I am leaving the pillar and I am saved! You also leave..."

The man must have been really intelligent – he understood. There was a shock for a moment, the way the question was answered, but in that very shock he could see the point. It penetrated to his very heart.

He touched the feet of Farid and said, "It is finished! I have asked the same question to many mahatmas, to many saints, and they gave me great discourses on it, and nothing happened. And your mad effort to answer me has immediately transformed something in me. Now I am not going back to my old world, I am going to be with you. I have found the man I was searching all my life. I needed a man like you who can hit me so hard, who could show me my stupidity."

You can drop your mind this very moment because the mind cannot hold you. Mind is just a mechanism, a machine; you can get out of it any moment. But you have invested so much in it that YOU cling to IT, and then you go on asking how to get out of it. The doors are open; there is nobody preventing you. You can come out of it! But rather than coming out of it you simply go on asking, "How to come out of it?" There is no question of "how."

Whenever anybody asked Gautam Buddha, "How to come out of my misery?" he always used to say that, "If your house is on fire, will you ask anybody how to come out of it? Will you wait for some learned answer? Will you consult scriptures? Or you will jump? If the door is not open, if the door is also aflame, you will jump from the window. You will not even bother that jumping out from the window will look a little odd. If you are in your bath room taking a bath and you are naked, you will not even bother to wrap around a towel; you will simply run out naked. And you will not think that this is not mannerly, against etiquette, running out naked; you won't bother at all. If you understand that the house is on fire you will find the way. But you are simply talking, talking how to get out of misery; you are not aware of the misery."

If one is really aware of the misery, nobody can prevent you. And there is no need to postpone. Postponement means that you have a very mediocre mind. The intelligent person acts immediately because who knows about the next moment? The tomorrow never comes.

The second question:

Osho,
What is wrong with marriage? Why do you speak always against it?

Marriage is a great institution. Without marriage life will be very empty. Without marriage you will be all Buddhas! It is marriage that keeps the world going on; it keeps things running. It keeps all kinds of things moving, alive. In fact, without marriage there will be no religion at all.

Religion exists not because of God or for God; it is because of marriage. Marriage creates so much misery that one has to meditate; meditation is a byproduct. Without marriage, who will bother to meditate? For what? You will be already blissful! Without marriage there will be no renunciation, Buddha would not have left the world – for what? His wife, Yashodhara, must have created the situation – Mahavira would not have escaped to the mountains. Without marriage there would have been no Buddha, no Mahavira. Just think: the history would have been very flat, without any salt, tasteless. Marriage keeps this whole "sorry-go-round" on and on. People call it "merry-go-round"....

I am not against marriage – without marriage, ninety-nine per cent jokes will disappear from the world. How I can be against marriage? I am all for it.

Marriage makes many things possible.

"Marriage is the process of finding what kind of man your wife would have preferred!" It is a mirror.

Drinking in a bar, two friends are chatting about life.

"Who introduced you to your wife?" asks one.

The other says, "We met casually. I can't blame anyone else."

Two women are chatting at the hairdresser.

One says, "My husband travels a lot. He spent one month at home out of the whole year!"

"One month?" exclaims the other. "That must be very annoying to you."

"No...a month goes by fast!"

The doctor and his wife are walking down the street when they are passed by an incredibly beautiful woman. She has big tits, a nice body and a beautiful face. She seems a little self-conscious of her beauty and as she passes by the doctor she smiles a familiar smile.

"Who is that lady?" asks the wife.

A little shy, the doctor answers, "A client."

"I know," the wife replies, "but is she your client or are you hers?"

In a small city in the interior of Brazil, a couple is sitting on a bench outside the house enjoying the moonlight. Maria turns to Ze and says, "Ze, do you know something? Tomorrow it is going to be twenty-five years that we have been married!"

And Ze answers, "Yeah!"

"Twenty-five years...Uau! Ze, it is a lot!"

"Yeah!"

"Look, Ze, why don't we catch some of the chickens in the yard and kill them for tomorrow?"

"Why, Maria? Poor chickens...it is not their fault!"

"Hey!" cried Satan to the arrival. "You act as if you own the place."

"I do," came the reply. "My wife gave it to me before I died."

Now, without marriage all these jokes will disappear, without marriage there will be no misery – and no laughter either. There will be so much silence...it will be Nirvana on the earth! Marriage keeps thousands of things going on: the religion, the state, the nations, the wars, the literature, the movies, the science; everything, in fact, depends on the institution of marriage.

I am not *against* marriage; I simply want you to be aware that there is a possibility of going beyond it too. But that possibility also open up only because marriage creates so much misery for you, so much anguish and anxiety for you, that you have to learn how to transcend it. It is a great push for transcendence. Marriage is not unnecessary; it is needed to bring you to your senses, to bring you to your sanity. Marriage is necessary and yet there comes a point when you have to transcend it too. It is like a ladder. You go up the ladder, it takes you up, but there comes a moment when you have to leave the ladder behind. If you go on clinging to the ladder, then there is danger.

Learn something from marriage. Marriage represents the whole world in a miniature form: it teaches you many things. It is only the mediocre ones who learn nothing. Otherwise it will teach you that you don't know what love is, that you don't know how to relate, that you don't know how to communicate, that you don't know how to commune, that you don't know how to live with another. It is a mirror: it shows your face to you in all its different aspects. And it is all needed for your maturity. But a person who remains clinging to it forever remains immature. One has to go beyond it too.

Marriage basically means that you are not able yet to be

alone; you need the other. Without the other you feel meaningless and with the other you feel miserable. Marriage is really a dilemma! If you are alone you are miserable; if you are together you are miserable. It teaches you your reality, that something deep inside you needs transformation so that you can be blissful alone and you can be blissful together. Then marriage is no more marriage because then it is no more bondage. Then it is sharing, then it is love. Then it gives *you* freedom and you give the freedom needed for the other's growth.

The ordinary marriage is an unconscious bondage: you cannot live alone so you become dependent on the other; the other cannot live alone so he or she becomes dependent on you. And we hate the person on which we are dependent; nobody likes to depend on anybody. Our deepest desire is to have freedom, total freedom – and dependence is against freedom. Everybody hates dependence, and that's why couples are continuously fighting, not knowing why they are fighting. They have to meditate over it, they have to contemplate over it, why they are fighting. Everything is just an excuse to fight. If you change one excuse, another excuse will be found; if no excuse is left then excuses will be invented, but somehow the fight has to be there.

The fight has a fundamental reason which has nothing to do with anything else. The fundamental reason is you hate the person you have to depend upon. You don't want to recognize it – you don't want to recognize the fact that you hate the person you believe you love. You hate simply because it is the other that hinders, defines your territories, keeps you confined, makes you feel limited from every side. Your freedom is crippled and paralyzed. How can you love the other person? And the same you are doing to the other. How can the other person love you?

Marriage is a great teaching; it is an opportunity to learn something: to learn that dependence is not love, that to depend means conflict, anger, rage, hatred, jealousy, possessiveness, domination. And one has to learn not to depend. But for that you will need great meditativeness so that you can be so blissful on your own that you don't need the other. When you don't need the other, the dependence disappears. Once you don't need the other you can share your joy – and sharing is beautiful.

I would like a different kind of relationship in the world. I call it relating just to make it different from your old kind of relationship. I would like a different kind of marriage in the world. I will not call it marriage because that word has become poisoned. I would like to call it just a friendship; no legal bondage, just a loving togetherness; no promise for tomorrow – this moment is enough. And if you love each other this moment and if you enjoy each other this moment, if you can share with each other this moment. the next moment will be born out of it; it will become more and more enriched. As time passes by, your love will become deeper, it will start having new dimensions, but it will not create any bondage.

Hence *my* vision of a new humanity does not have any place for the old kind of marriage or old kind of family because we have suffered enough. I know perfectly well that man and woman will need to be together, but not out of need, but out of overflowing joy; not out of poverty but out of richness – because you have so much that you have to give. Just like when a flower opens, its fragrance is released to the winds because it is so full of fragrance it *has* to release it. Or when a cloud comes in the sky it showers; it has to shower – it is so full of rain water it has to share.

Up to now we have not helped man to know what love is; on the contrary we have been forcing him to get married. Marriage has to be the first thing and then love will come on its own accord. That whole idea has proved totally wrong. Man has lived in hell for centuries. He has become accustomed, that is true, in fact so much accustomed that the very idea of a world without marriage shocks him.

Just the other day I received a letter that, "If marriage disappears and the family disappears, what will happen to children?" What has happened to children with the marriage and with the family? All children are born so beautiful, so innocent, so intelligent, and the family and the marriage destroy them. They start seeing their mothers and fathers continuously quarreling, nagging. They become accustomed of it and they will repeat the same pattern in their life.

I would like marriage to be replaced by relating and family to be replaced by small communes. For example, this commune: a few hundred people living together, working together, producing together, creating together. The children will not be confined to the small families, the children will belong to the whole commune. Not that they will not get affection from their father and mother – they will get *more* affection from their father and mother, because father and mother will also not feel burdened with the children, and they will also get affection from everybody else.

This whole idea of "my child" is also egoistic. Children should belong to the commune. And the commune should decide how many children are needed; it cannot be left now to individual families, otherwise the world will become more and more of a hell. And the commune should also decide that who are the right persons to parent children, to give birth to children. It will decide scientifically the man who can become a father, the woman who can become a mother. All men need not be fathers, all women need not be mothers, but they can mother the children of the whole commune, they can father the children of the whole commune.

We can have better children, more healthy, more intelligent, more talented, more beautiful, if we use a little science, which is available now. Now, going on producing like animals is very primitive, it is absolutely absurd. And there is no need also that two persons who are in love should produce the child, because now there are scientific ways. If you can get your son to be as intelligent as Albert Einstein then why bother that you should give birth from your own chromosomes? Why not he can be given birth through Albert Einstein's cells? Just as people dying donate their eyes they can donate their chromosomes, which will be beautiful. Those chromosomes can be preserved for thousands of years; there is no problem in it. And we can go on improving on human race. We are doing it as far as animals are concerned; you can see the difference.

In India, you look at the cows.. . and the foolish Indians think that they respect the cows. Just they call them mothers, that's all; otherwise the poorest cows in the world are the Indian cows, starving, ill, giving so little milk that it is uneconomical, absolutely uneconomical, to preserve them. But all over the world wherever science has entered, better cows, better bulls, better dogs, better animals have become available.

The same is possible with man. There is no need to go on hanging around old ideas. We can stop people like Adolf Hitler, Genghis Khan, Nadir Shah from being born because the first cell of the father is decisive, the egg of the mother is decisive. Now it can be decided that what kind of child will be born. Will he be an Adolf Hitler or an Albert Einstein? His whole future can be read – it can almost be predicted.

Only one thing will remain unpredictable forever, that is his enlightenment; that will remain unpredictable. Otherwise everything will be predictable. But we can give birth to people who are more intelligent, more healthy. Of course then there is more possibility of their becoming enlightened, of their becoming Buddhas.

We have to change the whole structure of humanity from the very roots. Marriage has to go the way it has existed up to now and a totally new concept has to be introduced. Only then a new man can be born on the earth.

The third question:

Osho,
Do you know Italian language?

Michael Potato,
I don't know much Italian language, but the little bit that I know is so beautiful that I would like to know it more. But I am a lazy person – I cannot learn anything. In fact, whatsoever I am, I am because I have learned only one thing: how to go on unlearning. Whatsoever I am, I am through the process of unlearning. I would have loved to know Italian language; it seems to be beautiful. But now there is no possibility. Just a little bit – which is not much...

An old Italian and a young Italian are sitting in an outdoor cafe watching the women go by.

The old Italian asks the young one, "Hey, Giuseppe, you like big-a fat-a ass-a?"

The young man answers, "No, I like nice small-a ass-a!"

Some time goes by and the old Italian asks, "You like big-a saggy tits-a?"

"No," answers the young Italian, "I like nice little tits-a".

Some time passes again and the old man asks, "You like garlic-a breath-a?"

"No, I like nice sweet-a breath-a."

Then the old Italian says, "If you don't-a like-a big-a, fat-a ass-a, you don't-a like-a big-a saggy tits-a, and you don't-a like-a garlic-a breath-a, then how come you keep-a fucking my wife-a?"

This much Italian... not more than that! But this is enough for my purposes.

The fourth question:

Osho,

What you are talking and doing here does not seem to be philosophy or religion to me at all.

Reverend Banana,

Once, for a change, you are right, sir. It is not philosophy, it is not religion, it is a totally different phenomenon. I am not interested in philosophy at all because philosophy has not done any service to humanity, it has only filled people's minds with unnecessary chattering and noise. It has not given man any radical transformation, it gives you only a false feeling of knowing. It is a pseudo phenomenon and it prevents you from searching the real truth because you become so addicted with words, you forget totally that truth is not a word, that God is not a word, that love is not a word. The philosopher becomes more and more wordy. He becomes so full of words, he forgets completely his being. He is surrounded with the crowds of words, clouds of theories, hypotheses, which all pretend to be conclusive, but none of them is conclusive.

Philosophy has not reached to any conclusion and it will never reach – it is an exercise in utter futility. It is a good game if you want to play an intellectual game, an intellectual gymnastics; it is hair splitting.

But I am not interested in it at all – and I know it from the inside: I have been a student of philosophy and a professor of philosophy too. I know it as an insider that the most useless activity in the world is philosophy, the most uncreative, the most pretentious – but very ego-fulfilling, gives you great ideas of knowledgeability without making you wise at all.

When P.D. Ouspensky met George Gurdjieff for the first time he was already a world-famous philosopher, mathematician. He has written his most important book, *Tertium Organum*. The book is really tremendously beautiful; if you are interested in philosophy, then it is unique. A man who is interested in philosophy, if he misses P.D. Ouspensky's *Tertium Organum*, he misses something very significant.

Ouspensky presented his book, *Tertium Organum*, to Gurdjieff. He just looked for five minutes here and there, threw the book and said to Ouspensky, "You take this piece of paper, go in the other room. On the one side you write what you exactly know and on the other side what you exactly don't know. If you know God, write it on the one side; if you don't know God, write it on the other side. And so about truth, love, enlightenment, immortality."

Ouspensky was a little puzzled, a little shocked, offended too, because his great book was thrown as if it was just disgusting. And I can understand: he must have felt very wounded. But now that he had come to see this strange man he wanted to try what he was asking. He went into the other room with a pencil and the paper. For the first time in his life, he says, "I became aware that I don't know anything at all. It was a cold Russian night; snow was falling outside. Even inside the room it was below zero..." But he started perspiring. A man of world fame could not write a single word – love, enlightenment, truth, God – on the side that Gurdjieff has told, "Write on this side if you know" – not a single word!

After one hour he came out with the empty paper, gave it back to Gurdjieff and said, "I am sorry, but you are really a strange man! You have already done a miracle! It is for the first time that I realize I know nothing."

Gurdjieff started laughing and he said, "How you have been writing such beautiful books? It is easy to write a beautiful book, it is easy to philosophize; it is far more easy if you don't know. If you know, it becomes more difficult."

Ouspensky became a disciple of Gurdjieff, accepting his ignorance.

Gurdjieff said that is the first condition to be fulfilled by a disciple: that he should accept his ignorance; only then things can be done, only then there is any possibility of inner growth. The false has to be known as false; only then the real can be understood as real

I am not a philosopher. My people here are not philosophers either. Yes, once in a while we joke about philosophy, that's all...

A man walked into a pub, crossed the room, walked up the far wall, then across the ceiling, back down the wall by the door and left again without saying a word.

"Did you see that? It was incredible!" said the stupefied bartender to a local philosopher.

"Sure, I saw it – it was really horrible!" said the philosopher. "He was wearing yellow shoes with pink socks!"

The corporal calls his soldiers to attention and asks for a volunteer to accomplish a dangerous mission.

After a few moments he goes up to a soldier and says, "Congratulations, my brave man! I have heard about you, that you are a great philosopher. You are the only one who has stepped forward! Now you have proved your courage and your mettle to me."

The philosopher-soldier looks around in surprise, then answers, "Well, the truth is – the others have all taken a step backwards!"

The philosophers live in a kind of deep sleep, a slumber. He was not aware that everybody has moved back. He must not have been there; he must have been somewhere else.

Wendel Holmes, a Justice of the Supreme Court of America, was known, very much well known in America for his philosophic attitude towards life. One day he left his courtroom and made his way to the railway station where he boarded an express train. An hour later, as the train crossed the Maryland countryside, the ticket inspector entered his compartment and asked to see his ticket. Holmes searched through all his pockets and his wallet, but was unable to find the ticket. A look of anxiety passed across his face.

The ticket inspector, who had recognized Holmes from newspaper reports, said, "Well, there is no need to worry about the ticket, Mr. Holmes. I am sure you forgot to buy one at the station. I can issue you one now."

Holmes' look of worry had deepened. In a perplexed voice he said, "It is not the ticket that worries me. I just realized I don't know where I am going."

Philosophers have never known where they are going.

Reverend Banana, I can understand your concern that things here don't seem to be philosophical – they are not. It is an existential commune. We trust in existence, not in philosophy.

And you say it does not seem religion, too.

That too is true. It is not religion in the sense Christianity is, it is not religion in the sense Hinduism is, it is not religion in the sense Mohammedanism is. It is not fanaticism: there is no dogma, there is no belief It is religion in the sense Buddha is religious, it is religion in the sense Jesus is religious, it is religion in the sense Ko Hsuan is religious. It is not religion but a religiousness, not a question of belief but a question of living.

Religion to me is not ritual. If you are looking for any ritual, no ritual exists here. To me religion is an insight, insight into the beauty of existence, insight into the tremendous mystery that surrounds us, insight into your own being and into the beings of others. It has nothing to do with any dogma, any belief, any creed, any cult – it is not a cult at all – it is just a totally different phenomenon.

We are trying to live a meditative life, working in the ordinary way but working it with a different quality.

People are working in the kitchen, cleaning the toilets, or in the carpentry shop or in the boutique or in the bakery or in the garden – just the ordinary kind of activities, but with a different quality: with a joy, with silence, with love, with bliss, with a dance in their heart, with celebration.

To me, that is true religion: to be able to celebrate life is religion. In that very celebration you come close to God. If one is able to celebrate, God is not far away; if one is not able to celebrate life, then God does not exist for him. God appears only in deep celebration, when you are so full of joy that all misery has left you, all darkness has left you. When you are so full that there is no emptiness in you, that you have started feeling the significance of the ordinary, day-to-day existence, when moment to moment you live totally, intensely, passionately, then God is available.

God is not a person but just an experience, an experience of overwhelming mystery, unfathomable mystery. It is not philosophy in the ordinary sense, it is not religion in the ordinary sense either. It is philosophy in the truest sense of the word – philosophy means love for wisdom; then it is philosophy. Religion, the word, very word, means to be in tune. It comes from *religere*: to be in deep harmony with the whole, to be married with the whole, to be related with the whole, to forget your ego and your separation. Then it is religion.

The last question:

Osho,
Please tell us few jokes about Jesus Christ which are only recorded in the Akashic records.

Okay.

It is a little known fact that Jesus Christ was nearly called Manny shortly after his birth. Just before he was, however, someone walking past the stable peeked a look inside to see what was going on. Hitting his toe on a sharp stone he cried out, "Jesus!"

"Oh, that's a good name," said Mary. "We will call him that."

Jesus walks into a hotel, throws some nails onto the counter and says, "Can you put me up for the night?"

Jesus was resting on the shores of Lake Galilee. A group of children nearby were laughing, throwing water at him and making a lot of noise.

Peter, annoyed, shouted at them, but Jesus stopped him and said, "Let the children come to me..."

The noise, the throwing of water, et cetera, continued even more than before. Finally, Peter, tired and very annoyed, tried to shove them away, but again Jesus stopped him and said, "Peter, I told you to let the children come close to me – so that I can kick them in the ass!"

Religion: The Ultimate Luxury

The first question:

Osho,
I wish you would say something about the Eastern indifference to what you are doing, and the Western attraction.

It is a very natural phenomenon. Religion is the ultimate luxury.

Man lives on three planes. If his bodily needs are fulfilled, only then psychological needs become significant; otherwise not. A hungry man will not be interested in the music of Beethoven, Mozart, Wagner. He will not be interested in the paintings of Michelangelo, Vincent Van Gogh, Picasso. It is natural. His first basic needs are not fulfilled. Once his bodily needs are fulfilled, immediately his consciousness shifts from the physical plane to the psychological. Consciousness remains attached to the plane where it is needed most. You know it in ordinary day-to-day existence too. If your leg is hurting you forget the whole body, your consciousness becomes focused on the leg. If you have a headache, only then you become aware of the existence of the head; otherwise, you remain absolutely unaware of its existence. It goes on functioning silently, your attention is not needed.

Body is the foundation, and the East is suffering from physical needs. Its physical needs are tremendous, so whatsoever goes on in the name of religion is not really religion in the East – it cannot be – it is something else. People gather around Satya Sai Baba, or persons like him, not for spiritual needs, but for physical needs. Somebody is ill and would like a miracle to happen so that he can be cured. Somebody is blind, somebody has no children, somebody has no employment, and they are hoping that by going to the saints, by the blessings of the saints, or by praying into the churches, into the temples, in the mosques, in the *gurudwaras*, their needs will be fulfilled. This is hoping in vain, but the poor man cannot help. He goes on hanging around these illusions. It is a vicious circle: he hangs around illusions in the hope that his needs will be fulfilled, and because he hangs around illusions he does not make any real effort to fulfill his needs. Those needs go on growing bigger and bigger. Then he goes on moving more and more into the illusory. His religion is more of wish-fulfillment – not of growth, not of maturity not of spiritual flight, but of dreaming, hallucinating.

You go for a long fast and you will start fantasizing about food – twenty-four hours you will fantasize about food. You go into loneliness and after the third week you will start talking to yourself. The need is such that you will start living in an illusion, as if there is somebody with whom you are having a dialogue.

The poor man creates a poor God, a God which is nothing but his imagination, a God which exists nowhere. The East has known one day the true religion, now only footprints are left. Buddha knew true religion, Mahavira knew true religion, Krishna knew true religion. They had touched the ultimate peaks of consciousness, but only now echoes are there in the atmosphere. The reality has disappeared long before, we are worshipping the foot-prints.

So people in the East become interested into a kind of religion which I call pseudo, false, basically illusory – and not only that, but positively harmful, because it prevents scientific growth.

If you are hungry you need better technology, not better prayers, not *yagnas*, not offerings to the fire god – that is utter stupidity. You are already poor and you are wasting money, food, purified butter in the fire, in the hope that gods will bless you. How long you have been hoping this way? And those gods have not heard at all. And how long you are going to be deceived by yourself? But just as I said, it is a vicious circle.

The hungrier, the more starving, the more undernourished, the more crowded you become – the more your problems become unmanageable – the more you start hoping, wishing, imagining, dreaming, the more you start going to some stupid people in the hope that miracles will be done. They have never been done and they will never be done. Miracles don't exist.

Miracles are absolutely non-existential, but the poor man's religion remains focused on the possibility of a miracle.

Have you heard about the latest miracle performed by the Polack Pope? He has made a blind man deaf.

Once a couple were thinking about having a baby one evening after an especially good session of love-making.

The woman joyfully exclaimed, "Ah, dear, I think that did it! Ah, I am so happy. What will we call it?"

The husband smiled, removing the unnoticed condom from himself, and said, "We will call him Houdini."

A madman went to the local Jewish tailor who was a kind of philosopher, to try on his new uniform. He dressed in the uniform and went to look in the mirror.

"Wow!" he shouted, "Look at that, Mr. Tailor! You made me a jumpsuit with three sleeves."

"Well," said the tailor, "you never told me how many you wanted."

Mad people going to mad people.

But these mad people are known as *mahatmas* in the East, and the East is full of *mahatmas*. When *you* get tired of one *mahatma* there are other *mahatmas*, and you go on moving from one shop to another shop. And life is short, you can go on remaining in illusion.

The poor man's religion is that of miracles, that's why Christianity has a deep attraction for the eastern man. You can see it happening.

Buddhism has great appeal in the West. Hundreds of Buddhist monasteries are opening up in America, in Europe, in Holland, in Germany; and in India, thousands of people are converting themselves every day into Christianity. What is this mathematics? How it is happening? – for the simple reason, the religion of Gautam the Buddha is appealing only to those whose all needs are fulfilled. It is the highest quality of religion, it is like an Everest.

Jesus has appeal – not because people understand Jesus – he has appeal only because of his miracles. Take the miracles away and people will stop getting into Christianity, they will lose all interest. Hence the Christian theologians, the Christian missionaries go on emphasizing the miracle part, which is just a mythology, which is not true, which is absolutely false – but it is not new. It has been in the air for long, for the simple reason because Jesus also was working in poor people. He was a poor man's son. All his friends, followers were poor people. They can understand only a language which appealed to their needs. *All* his followers were either farmers, gardeners, fishermen, carpenters, or people like these – uneducated, uncultured, unsophisticated. They must have created these stories about him, otherwise they would not have remained with him. These miracle stories function like glue. And for two thousand years that has been the appeal of Christianity.

It always appeals the poor. In India also you will not see Jainas being converted into Christianity – they are rich enough for that. You will not see *brahmins* being converted to Christianity – they are rich enough for that. Then who are the people who are being converted to Christianity? The very poor people, the oppressed, the downtrodden, the aboriginals, the untouchables, the hungry, the starving, the crippled, the paralyzed, the blind, the deaf, the ill, the orphans – these are the people who become interested in Christianity.

Now what they have to do with meditation? They need miracles; they don't want any inward eye, they don't want any spiritual nourishment. That is the first and the most important reason that people are not interested towards my vision, particularly in the East. But about that too, one condition has to be remembered.

In the East too, Japanese are interested in me; because that is the only country which is rich. You will find hundreds of Japanese here. Many centers are opening in Japan for me, many books are being published in Japan. There is great stir in Japan, and I have been really surprised Whenever people come to me I ask, "How long you are going to stay?" Germans almost always stay for three months, four months. Japanese always stay for six months, nine months, twelve months, two years. Japan is the only country which has come to a level of affluence which is rich, and their needs are now totally different. They will not go to Satya Sai Baba, they will not be interested there at all.

India is too poor to understand me, to be interested in me. Indians come here to stay for one day, two days – at the most three days. They come here only for one day, but they want to be treated like others They feel very shocked when they come to know that I will not be initiating them myself, that some of my disciples will initiate them. They feel very shocked: Why this treatment with us? But you are staying only one day here. In the morning you come, you want sannyas in the evening, and tomorrow you are gone. And the people who have been here for six months meditating, going through dozens of growth groups, working hard, you want that you should be treated exactly like them. You may stay the same way, you go through the same processes, you risk as much as they risk – for that they are not ready. But they feel offended, that they should be given the same opportunity.

Again and again they write to me, "Westerners are sitting in front of you and we are told to sit at the back." You should be happy that even you are allowed to sit at the back. Soon there will be no space at the back. You have to earn it. The people who are sitting in front of me have been here for six years, seven years. There are people who have come once and never gone again. They deserve it, they have earned it.

This is the first reason that I am talking about the highest form of religion; because I am talking about the whole world. To me, nations don't mean anything, races don't mean anything, colors don't mean anything. I am talking about a New Man, which is going to be born, which has become almost an absolute necessity because without the New Man the humanity cannot survive anymore. The old is rotten, and we have to get rid of it; but before we get rid of the old the new has to be brought on the scene. My work here consists in giving birth to the New Man, to a new humanity.

The second reason why the Indians are afraid is that Indians already think they know, and they know nothing. They are simply carrying a dead heritage. They are very knowledgeable, they can recite the Gita and the Vedas and the Upanishads, parrotlike, not knowing what they are saying. They have not experienced those truths, but they can recite them like gramophone records. And because of this, they think they know what religion is. Why they should come here?

The West in that way is innocent, is not knowledgeable. It has a tremendous inquiry, but no blocks; it is ready to explore. The knowledgeable person is always willing to explore; he is always afraid because something may go against his knowledge. He would like truth to be according to him, not vice versa. He is not ready to be according to the truth – which needs guts, which needs an open mind.

In the East, particularly in India, people don't have open mind at all. They have very closed minds. They are so full of holy cow dung that there is no space inside.

I can have an appeal only to those who are explorers, adventurers, inquirers, who are in a way innocent.

And the third reason...The third reason is concerned with those people who are neither poor nor knowledgeable. Why they are not coming here? There are rich people in this country. This is a country of contrasts: ninety-eight per cent people are very poor, two per cent people are very rich. Those two per cent rich people are afraid to come, for the simple reason: just to be associated with my name is a danger. They write to me that, "We would like to come, but we are afraid." Just to be associated with my name is dangerous. People will start talking to them, "So you have also become a victim? So you are also hypnotized? We had never thought that you are so mad, so crazy!"

And then, coming to listen to me does not mean just listening, as it means when you go to listen to Krishnamurti. You can listen and go home. Here listening means slowly, slowly getting committed. It is involvement, and involvement means your whole life will change with it. Your family life, your personal life, your social life, your business life – everything will be affected by it. You can go and listen to Krishnamurti, there is no problem in it, you remain outside of any commitment. With me, you become committed.

To listen to me is dangerous for two reasons: one, the fear that you may get involved into it, and then where it will lead? Secondly, you will be condemned by everybody and criticized by everybody. That keeps people holding themselves back. They read, they listen to the tapes – thousands of people listen to the tapes, thousands of people read the books, and millions of people talk and discuss about me, for and against. In fact, anybody who has any intelligence is already divided by me: either for me or against me.

But to come here, to enter the gate needs some courage which Indians have lost long before; otherwise they would not have been slaves for two thousand years. They don't have any courage, the backbones are missing, they have no spine. How they manage to walk and live is a miracle.

And there are people who are not knowledgeable either, who cannot say that they are scholars or pundits or they know anything of Vedas or Upanishads; but then their craze is to imitate the West. Their whole craze is...They have the money, they have the opportunity, they go on rushing towards the West. They go on for world tours they want to have all kinds of gadgets that the West is enjoying. They are not interested in religion, in spirituality. They may show lip service to religion and spirituality, because that is a traditional thing, conventional. But it is only lip service; their hearts are for absolute materialistic values.

These are the reasons why the eastern people, particularly Indians, are not interested here; but the whole world is interested.

And they are also imitators. Just wait a little. When more and more people from the world will be coming here, they will start following them. They are imitators. They are carbon copies. They always have been imitating for two thousand years. They cannot take any step on their own. If they see the West is coming, they will come; but I don't pay any respect to such people. I don't have any place in my heart for such people who are imitators.

You can see it happen everywhere. Rabindranath Tagore got

the Nobel Prize. Before he got the Nobel Prize his book was already published for years – the book on which he got the Nobel Prize, *gitanjali* – but nobody has praised it. Once he got the Nobel Prize, the whole India was praising him, and he could see. He refused the invitation of Calcutta Corporation. They wanted to honor him. He said, "I won't come. I refuse this honor, because the book has been published for many years in the original, and you have never honored me." In fact, no note was taken of his book, and it is one of the greatest books ever written. On the contrary, people were criticizing it, criticizing it because it was not according to the old pattern of Indian poetry. It has something original, and the Indian mind cannot understand anything original; it needs repetitive things, then it praises. But when the whole West started praising him, the whole India was ready to praise him. He became a great "son of the country"; otherwise nobody was bothering about him.

Just now you have seen it happen again. Mother Teresa was here her whole life, working. Nobody was bothering, nobody has really ever heard of her name. Once she got the Nobel Prize, the whole India is agog.

These are imitators. These people don't have any intelligence of their own. They are ready to do anything, whatsoever is being done by the whole world – any stupid thing they will be ready to do.

So just wait. Let more and more people come – and they are coming, they are on the way. My invitation has reached to the farthest corner of the world, and I have stirred millions of hearts and they will be coming. And they are my people, because their bodily needs are fulfilled, so they don't come here asking for some stupid miracle. They don't come here for any psychological needs either. If they have any psychological needs I have got one hundred therapies going on here, so those needs can be fulfilled. My work starts only when your bodily and psychological needs are fulfilled. Then only you can look a little beyond to the spiritual realm.

So whosoever is able to look beyond the body-mind complex belongs to me. Whether he is born in the East or in the West, is black or white, does not matter at all. Whether he is man or woman does not matter at all. I am creating world citizens. And

I am not creating any religion. It is only a religiousness, a diffused kind of religiousness, not very tangible. You cannot make a creed out of it, you cannot make a church out of it – impossible! I am not leaving a single Bible or Koran or Gita so you can make a church out of it. When I will leave the world I will leave at least one thousand books, so contradictory to each other that anybody trying to make out any dogma out of them will go crazy.

It is impossible to make any dogma out of my ideas, but you can transform your being through them. Forget about this East and West business; don't waste my time about these things again and again.

The second question:

Osho,
If an enlightened person cannot lose his Buddhahood, how does a baby born as a Buddha lose his?

Each child is born a Buddha, but cannot remain a Buddha for long. That is part of growth: he has to lose it.

Unless he loses it, he will never be able to understand its value. It is like a fish in the ocean...The fish is born in the ocean, lives in the ocean; but knows nothing of the ocean, cannot know. There is no separation, there is no space, there is no gap between the two. Fetch the fish out of the ocean, throw it on the shore, and immediately there is great understanding in the fish. Now the fish knows for the first time the beauty of the ocean, the joy of the ocean. Now the fish longs for it. Let the fish slip back into the ocean again and see its rejoicing, see its joy.

That's exactly the meaning of the biblical story. Adam and Eve have to leave paradise just to regain it – that's the only way to regain it. Paradise has to be lost. Only then there is awareness. Innocence is one thing – every child is innocent – but to be aware of innocence is a totally different thing. Only a Buddha is aware of innocence; hence the Buddha cannot lose it, because he is aware. The child has to lose it, he is not aware – he cannot be in the very nature of things; he has never lost it.

One morning little Johnny comes down in tears. "Mommy, Mommy," sobs Johnny, "I got so frightened. I woke up, ran to your bed and you were not there. Then I ran to Dad's bed and he was not there. Then I ran into my bed and I was not there!"

This experience is needed. Everything has to get lost. Suddenly there is only emptiness, meaninglessness, darkness, and the search starts again for that which is lost.

Meditation is only a way back home. It is not a search for something new; it is a search for something that was intrinsically our own, but we were bound to be unaware of it.

On the first day of kindergarten, Tommy was nervous and upset and wanted to talk to his mother. A teacher helped him place a telephone call to his home, but when the mother answered, Tommy was too nervous to speak right away.

"Hello," the mother said, "who is this?"

"This is your son," said Tommy, bursting into tears. "Have you forgotten me already?"

Children are innocent, but their innocence is not the innocence of a Buddha. The difference is tremendous. It is unconscious innocence, and because it is unconscious it has no virtue. That's why Jesus says, "Unless you are like small children" – note the word: unless you are *like* the small children – "you shall not enter into the kingdom of God." He is not saying unless you are children; he cannot say that, otherwise every child will enter into the kingdom of God. He is saying unless you are *like* the small children. The difference is great. To be *like* the small children certainly means you are *not* children, and yet you are *like* the children. There is some similarity and some dissimilarity – something common between the two, and something not common.

Little Jeffrey was sad when he found his pet turtle lying on its back on the bank of the pond.

"Never mind," said his father, "we will have a fine funeral for him. I will make a little coffin for him and mother will wrap him in silk. We will buy a white picket fence to put around his grave. After we bury him we will go down to Hagen Dazs and I will buy a big ice-cream cone."

Suddenly the turtle turned over and headed for the water.

"Jeff, look!" shouted his father. "Your turtle is not dead after all."

"Daddy, let's kill it!"

This is innocence, but not Buddha-like. Now the child has become so much interested in the grave and the white fence and the ice-cream, that who cares for the turtle now? Now all that ceremony...

But there is no sin either. There is no virtue, no sin; he is simply unaware. You cannot say that he is violent or murderous, no, not at all. He is simply unconscious.

Innocence plus consciousness is equal to Buddhahood. Innocence minus consciousness is equal to childhoodness. And how one can be conscious? The only way – and let me emphasize – the *only* way is to lose it and gain it again.

You ask me: *"If an enlightened person cannot lose his buddhahood, how does a baby born as a buddha lose his?"*

The enlightened person has lost it and found it. The baby has not lost it, and has not yet found it; he is born with it, oblivious of it. Hence you will see in the eyes of small children something of the saints, something of the same beauty; but also a deep ignorance. The innocence is there but full of ignorance. The saint is innocent but full of awareness, knowing. His innocence is not mixed with ignorance; it is wisdom.

And the children are bound to lose their innocence. The sooner, the better. The more intelligent children will lose it sooner; the stupid children will lose it a little later; the retarded children may not lose it ever. More intelligent the child is, the quicker he will lose his innocence, because he will start inquiring, exploring. He would like to know more and more, he will be very curious, he will ask thousand-and-one questions – questions which even his father, his mother, his teachers can't answer.

RELIGION: THE ULTIMATE LUXURY

A child was walking with his father, and he asked "Why the roses are red?"

And the father said, "I don't know."

A little afterwards, he asked, "Why the river always flows downward? Why not upward?"

The father said, "Shut up! I don't know! Don't bother me!"

After few seconds, again he asked, "Where are the stars in the daytime?"

And the father said, "I don't know." And the father mumbled to himself, "What would have happened if I had asked all these questions to my father?"

The child said, "Then you would have been able to answer me." But then the child remained silent.

The silence was so long that the father became worried – it was so rare, because he was constantly asking – A very intelligent child he must have been – that he asked, "Why are you not asking anything?"

The child said, "What is the point?"

And the father said, "Then how you going to learn?"

We want children to ask, we want children to inquire although we don't have answers ourselves. We want them to become knowledgeable, informed, because it will be needed in their life, but we are not very authentic, very true. Even with our small children we are false. A really loving father, a loving mother, a loving teacher, will always say what he knows and what he does not know. He will not pretend.

If the child asks, "Who made the world?" he will not say, "God" because he does not know. He will say, "I have been inquiring, I have not found the answer yet. You also inquire. If you find before me, tell me. If I find before you I will tell you; but I have not found." And there will arise a great friendship and a great understanding between the child and the father. And the child will respect such a father his whole life; otherwise sooner or later he will discover that all your answers were just bullshit. You were pretending that you know; you know nothing. Then all his respect will disappear.

Two boys were talking about their dogs. "I can't figure it out," complained one. "How can you teach your dog all those tricks? And I can't teach my dog anything!"

"Well," said the other boy, "to begin with you have to know more than your dog."

Naturally, children have to learn, and learning means conditioning. From whom they are going to learn? From people who are not Buddhas, from people who have not arrived, from people who are themselves groping in the dark, from people whose inner being is a dark continent, from people who have no light of their own – they will learn things from these people, they will become just like these people. They will be lost into the jungle of the world, unless one day they are intelligent enough to see what has happened – how they have lost those beautiful, wonderful, awe-inspiring days, how they have lost the purity, the innocence of their childhood – and they start searching for it again. That is the moment when meditation begins. That is the moment when religion is born.

Religion is not Christianity, Hinduism, Mohammedanism; religion is the beginning of going back to your original source, trying to find out your innermost core that you had brought from the unknown, and that is still there wrapped around with information, knowledge – all kinds of things. You will have to peel it like an onion. You will have to go on peeling, because there are layers and layers, and you have learned so many lies. You have been told to learn lies, you have been brought up in lies – Christian lies, Hindu lies, Mohammedan lies. Beautiful lies – very appealing, but they are not true. Truth has to be discovered within one's own being.

A brother and sister are making love...

It must have happened in France; it cannot happen anywhere else!

The brother says, "Mm, you are better than Mum."

"Yes," answers the sister. "Daddy told me this morning."

Now these children will be corrupted by you. They are corrupted; in thousand-and-one ways we corrupt them. We are also helpless, because we have been corrupted by others; that's our heritage – corruption. That's what we get from one generation to another, and we go on handing to the new generation.

But the intelligent child sooner or later will discover all this corruption and all this deception, and will be able to get out of it. That's my definition of sannyas: getting out of all that has been told, taught, that has been given to you by others, discarding it all in total, so that you can regain your innocence again. Then one becomes a Buddha. Now you cannot lose this, because this is your achievement. Now you are fully aware of it. Now nobody can destroy it, because there is nothing more valuable than this.

The child was unaware; it was bound to happen. So the child cannot be protected, the child cannot be prevented. All that loving parents can do is to go on making him aware that whatsoever is being told to you, taught to you, is only hypothetical; it is not truth. Remember it. It is utilitarian, it is the best lie that we have discovered up to now, but it is not the truth. Truth you will have to discover on your own, you will have to discover within your own being. You will have to become a light unto yourself.

The third question:

Osho,
I am homosexual. What should I do about it?

It is good that you have confessed it. It is good that you are truthful about it. It is good that you are not hiding it, because whenever you expose yourself in totality, it is the beginning of a transformation. Don't be worried. One has to go beyond sex one day, whether it is homosexuality or heterosexuality or bisexuality – it does not matter much. Sex is sex, these are only preferences, differences of liking. Don't feel much guilty about it, and this is not your fault.

Homosexuality has come into existence because of repressive measures, because of repressive moralities, because of thousands of years of separating man and woman into separate camps. In the colleges, in the schools, in the army, in the monasteries – everywhere men and women are kept apart.

The natural outcome is going to be homosexualism, lesbianism, because the natural energy will try to find out some outlet.

Homosexuality is a byproduct of your so-called religions. The first homosexual must have been born in a monastery, that is almost certain. We don't know his name, but a memorial should be made dedicated to the unknown – the first homosexual. He must have been a monk.

It is a well known fact that Christian monasteries, Buddhist monasteries have been full of homosexuality. It was bound to happen because you don't give them the science of transcending sex, and you simply tell them to repress the energy. Now the energy starts moving into perverted ways.

And don't take offense at the word *perversion*. It simply means unnatural, it simply means not as it was prescribed by the biology. The biological route is heterosexual. If you prevent it...It is like a small stream is flowing: you put a rock in its way, it will start flowing from some other side, it will go by passing the rock, it will become two streams instead of one. You can go on preventing it and it will go on splitting into many streams. It will find out some way. It has a source of water that has to be taken to the ocean.

Don't be worried about it, because worrying won't help. Accept it. Just as repression has created it, a deep acceptance can dissolve it. Accept it. You are a victim of a thousands of years conditioning.

Friendship is born at the moment when one person says to another, "What! You too? I thought I was the only one."

People go on hiding it, but sooner or later you have to find out somebody, and there are ways how homosexuals indicate. They walk differently – they may not say, but they walk differently. They look differently, they talk differently, their gestures are different, and other homosexuals immediately understand the language.

And it is not a small minority, remember. Ten per cent people all over the world are homosexuals. Out of ten, one person is a homosexual; it is a big number. And this is increasing every day, because the women's liberation movement is creating lesbianism. "Why depend on men, even for love? Sisterhood is beautiful. Love your sisters." The natural outcome will be that many brothers will be left alone.

The new bride, frustrated by her groom's indifference, could not contain herself anymore. "Listen," she said, "if you are gonna keep on reading these newspapers, I am going downtown to get myself a man."

"Far out!" he said. "Would you get me one too?"

A homo and a hetero went into the desert.

"Ah," said the horny hetero, "even if there was a fly here, I could screw it."

"Z-z-z-z," replied the homo.

In a bar two homosexuals are drinking their martinis with chips and olives. Suddenly one of them pricks his lip with the toothpick. At the sight of the blood he exclaims, "Ah, my, I have got my period."

A little bit perverted, but so what. Nothing to be worried. Accept it.

My fundamental principle is acceptance – *tathata*. Whatsoever is the situation, you accept it. From there things can begin. Don't reject it. It is out of rejection that the problem has arisen, so only with acceptance...Relax into it and you will be surprised. If you can accept it without any guilt, slowly, slowly your homosexuality will turn into heterosexuality again. Why? – because guilt is also a religious phenomenon, and homosexuality too. They are joined together, they are tied together. If you go on feeling guilty, you will remain homosexual. Drop the guilt, accept it. Nothing is wrong, just you are carrying the whole ugly past of humanity. What can you do? You have come a little late, people have preceded before. They have dirtied the whole beach. So we have to clean it.

But what is the point of crying and weeping and feeling guilty? There is no need to waste energies in that. Accept it with no guilt at all. And with the disappearance of the guilt you will be surprised: if you are a Christian your Christianity disappears; if you are a Jew your Judaism disappears; if you are a Hindu your Hinduism disappears. This is really a miracle:

when the guilt is dropped your religions disappear. And when religions disappear you become a far more natural being. You can start seeing things clearly. In fact, what you are seeking into the other man, you cannot find in him. There will be frustration. What the other man is trying to find in you, he cannot find in you; there will be frustration.

Friendship is possible, but love is not possible, and friendship and love are different dimensions. Friendship has its own beauty. Love needs polar opposites, only then there is attraction, only then there is tension enough. Love needs a subtle dialectics, it is a process of dialectics. The man and woman relationship is a dialectical process full of hazards, adventures, fights. It is a kind of intimate enmity. In the morning the fight, in the evening the love, in the morning again the fight, and it goes on moving from one polarity to the other.

But this is how it keeps itself alive. It is Hegelian dialectics: thesis, antithesis, synthesis, and again synthesis becomes the thesis. Just the other night you had reached to a treaty, a peaceful state, and in the morning it disappears. And you were thinking, "Now, things are going smooth." But from the same point, in the morning the argument starts, and by the evening the same point leads you to lovemaking.

In fact, unless you fight before, you will not be able to make love really, tremendously. A good fight before making love gives you zest, gusto – just a good fight and you become hot; otherwise, civilized people have become cool. Just a good fight – shouting, throwing things, exchange of pillows, and then relaxing into each other in the warmth of each other. The fight creates the distance. The farther away you are – it is a kind of mini-divorce, then comes a mini-honeymoon.

It can't happen in a homosexual relationship. That's why homosexuals are called gay; there is no dialectics, they are always smiling. But their smile seems to be shallow; it cannot be very deep. They are smiling because there is not any possibility of tears, and they understand each other. They are both men or both women, so they understand each other. With understanding there is no fight. A man and woman never understand each other, they cannot. If they understand, immediately all is finished, they both have become Buddhas.

The fourth question:

Osho,
Cannot I wait a little before taking the jump into sannyas? I don't feel fully ready yet.

I know you are a mathematician and a Jew and also an Italian. It is a rare combination. The mathematician is always calculating, but he can never take the jump. Calculation will not allow you to take the jump, it is impossible for the calculating mind. And you will never be fully ready. How you will be fully ready? There are things you become ready only when you have entered in them.

No two lovers are fully ready before they enter into a love relationship. If they want to be fully ready, then there will never happen any love relationship. Where they are going to get ready for it? And why this readiness? Is it not out of fear? – something may go wrong...

But your whole life what have you done? You have been calculating, calculating, living in a very businesslike way. What have you achieved? Sometimes taking risks has a beauty of its own. In fact, all great radical changes happen only when you move into some dimension without any calculations.

Sannyas is a love affair; it is not mathematics.

A mathematician passing through the security check at an airport is discovered to have a bomb in his hand luggage.

"You are arrested," said the security officer.

"Arrested? What for? I am not a hijacker, I am a mathematician."

"Then what is this bomb doing in your bag?"

"Why, it is a matter of security."

"I don't understand," replied the security officer.

"Well, my man, consider. If the possibility of one bomb being on board the plane is removed, then the possibility of two bombs being on board the same plane is practically non-existent."

This is calculation. He is going very mathematically.

Sannyas will never happen to you. It is not mathematics; it is poetry, it is music, it is dance, it is celebration. It is a mad, mad love affair. And you are a Jew too. Maybe it is because of your Jewishness that you have become a mathematician. Jews are good mathematicians. It is no wonder that Albert Einstein proved to be the greatest mathematician of the world. Who else can be the greatest mathematician than a Jew?

Aaron Silberstein called his little son Moise, gave him a ruble and said, "Moise, go to the grocer and get two pounds of butter."

Moise went off, taking the little dog of the Silberstein family along. On the way to the grocer's he decided to make better use of his father's money. Instead of getting two pounds of butter, he bought two pounds of sweets from the grocer. After he had hidden the sweets in the barn, Moise put on a sad face and went in to meet his father.

"What happened?" asked the father. "Where is the butter?"

"The dog," said little Moise, "the fucking beast snatched the butter away from me and ate it all up."

Silberstein grabbed the little dog and put it on the scale. The scale indicated exactly two pounds. He turned to his son and said, "Okay, son. This is the butter, now where is the dog?"

Take a jump out of your Jewishness, out of your mathematics. I say you are fully ready; I can certify.

Do you think all of my sannyasins were fully ready before they took the jump? They dared! And it is not a question of being fully ready. How you are going to measure? How you are going to weigh? At what point you are fully ready? What is the criterion? You can ask me.

The very question says that a deep desire has arisen in you, but your mind is holding you back. Your spirit wants to take the jump, but your mind is not willing. The mind says, "First get ready," because the mind knows perfectly well one is never ready.

The great mathematician was getting old and his health was deteriorating every day. He went to his physician. After a

RELIGION: THE ULTIMATE LUXURY

complete check the doctor took a deep breath and began.

"Dear sir, in a case like this it is better to be frank and tell you the whole truth."

"Tell me, doctor, whatever it is."

"It is difficult."

"Tell me the truth, doctor. How long do I have to live? A year?"

"Less."

"Less? Well, better I should know. Six months, then?"

"Less."

"Okay, okay. I can take it. One month?"

"I am sorry to have to say it but..."

"It is okay, doctor, I accept." So saying he left the room. The doctor was very much impressed at the way the man had taken the news, and he went to the window to take a last look at him.

He was standing on the pavement about to cross the road. Just then a hearse passed by, at which he raised his hand and shouted, "Taxi! Taxi!"

Tomorrow is not certain. Who knows? – tomorrow may come, may not come. If you are feeling an urge, a deep longing, then take the jump, and don't be so afraid. Gather a little courage. Sannyas has to be a discontinuity with your past. If it is not a discontinuity with the past, it is not sannyas at all. And if you are fully ready it will not be a discontinuity; it will be continuous. You were ready and will come out of that readiness, it will remain part of your past.

Sannyas has to be a discontinuous thing. The past simply disappears as if it had existed never. You start anew, fresh.

And you are burdened with problems, I can see: mathematician, and a Jew, living in Italy...

In a concentration camp it is Christmas Eve, and the general calls all the prisoners into the courtyard and lines them in three rows.

"Christmas makes me feel good," says the general, "and I want to ease your sufferings. The first row one step forward." The first row does as it is told. The general shouts, "Fire!" and they are all killed. The same happens with the second row. Then again the general shouts, "One step forward, the third row." All the prisoners step forward except two; they are Italians.

They look at each other and then one says, "Ah well, let us step forward, otherwise he gets pissed off."

You ask me: "Cannot I wait a little before taking the jump into sannyas?"

You can wait as long as you want, but how long it will take? And death can always end the game. Even the next moment is not certain. All that is certain is this moment, and I can feel a longing. Whenever I see the longing that is enough proof that one is prepared. And don't ask for perfection. Nobody is ever perfect. Don't be a perfectionist. Perfectionists are all neurotics. Become a sannyasin the way you are, as you are. Don't wait any more. You have waited enough. You have been here at least for six to seven weeks, asking me again and again. Now I think it is time.

And this longing is not going to leave you. It will become stronger and stronger. If you leave without becoming a sannyasin, you will have to come back. It will haunt you wherever you are. I will follow you.

The boss calls for the Jewish accountant, and the secretary says, "He went out, boss. He went to play the sports lottery."

The next day at the same time the boss calls for the accountant again. "He went out, boss. He went to play the horses," answers the secretary.

The third day the boss calls for the accountant again. The secretary explains, "He went out, boss. He went to play the lottery again."

"What is this?" exclaims the boss. "Is he mad? Every day he is going out at work time to play."

The secretary said, "It is the last chance he has to balance the books this month."

That's all I can say to you. This is the last chance. I may not meet you again. You may not find a madman like me again. Buddhas will be there always, but rarely a Buddha like me who will accept all kinds of crazy people.

Gautam Buddha was very particular. You had to go through

a long initiation process. There were many steps to be fulfilled. But once a man came to him – his name was Sariputta – who became one of his greatest disciples. Sariputta touched Buddha's feet and said, "Please initiate me." Buddha said, "First you have to fulfill many other things."

Sariputta said, "I will fulfill everything afterwards, but first initiate me."

Buddha said, "You have not even fulfilled the ordinary formality" – of going three times around Buddha, touching his feet three times, and asking three times, "Lord, initiate me."

Sariputta said, "If I die doing all this ritual, will you be responsible for me? If I miss this opportunity, will you be responsible for me? Then I am ready. I will do three hundred rounds around you, I will touch three hundred times your feet – or as many times as you want. But are you ready to take my responsibility? Because who knows – I may not be here, you may not be here..."

Buddha looked at Sariputta, smiled, and Sariputta was the first disciple who was initiated without any requirements fulfilled by him. His other disciples were angry, and they said, "We had to go through years of training. What this man has done?"

Buddha said, "I looked into his eyes. I saw his longing – a pure flame. I can agree with him, he can fulfill all these things later on; these are formalities, these are for fools. But he is not a foolish man, he has tremendous intelligence."

Bodhidharma, one of Buddha's greatest inheritors, went around this country but could not find a single man to initiate, because nobody was able to fulfill his conditions. His conditions were impossible; hence, he had to go to China in search of a disciple. And there too, thousands came but he refused. And he sat facing the wall for nine years, and told that "Unless the right person turns up, I am not going to look at his face."

And then a disciple turned – out of hundreds, thousands who came and went away, and he will not look back. And this disciple cut his hand, threw it before Bodhidharma, and said, "Turn towards me! Otherwise I will cut my head!"

And he had to turn immediately, a hundred-eighty-degree turn, and he said, "Wait, don't be in such a hurry. I have been waiting for you." He initiated only four persons in China.

There are different kind of Buddhas. You will not find a man like me again – it is very rare. It has never been before and I don't think there is going to be a man like me again.
So, I don't think it is good, wise, Jewish to miss.

The last question:

Osho,
Why are you called the Master of Masters?

Reverend Banana, Michael Potato Singh, Michael Tomato; dear gentlemen or ladies as the case may be...Because nobody has yet been able to decide whether these fellows are gentlemen or ladies.

It is a difficult question. I had to look in the Akashic records, and not in the past Akashic records – because it is not recorded there – but in the future Akashic records. This is a future story. Listen carefully.

It happened in Moksha, the ultimate resting place of the awakened ones. A journalist for the local newspaper, *The Nirvana Timeless*, was desperately seeking material to fill up the center page of the next edition which was due to appear in twenty-five hundred years. There was not much news around in Moksha, and soon he realized that he would have to make something up himself if the center page was not to be left empty again, as it had been for countless ages.

Finally, he hit on the idea of choosing which of the many Buddhas, *Arhatas*, Bodhisattvas, Christs, *Kutubs* and other enlightened beings abounding in the lotus paradise was the master of masters – in short, a spiritual Mr. Universe competition.

He summoned all the enlightened ones together and asked them to encapsulate in a short phrase the essence of their teaching, which would entitle them to the title of master of masters. There was, as usual, a deep silence which lasted a few hundred years. Finally a Zen master stood forward and hit the journalist hard on the head. This was considered to be well deserved, but not very original.

Another hundred years passed and then a Sufi stood up and

began to whirl. Unfortunately he was out of training, and after a couple of months he fell flat on his face, causing some merriment among the Hassidic masters, who had been surreptitiously pouring oil on the floor to bring the uppity Arab down.

After some goading by Manjushree and Subhuti, Buddha slowly stood up and addressed the gathering in the following way: "There is no teaching and no one to be taught. There is no master and nothing to master. Nothing can be said; there is no one to hear it." Then he held up a flower and Mahakashyap giggled as usual. Many applauded the Buddha, but to the journalist it did not appear like the kind of news which would help him to sell his paper.

One after another the enlightened ones came forward to make their bids for the title. Moses gave a few new commandments. Bodhidharma stared at a wall for ninety years. Jesus made a mountain out of a molehill, and delivered a sermon from it. Diogenes displayed his suntan. Shiva and Parvati ran through one hundred twelve new positions they had invented. Gurdjieff drank twenty bottles of brandy, then walked on his hands on a tightrope over the plenum void, smiling with the left side of his face and grimacing with the right. Lao Tzu had a good belly laugh at all these antics. Mansoor would not stop shouting, "Ana'l Haq! Ana'l Haq!" and finally had to be put in a straitjacket and given a couple of Valium. Vatsyayana gave himself a blow job to demonstrate existentially that sex and samadhi were manifestations of the same energy – and so on.

It proved impossible to choose which of the awakened ones was the master of masters, since even the journalist had attained to choiceless awareness long ago. But the day seemed saved when Teertha, a relative newcomer from England, stood up and declared with typical British diplomacy, "The greatest master is the one who has yet to come." Suddenly an Indian mahatma jumped to his feet and cried triumphantly, "Then that must be me – for I have been celibate for eighty-four million lives."

By unanimous agreement the awakened ones decided that the mahatma's samadhi was not yet "seedless," and he was dispelled back to sansara to spill his seed once and for all.

Just as the mahatma disappeared from sight, Osho came out of his room, where he had been sitting all this time, and made his way towards a small marble podium in the corner of the hall. A deathly hush gripped the audience, and even Mansoor shut up. If a look of dread could be said to cloud those tranquil eyes, this is what happened to the gathering.

As Osho sat down and leaned towards the microphone, a cry arose from Mahavira, "Wait! Wait! We proclaim you master of masters! Now please go back to your room."

Osho smiled innocently and left the hall. There was a sigh of relief.

The journalist turned to Mahavira in consternation: "I don't understand. Why did he get the title? What did he do?"

"Nothing," said Mahavira, "but last time he spoke here it took us seven hundred years to get him to stop, and send him to Pune!"

About Osho

Osho defies categorization, reflecting everything from the individual quest for meaning to the most urgent social and political issues facing society today. His books are not written but are transcribed from recordings of extemporaneous talks given over a period of thirty-five years. Osho has been described by the *Sunday Times* in London as one of the "1000 Makers of the 20th Century" and by *Sunday Mid-Day* in India as one of the ten people – along with Gandhi, Nehru and Buddha – who have changed the destiny of India.

Osho has a stated aim of helping to create the conditions for the birth of a new kind of human being, characterized as "Zorba the Buddha" – one whose feet are firmly on the ground, yet whose hands can touch the stars. Running like a thread through all aspects of Osho is a vision that encompasses both the timeless wisdom of the East and the highest potential of Western science and technology.

He is synonymous with a revolutionary contribution to the science of inner transformation and an approach to meditation which specifically addresses the accelerated pace of contemporary life. The unique Osho Active Meditations™ are designed to allow the release of accumulated stress in the body and mind so that it is easier to be still and experience the thought-free state of meditation.

Osho International Meditation Resort

Osho International Meditation Resort has been created so that people can have a direct experience of a new way of living – with more alertness, relaxation, and humor. It is located about 100 miles southeast of Mumbai in Pune, India, on 40 acres in the tree-lined residential area of Koregaon Park. The resort offers a variety of programs to the thousands of people who visit each year from more than 100 countries. Accommodation for visitors is available on-campus in the new Osho Guesthouse.

    The Multiversity programs at the meditation resort take place in a pyramid complex next to the famous Zen garden park, Osho Teerth. The programs are designed to provide the transformation tools that give people access to a new lifestyle – one of relaxed awareness – which is an approach they can take with them into their everyday lives. Self-discovery classes, sessions, courses and meditative processes are offered throughout the year. For exercising the body and keeping fit, there is a beautiful outdoor facility where one can experiment with a Zen approach to sports and recreation.

    In the main meditation auditorium the daily schedule from 6:00 A.M. up to 11:00 P.M. includes both active and passive meditation methods. Following the daily evening meeting meditation, the nightlife in this multicultural resort is alive with outdoor eating areas that fill with friends and often with dancing.

    The resort has its own supply of safe, filtered drinking water and the food served is made with organically grown produce from the resort's own farm.

    An online tour of the meditation resort, as well as travel and program information, can be found at: www.osho.com

This is a comprehensive website in different languages with an online magazine, audio and video webcasting, an Audiobook Club, the complete English and Hindi archive of Osho talks and a complete catalog of all Osho publications including books, audio and video. Includes information about the active meditation techniques developed by Osho, most with streaming video demonstrations.

The daily meditation schedule includes:

Osho Dynamic Meditation™: A technique designed to release tensions and repressed emotions, opening the way to a new vitality and an experience of profound silence.

Osho Kundalini Meditation™: A technique of shaking free one's dormant energies, and through spontaneous dance and silent sitting, allowing these energies to be redirected inward.

Osho Nadabrahma Meditation™: A method of harmonizing one's energy flow, based on an ancient Tibetan humming technique.

Osho Nataraj Meditation™: A method involving the inner alchemy of dancing so totally that the dancer disappears and only the dance remains.

Vipassana Meditation: A technique originating with Gautam Buddha and now updated for the 21st Century, for dissolving mental chatter through the awareness of breath.

No Dimensions Meditation™: A powerful method for centering one's energy, based on a Sufi technique.

Osho Gourishankar Meditation™: A one-hour nighttime meditation, which includes a breathing technique, gazing softly at a light and gentle body movements.

Books by Osho in English Language

Early Discourses and Writings
A Cup of Tea
Dimensions Beyond The Known
From Sex to Super-consciousness
The Great Challenge
Hidden Mysteries
I Am The Gate
The Inner Journey
Psychology of the Esoteric
Seeds of Wisdom

Meditation
The Voice of Silence
And Now and Here (Vol 1 & 2)
In Search of the Miraculous (Vol 1 &.2)
Meditation: The Art of Ecstasy
Meditation: The First and Last Freedom
The Path of Meditation
The Perfect Way
Yaa-Hoo! The Mystic Rose

Buddha and Buddhist Masters
The Book of Wisdom
The Dhammapada: The Way of the Buddha (Vol 1-12)
The Diamond Sutra
The Discipline of Transcendence (Vol 1-4)
The Heart Sutra

Indian Mystics
Enlightenment: The Only Revolution (Ashtavakra)
Showering Without Clouds (Sahajo)
The Last Morning Star (Daya)
The Song of Ecstasy (Adi Shankara)

Baul Mystics
The Beloved (Vol 1 & 2)
Kabir
The Divine Melody
Ecstasy: The Forgotten Language
The Fish in the Sea is Not Thirsty
The Great Secret
The Guest
The Path of Love
The Revolution

Jesus and Christian Mystics
Come Follow to You (Vol 1-4)
I Say Unto You (Vol 1 & 2)
The Mustard Seed
Theologia Mystica

Jewish Mystics
The Art of Dying
The True Sage

Western Mystics
Guida Spirituale (Desiderata)
The Hidden Harmony (Heraclitus)
The Messiah (Vol 1 & 2) (Commentaries on Khalil Gibran's The Prophet)
The New Alchemy: To Turn You On (Commentaries on Mabel Collins' Light on the Path)
Philosophia Perennis (Vol 1 & 2) (The Golden Verses of Pythagoras)
Zarathustra: A God That Can Dance
Zarathustra: The Laughing Prophet (Commentaries on

Nietzsche's Thus Spake Zarathustra)

Sufism
Just Like That
Journey to the Heart
The Perfect Master (Vol 1 & 2)
The Secret
Sufis: The People of the Path (Vol 1 & 2)
Unio Mystica (Vol 1 & 2)
The Wisdom of the Sands (Vol 1 & 2)

Tantra
Tantra: The Supreme Understanding
The Tantra Experience
 The Royal Song of Saraha
 (same as Tantra Vision, Vol 1)
The Tantric Transformation
 The Royal Song of Saraha
 (same as Tantra Vision, Vol 2)
The Book of Secrets: Vigyan Bhairav Tantra

The Upanishads
Behind a Thousand Names
(Nirvana Upanishad)
Heartbeat of the Absolute
(Ishavasya Upanishad)
I Am That (Isa Upanishad)
The Message Beyond Words
(Kathopanishad)
Philosophia Ultima (Mandukya Upanishad)
The Supreme Doctrine (Kenopanishad)
Finger Pointing to the Moon
(Adhyatma Upanishad)
That Art Thou (Sarvasar Upanishad, Kaivalya Upanishad, Adhyatma Upanishad)
The Ultimate Alchemy, Vol 1&2
 (Atma Pooja Upanishad Vol 1 & 2)
Vedanta: Seven Steps to Samadhi (Akshaya Upanishad)
Flight of the Alone to the Alone

(Kaivalya Upanishad)

Tao
The Empty Boat
The Secret of Secrets
Tao:The Golden Gate (Vol 1&2)
Tao:The Pathless Path (Vol 1&2)
Tao: The Three Treasures (Vol 1-4)
When the Shoe Fits

Yoga
The Path of Yoga (previously Yoga: The Alpha and the Omega Vol 1)
Yoga: The Alpha and the Omega (Vol 2-10)

Zen and Zen Masters
Ah, This!
Ancient Music in the Pines
And the Flowers Showered
A Bird on the Wing
Bodhidharma: The Greatest Zen Master
Communism and Zen Fire, Zen Wind
Dang Dang Doko Dang
The First Principle
God is Dead: Now Zen is the Only Living Truth
The Grass Grows By Itself
The Great Zen Master Ta Hui
Hsin Hsin Ming: The Book of Nothing
I Celebrate Myself: God is No Where, Life is Now Here
Kyozan: A True Man of Zen
Nirvana: The Last Nightmare
No Mind: The Flowers of Eternity
No Water, No Moon
One Seed Makes the Whole Earth Green
Returning to the Source
The Search: Talks on the 10 Bulls of Zen
A Sudden Clash of Thunder
The Sun Rises in the Evening
Take it Easy (Vol 1 & 2)

This Very Body the Buddha
Walking in Zen, Sitting in Zen
The White Lotus
Yakusan: Straight to the Point of Enlightenment
Zen Manifesto : Freedom From Oneself
Zen: The Mystery and the Poetry of the Beyond
Zen: The Path of Paradox (Vol 1, 2 & 3)
Zen: The Special Transmission
Zen Boxed Sets
The World of Zen (5 vol.)
Live Zen
This. This. A Thousand Times This
Zen: The Diamond Thunderbolt
Zen: The Quantum Leap from Mind to No-Mind

Zen: The Solitary Bird, Cuckoo
of the Forest
Zen: All The Colors Of The Rainbow (5 vol.)
The Buddha: The Emptiness of the Heart
The Language of Existence
The Miracle
The Original Man
Turning In

Osho: On the Ancient Masters of Zen (7 volumes)*
Dogen: The Zen Master
Hyakujo: The Everest of Zen–
With Basho's haikus
Isan: No Footprints in the Blue Sky
Joshu: The Lion's Roar
Ma Tzu: The Empty Mirror
Nansen: The Point Of Departure
Rinzai: Master of the Irrational
*Each volume is also available individually.

Responses to Questions
Be Still and Know
Come, Come, Yet Again Come
The Goose is Out

The Great Pilgrimage: From Here to Here
The Invitation
My Way: The Way of the White Clouds
Nowhere to Go But In
The Razor's Edge
Walk Without Feet, Fly Without Wings and Think Without Mind
The Wild Geese and the Water
Zen: Zest, Zip, Zap and Zing

Talks in America
From Bondage To Freedom
From Darkness to Light
From Death To Deathlessness
From the False to the Truth
From Unconsciousness to Consciousness
The Rajneesh Bible (Vol 2-4)

The World Tour
Beyond Enlightenment (Talks in Bombay)
Beyond Psychology (Talks in Uruguay)
Light on the Path (Talks in the Himalayas)
The Path of the Mystic (Talks in Uruguay)
Sermons in Stones (Talks in Bombay)
Socrates Poisoned Again After 25 Centuries (Talks in Greece)
The Sword and the Lotus
(Talks in the Himalayas)
The Transmission of the Lamp
(Talks in Uruguay)

Osho's Vision for the World
The Golden Future
The Hidden Splendor
The New Dawn
The Rebel
The Rebellious Spirit

The Mantra Series
Hari Om Tat Sat
Om Mani Padme Hum

Om Shantih Shantih Shantih
Sat-Chit-Anand
Satyam-Shivam-Sundram

Personal Glimpses
Books I Have Loved
Glimpses of a Golden Childhood
Notes of a Madman

Interviews with the World Press
The Last Testament (Vol 1)

Intimate Talks between
Master and Disciple – Darshan Diaries
A Rose is a Rose is a Rose
Be Realistic: Plan for a Miracle
Believing the Impossible Before Breakfast
Beloved of My Heart
Blessed are the Ignorant
Dance Your Way to God
Don't Just Do Something, Sit There
Far Beyond the Stars
For Madmen Only
The Further Shore
Get Out of Your Own Way
God's Got A Thing about You
God is Not for Sale
The Great Nothing
Hallelujah!
Let Go!
The 99 Names of Nothingness
No Book, No Buddha, No Teaching, No Disciple
Nothing to Lose but Your Head
Only Losers Can Win in This Game
Open Door
Open Secret
The Shadow of the Whip
The Sound of One Hand Clapping
The Sun Behind the Sun Behind the Sun

The Tongue-Tip Taste of Tao
This Is It
Turn On, Tune In and Drop the Lot
What Is, Is, What Ain't, Ain't
Won't You Join The Dance?

Compilations
After Middle Age: A Limitless Sky
At the Feet of the Master
Bhagwan Shree Rajneesh: On Basic Human Rights
Jesus Crucified Again, This Time in Ronald Reagan's America
Priests and Politicians: The Mafia of the Soul
Take it Really Seriously

Gift Books of Osho Quotations
A Must for Contemplation Before Sleep
A Must for Morning

Contemplation
India My Love

Photobooks
Shree Rajneesh: A Man of Many Climates, Seasons and Rainbows
through the eye of the camera
Impressions... Osho Commune International Photobook

Books about Osho
Bhagwan: The Buddha for the Future by Juliet Forman
Bhagwan Shree Rajneesh: The Most Dangerous Man Since Jesus Christ by Sue Appleton

Bhagwan: The Most Godless Yet the Most Godly Man by Dr. George Meredith
Bhagwan: One Man Against the Whole Ugly Past of Humanity by Juliet Forman
Bhagwan: Twelve Days That Shook the World by Juliet Forman
Was Bhagwan Shree Rajneesh Poisoned by Ronald Reagan's America? by Sue Appleton

Diamond Days With Osho
by Ma Prem Shunyo

For any information about Osho Books & Audio/Video Tapes please contact:

Sadhana Foundation
17 Koregaon Park, Pune–411001, MS, India
Phone: 020 4019999 Fax: 020 4019990
E-mail: distrib@osho.net Website: www.osho.com